The Maine Woods

A THOREAU TRILOGY
Illustrated by Henry Bugbee Kane

THE MAINE WOODS
Introduction by Dudley C. Lunt

CAPE COD
Introduction by Henry Beston

WALDEN
Introduction by Basil Willey

Henry David Thoreau

THE

MAINE WOODS

Arranged with Notes by DUDLEY C. LUNT

Illustrated by Henry Bugbee Kane

BRAMHALL HOUSE ● *New York*

The mountainous region of the State of Maine stretches from near the White Mountains, northeasterly one hundred and sixty miles, to the head of the Aroostook River, and is about sixty miles wide. The wild or unsettled portion is far more extensive. So that some hours only of travel in this direction will carry the curious to the verge of a primitive forest, more interesting, perhaps, on all accounts, than they would reach by going a thousand miles westward.

*This edition published by Bramhall House, a
division of Clarkson N. Potter, Inc., by
arrangement with W. W. Norton & Company, Inc.*

J

Contents

Introductory Note

"On the 31st of August, 1846, I left Concord in Massachusetts for Bangor and the backwoods of Maine. . . ." With this simple statement Thoreau opens his account of the first of his three excursions in the Maine woods.

From Bangor he went on up the Penobscot where an old Indian, pointing, had told him—"two or three mile up the river, one beautiful country." Here in company with his relative, George A. Thatcher, two friends from Bangor, and two boatmen—George McCauslin, "Uncle George," and Tom Fowler—he climbed Ktaadn. The river trip up and the return down the West Branch of the Penobscot was made in a batteau. His account of this excursion first appeared in five installments in 1848 in *The Union Magazine* (New York) under the title, "Ktaadn and the Maine Woods."

The purpose of his next trip in mid-September, 1853, was primarily to accompany his relative, in his phrase, "a-moose-hunting." This time he went overland from Bangor to Moosehead Lake, across Northeast Carry and down the West Branch—where they hunted—to Chesuncook Lake, returning by the same route to Bangor. On the West Branch they used a birch, that is a birch-bark canoe, and were paddled by an Indian guide, Joe Aitteon. The account of this appeared in the *Atlantic Monthly* in June, July, and August, 1858, under the title, "Chesuncook."

11

Thoreau's last venture was made in the midsummer of 1857, and of it he wrote:

We had at first thought of exploring the St. John from its source to its mouth, or else to go up the Penobscot by its East Branch to the lakes of the St. John, and return by way of Chesuncook and Moosehead. We had finally inclined to the last route, *only reversing the order of it,* going by way of Moosehead, and returning by the Penobscot, otherwise it would have been all the way up stream and taken twice as long.

Here was a real river trip, swinging northwestward from Bangor again, over the length of Moosehead Lake, which they traversed in a birch, then across Northeast Carry into the West Branch and on down to Chesuncook Lake, up Umbazookskus Stream, over Mud Pond Carry into the Allegash waters—Chamberlain, Eagle, and Telos Lakes—and finally returning by Webster Stream and the East Branch down the Penobscot to Bangor. In this fashion they completely encircled Ktaadn which rises within the yoke formed by the East and West Branch.[1]

His friend Edward Hoar of Concord was his companion and the Penobscot Indian, Joe Polis of Oldtown, was their guide. His journal account did not appear in his lifetime—Thoreau died in 1862—but was first published with the other accounts under the editorial direction of Sophia Thoreau and William Ellery Channing in 1864, bearing the title, "The Allegash and East Branch."

The traditional framework of *The Maine Woods* has been in the form of these three separate accounts—"Ktaadn" (1846), "Chesuncook" (1853), and "The Allegash and East Branch" (1857). There occurs inevitably not a little repeti-

---

[1] In the valley of the Penobscot the reference is always to the East Branch or to the West Branch, a usage which is followed by Thoreau. Those who live there are akin to the Prince Edward Islander whose query was—"Sure, is there any other Island?"

tion, some confusion, and a deal of what the Maine woodsman calls back-tracking. This is all caused by the accident of
chronological sequence given to these journalized accounts,
not by Thoreau himself, but evidently by others after his
death.

This then is the purpose of this edition.

It is to give to *The Maine Woods* a unity that is rooted
in Thoreau's swing around the great sweep of the Ktaadn
country. To this end a single account has been arranged,
using the route followed on the river trip in 1857 and dove-
tailing into it at the appropriate places the 1853 excursion to
Chesuncook—a-moose-hunting—and the ascent of Ktaadn in
1846. As these transitions occur, the reader's attention is
specifically drawn to them. In a manner akin to the first two
accounts published in Thoreau's lifetime, the whole is divided into sixteen chapters and an appendix, using titles
taken from the text. While a rearrangment of this nature has
necessarily entailed some minor omissions, they are confined
almost entirely to journalistic passages on the several journeys to and from the woods. The integrity of Thoreau's text
has been utterly respected.

On his visit to Oldtown on September 22, 1853, Thoreau
wrote in his Journal a meticulously accurate description of
the construction of a birch-bark canoe. This he condensed
to a single paragraph in the account entitled "Chesuncook."
The courtesy of Houghton Mifflin Company, publishers of
the Journal, is acknowledged in relation to this passage and
several others of striking import which were similarly condensed or omitted and have been included here.

A mark of the woodsman is his economy of exact expression in describing a locale. The duck pond, he will tell you,
pointing, lies in two pockets with the narrows between and
the thoroughfare beyond. What more is needed? You now
know the lay of the land and the direction of the stream. In

this as in other aspects Thoreau was, on the amateur scale, a good woodsman. It is a simple matter to follow his route on Hubbard's Map of Northern Maine (1879–1929), and to locate with ease his portages and camp grounds. This was the way Thoreau would have it. In ascending the West Branch toward Ktaadn, he said:

I am particular to give the names of the settlers and the distances, since every log-hut in these woods is a public house, and such information is of no little consequence to those who may have occasion to travel this way.

DUDLEY C. LUNT

Scarborough, Maine

1. The Avenue Road

AT FIVE P. M., September 13, 1853, I left Boston, in the steamer, for Bangor, by the outside course. It was a warm and still night,—warmer, probably, on the water than on the land,—and the sea was as smooth as a small lake in summer, merely rippled. The passengers went singing on the deck, as in a parlor, till ten o'clock. We passed a vessel on her beam-ends on a rock just outside the islands, and some of us thought that she was the "rapt ship" which ran

> "on her side so low
> That she drank water, and her keel ploughed air,"

not considering that there was no wind, and that she was under bare poles. Now we have left the islands behind and are off Nahant. We behold those features which the discoverers saw, apparently unchanged. Now we see the Cape Ann lights, and now pass near a small village-like fleet of mackerel-fishers at anchor, probably off Gloucester. They salute us with a shout from their low decks; but I understand their "Good evening" to mean, "Don't run against me, sir."

From the wonders of the deep we go below to yet deeper sleep. And then the absurdity of being waked up in the night by a man who wants the job of blacking your boots! It is more inevitable than sea-sickness, and may have something to do with it. It is like the ducking you get on crossing the line the first time. I trusted that these old customs were abolished. They might with the same propriety insist on blacking your face. I heard of one man who complained that somebody had stolen his boots in the night; and when he found them, he wanted to know what they had done to them,—they had spoiled them,—he never put that stuff on them; and the bootblack narrowly escaped paying damages.

Anxious to get out of the whale's belly, I rose early, and joined some old salts, who were smoking by a dim light on a sheltered part of the deck. We were just getting into the river. They knew all about it, of course. I was proud to find that I had stood the voyage so well, and was not in the least digested. We brushed up and watched the first signs of dawn through an open port; but the day seemed to hang fire. We

inquired the time; none of my companions had a chronome-
ter. At length an African prince rushed by, observing,
"Twelve o'clock, gentlemen!" and blew out the light. It was
moonrise. So I slunk down into the monster's bowels again.

The first land we make is Monhegan Island, before dawn,
and next St. George's Islands, seeing two or three lights.
Whitehead, with its bare rocks and funereal bell, is interesting. Next I remember that the Camden Hills attracted my
eyes, and afterward the hills about Frankfort. We reached
Bangor about noon.

We had hardly left the steamer, when we passed Molly
Molasses in the street. As long as she lives, the Penobscots
may be considered extant as a tribe. The succeeding morning, a relative of mine, who is well acquainted with the
Penobscot Indians, and who had been my companion in
my previous excursion into the Maine woods, took me in
his wagon to Oldtown, to assist me in obtaining an Indian
for this expedition. We were ferried across to the Indian
Island in a batteau. The ferryman's boy had got the key to
it, but the father, who was a blacksmith, after a little hesitation cut the chain with a cold-chisel on the rock. He told me
that the Indians were nearly all gone to the seaboard and to

Massachusetts, partly on account of the small-pox, of which they are very much afraid, having broken out in Oldtown, and it was doubtful whether we should find a suitable one at home.

The first man we saw on the island was an Indian named Joseph Polis, whom my relative had known from a boy, and now addressed familiarly as "Joe." He was dressing a deer-skin in his yard. The skin was spread over a slanting log, and he was scraping it with a stick, held by both hands. He was stoutly built, perhaps a little above the middle height, with a broad face, and, as others said, perfect Indian features and complexion.[1] His house was a two-story white one, with blinds, the best looking that I noticed there, and as good as an average one on a New England village street. It was surrounded by a garden and fruit-trees, single cornstalks standing thinly amid the beans.

We asked him if he knew any good Indian who would like to go into the woods with us, that is, to the Allegash Lakes, by way of Moosehead, and return by the East Branch of the Penobscot, or vary from this as we pleased. To which he answered, out of that strange remoteness in which the Indian ever dwells to the white man, "Me like to go myself; me want to get some moose;" and kept on scraping the skin. His brother had been into the woods with my relative only a year or two before, and the Indian now inquired what the latter had done to him, that he did not come back, for he had not seen nor heard from him since.

At length we got round to the more interesting topic again. The ferryman had told us that all the best Indians were gone

---

[1] Thoreau recorded in his Journal under date of July 31, 1857: P. (Polis) said that his mother was a Province woman and as white as anybody, but his father a pure-blooded Indian. I saw no trace of white blood in his face, and others, who knew him well and also his father, were confident that his mother was an Indian and suggested that she was of the Quoddy tribe (belonged to New Brunswick), who are often quite light-colored.

except Polis, who was one of the aristocracy. He to be sure would be the best man we could have, but if he went at all would want a great price; so we did not expect to get him. Polis asked at first two dollars a day, but agreed to go for a dollar and a half, and fifty cents a week for his canoe. He would come to Bangor with his canoe by the seven o'clock train that evening,—we might depend on him. We thought ourselves lucky to secure the services of this man, who was known to be particularly steady and trust-worthy.

I spent the afternoon with my companion, who had re-mained in Bangor, in preparing for our expedition, purchas-ing provisions, hard bread, pork, coffee, sugar, etc., and some India-rubber clothing.[1]

We had at first thought of exploring the St. John from its source to its mouth, or else to go up the Penobscot by its East Branch to the lakes of the St. John, and return by way of Chesuncook and Moosehead. We had finally inclined to the last route, only reversing the order of it, going by way of Moosehead, and returning by the Penobscot, otherwise it would have been all the way up stream and taken twice as long.

At evening the Indian arrived in the cars, and I led the way while he followed me three quarters of a mile to my friend's house, with the canoe on his head.[2] I did not know the exact route myself, but steered by the lay of the land,

---

[1] Thoreau's detailed description of his outfit will be found in the Appendix on page 333.

[2] A common sight in the Maine woods. The canoeman steps to the side of his canoe. He grasps the middle thwart with his right hand at the near gun-wale and his left hand at the far gunwale. Then he raises the craft until her bilge rests on his right thigh. Of a sudden there is a heave timed to a quick shift of stance to the left. The canoe is now bottom side up with the middle thwart sliding over his right shoulder. Now he is ready to "walk away with her." Thoreau at a later stage describes (p. 53) the Indian's ingenious method of toting his birch on the carries.

as I do in Boston, and I tried to enter into conversation with
him, but as he was puffing under the weight of his canoe,
not having the usual apparatus for carrying it, but, above
all, was an Indian, I might as well have been thumping on
the bottom of his birch the while. In answer to the various
observations which I made by way of breaking the ice, he
only grunted vaguely from beneath his canoe once or twice,
so that I knew he was there.

Early the next morning the stage called for us, the Indian having breakfasted with us, and already placed the
baggage in the canoe to see how it would go. My companion
and I had each a large knapsack as full as it would hold, and
we had two large India-rubber bags which held our provision and utensils. As for the Indian, all the baggage he had,
beside his axe and gun, was a blanket, which he brought
loose in his hand. However, he had laid in a store of tobacco
and a new pipe for the excursion. The canoe was securely
lashed diagonally across the top of the stage, with bits of
carpet tucked under the edge to prevent its chafing. The very
accommodating driver appeared as much accustomed to
carrying canoes in this way as bandboxes.

We went by the Avenue Road, which is quite straight
and very good, northwestward toward Moosehead Lake,
through more than a dozen flourishing towns, with almost
every one its academy,—not one of which, however, is on
my General Atlas, published, alas! in 1824; so much are they
before the age, or I behind it! The earth must have been
considerably lighter to the shoulders of General Atlas then.

It rained all this day and till the middle of the next forenoon, concealing the landscape almost entirely; but we had
hardly got out of the streets of Bangor before I began to
be exhilarated by the sight of the wild fir and spruce tops,

and those of other primitive evergreens, peering through the mist in the horizon. It was like the sight and odor of cake to a schoolboy. The beauty of the road itself was remarkable. The various evergreens, many of which are rare with us,—delicate and beautiful specimens of the larch, arbor-vitæ, ball-spruce, and fir-balsam, from a few inches to many feet in height,—lined its sides.

He who rides and keeps the beaten track studies the fences chiefly. Near Bangor, the fence-posts, on account of the frost's heaving them in the clayey soil, were not planted in the ground, but were mortised into a transverse horizontal beam lying on the surface. Afterwards, the prevailing fences were log ones, with sometimes a Virginia fence, or else rails slanted over crossed stakes,—and these zigzagged or played leap-frog all the way to the lake, keeping just ahead of us.

After getting out of the Penobscot valley, the country was unexpectedly level, or consisted of very even and equal swells, for twenty or thirty miles, never rising above the general level, but affording, it is said, a very good prospect in clear weather, with frequent views of Ktaadn,—straight roads and long hills. The houses were far apart, commonly small and of one story, but framed. There was very little land under cultivation, yet the forest did not often border the road. The stumps were frequently as high as one's head, showing the depth of the snows. The white hay-caps, drawn over small stacks of beans or corn in the fields on account of the rain, were a novel sight to me. We saw large flocks of pigeons, and several times came within a rod or two of partridges in the road. My companion said that in one journey out of Bangor he and his son had shot sixty partridges from his buggy.

The mountain-ash was now very handsome, as also the wayfarer's-tree or hobble-bush, with its ripe purple berries mixed with red. The Canada thistle, an introduced plant, was the prevailing weed all the way to the lake,—the roadside in many places, and fields not long cleared, being densely filled with it as with a crop, to the exclusion of everything else. There were also whole fields full of ferns, now rusty and withering, which in older countries are commonly confined to wet ground. There were very few flowers, even allowing for the lateness of the season. It chanced that I saw no asters in bloom along the road for fifty miles, though they were so abundant then in Massachusetts,—except in one place one or two of the Aster acuminatus,—and no goldenrods till within twenty miles of Monson, where I saw a three-ribbed one. There were many late buttercups, however, and the two fire-weeds, Erechthites and Epilobium, commonly where there had been a burning, and at last the pearly everlasting.

I noticed occasionally very long troughs which supplied the road with water, and my companion said that three dollars annually were granted by the State to one man in each school-district, who provided and maintained a suitable water-trough by the roadside, for the use of travelers,—a piece of intelligence as refreshing to me as the water itself. That legislature did not sit in vain. It was an Oriental act, which made me wish that I was still farther down East,—another Maine law, which I hope we may get in Massachusetts. That State is banishing barrooms from its highways, and conducting the mountain springs thither.

The country was first decidedly mountainous in Garland, Sangerville, and onwards, twenty-five or thirty miles from Bangor. At Sangerville, where we stopped at mid-afternoon to warm and dry ourselves, the landlord told us that he had found a wilderness where we found him. At a fork in the road between Abbot and Monson, about twenty miles from

Moosehead Lake, I saw a guide-post surmounted by a pair
of moose horns, spreading four or five feet, with the word

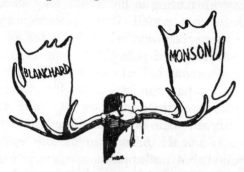

"Monson" painted on one blade, and the name of some other
town on the other.[1] They are sometimes used for ornamental
hat-trees, together with deers' horns, in front entries; but,
after the experience which I shall relate, I trust that I shall
have a better excuse for killing a moose than that I may hang
my hat on his horns. We reached Monson, fifty miles from
Bangor, and thirteen from the lake, after dark.

*In order to give as complete a picture as possible of the
Maine countryside as Thoreau saw it, the accounts of all three
of his trips have been drawn upon in the preceding pages.
On the last trip in July, 1857, he noted that this was the third
time he had passed over this route. From this point on, however, the text follows the account of this third trip on which
his companions were Edward Hoar and their Indian guide,
Joe Polis. Thoreau also remarked that it was raining steadily.
"The stage," he said, "was crowded all the way, and I attended the more to my fellow travelers." He continued:*

If you had looked inside this coach you would have
thought that we were prepared to run the gauntlet of a band

---

[1] This fork is known today as Moosehorns, and the antlers of a bull moose—
though not the original ones—still point the way.

of robbers, for there were four or five guns on the front seat, the Indian's included, and one or two on the back one, each man holding his darling in his arms. One had a gun which carried twelve to a pound. It appeared that this party of hunters was going our way, but much farther down the Allegash and St. John, and thence up some other stream, and across to the Ristigouche and the Bay of Chaleur, to be gone six weeks. They had canoes, axes, and supplies deposited some distance along the route. They carried flour, and were to have new bread made every day.

Their leader was a handsome man about thirty years old, of good height, but not apparently robust, of gentlemanly address and faultless toilet; such a one as you might expect to meet on Broadway. In fact, in the popular sense of the word, he was the most "gentlemanly" appearing man in the stage, or that we saw on the road. He had a fair white complexion, as if he had always lived in the shade, and an intellectual face, and with his quiet manners might have passed for a divinity student who had seen something of the world. I was surprised to find, on talking with him in the course of the day's journey, that he was a hunter at all,—for his gun was not much exposed,—and yet more to find that he was probably the chief white hunter of Maine, and was known all along the road. He had also hunted in some of the States farther south and west. I afterwards heard him spoken of as one who could endure a great deal of exposure and fatigue without showing the effect of it; and he could not only use guns, but make them, being himself a gunsmith.[1]

In the spring, he had saved a stage-driver and two passengers from drowning in the backwater of the Piscataquis in Foxcroft on this road, having swum ashore in the freezing water and made a raft and got them off,—though the horses

---

[1] This gentleman was Hiram L. Leonard, long famed among anglers for his excellent fishing rods.

were drowned,—at great risk to himself, while the only other man who could swim withdrew to the nearest house to prevent freezing. He could now ride over this road for nothing. He knew our man, and remarked that we had a good Indian there, a good hunter; adding that he was said to be worth $6000. The Indian also knew him, and said to me, "the great hunter." The former told me that he practiced a kind of still hunting, new or uncommon in those parts; that the caribou, for instance, fed round and round the same meadow, returning on the same path, and he lay in wait for them.

The Indian sat on the front seat, saying nothing to anybody, with a stolid expression of face, as if barely awake to what was going on. Again I was struck by the peculiar vagueness of his replies when addressed in the stage, or at the taverns. He really never said anything on such occasions. He was merely stirred up, like a wild beast, and passively muttered some insignificant response. His answer, in such cases, was never the consequence of a positive mental energy, but vague as a puff of smoke, suggesting no *responsibility,* and if you considered it, you would find that you had got nothing out of him. This was instead of the conventional palaver and smartness of the white man, and equally profitable.

Most get no more than this out of the Indian, and pronounce him stolid accordingly. I was surprised to see what a foolish and impertinent style a Maine man, a passenger, used in addressing him, as if he were a child, which only made his eyes glisten a little. A tipsy Canadian asked him at a tavern, in a drawling tone, if he smoked, to which he answered with an indefinite "yes." "Won't you lend me your pipe a little while?" asked the other. He replied, looking straight by the man's head, with a face singularly vacant to all neighboring interests, "Me got no pipe;" yet I had seen him put a new one, with a supply of tobacco, into his pocket that morning.

Our little canoe, so neat and strong, drew a favorable criticism from all the wiseacres among the tavern loungers along the road. By the roadside, close to the wheels, I noticed a splendid great purple-fringed orchis with a spike as big as an epilobium, which I would fain have stopped the stage to pluck, but the driver would probably have thought it a waste of time.[1]

When we reached the lake, about half past eight in the evening, it was still steadily raining, and harder than before; and, in that fresh, cool atmosphere, the hylodes [frogs] were peeping and the toads singing about the lake universally, as in the spring with us. It was as if the season had revolved backward two or three months, or I had arrived at the abode of perpetual spring.

We had expected to go upon the lake at once, and, after paddling up two or three miles, to camp on one of its islands; but on account of the steady and increasing rain, we decided to go to one of the taverns for the night, though, for my own part, I should have preferred to camp out.[2]

---

[1] The handsomest and most interesting flowers were the great purple orchises, rising ever and anon, with their great purple spikes perfectly erect, amid the shrubs and grasses of the shore. It seemed strange that they should be made to grow there in such profusion, seen of moose and moose-hunters only, while they are so rare in Concord. I have never seen this species flowering nearly so late with us, or with the small one.

[2] On his trip in 1853 Thoreau had reached Greenville at the foot of Moosehead Lake in the daytime. His description is set forth in the Appendix on page 321.

2. Crossing Moosehead in a Birch

ABOUT four o'clock the next morning, though it was quite cloudy, accompanied by the landlord to the water's edge, in the twilight, we launched our canoe from a rock on the Moosehead Lake. When I was there four years before, we had a rather small canoe for three persons, and I had thought that this time I would get a larger one, but the present one was even smaller than that. It was 18¼ feet long by 2 feet 6½ inches wide in the middle, and one foot deep within, so I found by measurement, and I judged that it would weigh not far from eighty pounds. The Indian had recently made it himself, and its smallness was partly compensated for by its newness, as well as stanchness and solidity, it being made of very thick bark and ribs.

Our baggage weighed about 166 pounds, so that the canoe carried about 600 pounds in all, or the weight of four men.

The principal part of the baggage was, as usual, placed in the middle of the broadest part, while we stowed ourselves in the chinks and crannies that were left before and behind it, where there was no room to extend our legs, the loose articles being tucked into the ends. The canoe was thus as closely packed as a market-basket, and might possibly have been upset without spilling any of its contents. The Indian sat on a cross-bar in the stern, but we flat on the bottom, with a splint or chip behind our backs, to protect them from the cross-bar, and one of us commonly paddled with the Indian. He foresaw that we should not want a pole till we reached the Umbazookskus River, it being either dead water or down stream so far, and he was prepared to make a sail of his blanket in the bows if the wind should be fair; but we never used it.

It had rained more or less the four previous days, so that we thought we might count on some fair weather. The wind was at first southwesterly. Paddling along the eastern side of the lake in the still of the morning, we soon saw a few sheldrakes, which the Indian called *Shecorways,* and some peetweets, *Naramekechus,* on the rocky shore; we also saw and heard loons, *Medawisla,* which he said was a sign of wind. It was inspiriting to hear the regular dip of the paddles, as if they were our fins or flappers, and to realize that we were at length fairly embarked. We who had felt strangely as stage-passengers and tavern-lodgers were suddenly naturalized there and presented with the freedom of the lakes and the woods.

Having passed the small rocky isles within two or three miles of the foot of the lake, we had a short consultation respecting our course, and inclined to the western shore for the sake of its lee; for otherwise, if the wind should rise, it would be impossible for us to reach Mount Kineo, which is about midway up the lake on the east side, but at its narrowest part, where probably we could recross if we took the western side. The wind is the chief obstacle to crossing the lakes, especially in so small a canoe. The Indian remarked several times that he did not like to cross the lakes "in littlum canoe," but nevertheless, "just as we say, it made no odds to him." He sometimes took a straight course up the middle of the lake between Sugar and Deer islands, when there was no wind.

Measured on the map, Moosehead Lake is twelve miles wide at the widest place, and thirty miles long in a direct line, but longer as it lies. The captain of the steamer called it thirty-eight miles as he steered. We should probably go about forty. The Indian said that it was called "*Mspame*, because large water." Squaw Mountain rose darkly on our left, near the outlet of the Kennebec, and what the Indian called Spencer Bay Mountain, on the east, and already we saw Mount Kineo before us in the north.

Paddling near the shore, we frequently heard the *pe-pe* of the olive-sided flycatcher, also the wood-pewee, and the

kingfisher, thus early in the morning. The Indian reminding us that he could not work without eating, we stopped to breakfast on the main shore, southwest of Deer Island, at a spot where the *Mimulus ringens* [monkey-flower] [1] grew abundantly. We took out our bags, and the Indian made a fire under a very large bleached log, using white-pine bark from a stump, though he said that hemlock was better, and kindling with canoe-birch bark. Our table was a large piece of freshly peeled birch-bark, laid wrong side up, and our breakfast consisted of hard bread, fried pork, and strong coffee, well sweetened, in which we did not miss the milk.

While we were getting breakfast a brood of twelve black dippers, half grown, came paddling by within three or four rods, not at all alarmed; and they loitered about as long as we stayed, now huddled close together, within a circle of eighteen inches in diameter, now moving off in a long line, very cunningly. Yet they bore a certain proportion to the great Moosehead Lake on whose bosom they floated, and I felt as if they were under its protection.

Looking northward from this place it appeared as if we were entering a large bay, and we did not know whether we should be obliged to diverge from our course and keep outside a point which we saw, or should find a passage between this and the mainland. I consulted my map and used my glass, and the Indian did the same, but we could not find our place exactly on the map, nor could we detect any break in the shore. When I asked the Indian the way, he answered "I don't know," which I thought remarkable, since he had said that he was familiar with the lake; but it appeared that he had never been up this side.

It was misty dog-day weather, and we had already penetrated a smaller bay of the same kind, and knocked the bot-

---

[1] The translation has been supplied from Thoreau's Lists of Flowers and Shrubs and of Plants, which he states: "I noticed in the Maine woods, in the years 1853 and 1857." Such interpolations in the text have been placed in square brackets.

tom out of it, though we had been obliged to pass over a small
bar, between an island and the shore, where there was but
just breadth and depth enough to float the canoe, and the
Indian had observed, "Very easy makum bridge here," but
now it seemed that, if we held on, we should be fairly em-
bayed. Presently, however, though we had not stirred, the
mist lifted somewhat, and revealed a break in the shore northward, showing that the point was a portion of Deer Island,
and that our course lay westward of it.

Where it had seemed a continuous shore even through
a glass, one portion was now seen by the naked eye to be
much more distant than the other which overlapped it,
merely by the greater thickness of the mist which still rested
on it, while the nearer or island portion was comparatively
bare and green. The line of separation was very distinct, and
the Indian immediately remarked, "I guess you and I go
there,—I guess there's room for my canoe there." This was
his common expression instead of saying we. He never addressed us by our names, though curious to know how they
were spelled and what they meant, while we called him Polis.
He had already guessed very accurately at our ages, and said
that he was forty-eight.

After breakfast I emptied the melted pork that was left
into the lake, making what sailors call a "slick," and watching
to see how much it spread over and smoothed the agitated
surface. The Indian looked at it a moment and said, "That
make hard paddlum thro'; hold 'em canoe. So say old times."

We hastily reloaded, putting the dishes loose in the bows,
that they might be at hand when wanted, and set out again.
The western shore, near which we paddled along, rose gently
to a considerable height, and was everywhere densely covered with the forest, in which was a large proportion of hard
wood to enliven and relieve the fir and spruce.

The Indian said that the usnea lichen which we saw hanging from the trees was called *chorchorque*. We asked him the names of several small birds which we heard this morning. The wood-thrush, which was quite common, and whose note he imitated, he said was called *Adelungquamooktum;* but sometimes he could not tell the name of some small bird which I heard and knew, but he said, "I tell all the birds about here,—this country; can't tell littlum noise, but I see 'em, then I can tell."

I observed that I should like to go to school to him to learn his language, living on the Indian island the while; could not that be done? "Oh, yer," he replied, "good many do so." I asked how long he thought it would take. He said one week. I told him that in this voyage I would tell him all I knew, and he should tell me all he knew, to which he readily agreed.

The birds sang quite as in our woods,—the red-eye, red-start, veery, wood-pewee, etc., but we saw no bluebirds in all our journey, and several told me in Bangor that they had not the bluebird there. Mount Kineo, which was generally visible, though occasionally concealed by islands or the mainland in front, had a level bar of cloud concealing its summit, and all the mountain-tops about the lake were cut off at the same height. Ducks of various kinds,—sheldrake, summer ducks, etc.,—were quite common, and ran over the water before us as fast as a horse trots. Thus they were soon out of sight.

The Indian asked the meaning of *reality*, as near as I could make out the word, which he said one of us had used; also of *"interrent,"* that is, intelligent. I observed that he could rarely sound the letter r, but used l, as also r for l sometimes; as *load* for road, *pickelel* for pickerel, *Soogle* Island for Sugar Island, *lock* for rock, etc. Yet he trilled the r pretty well after me.

He generally added the syllable *um* to his words when he could,—as pad*lum*, etc. I have once heard a Chippewa lecture, who made his audience laugh unintentionally by putting *ne* after the word *too,* which word he brought in continually and unnecessarily, accenting and prolonging this sound into *m ar* sonorously as if it were necessary to bring in so much of his vernacular as a relief to his organs, a compensation for twisting his jaws about, and putting his tongue into every corner of his mouth, as he complained that he was obliged to do when he spoke English. There was so much of the Indian accent resounding through his English, so much of the "bow-arrow tang" as my neighbor calls it, and I have no doubt that word seemed to him the best pronounced. It was a wild and refreshing sound, like that of the wind among the pines, or the booming of the surf on the shore.

I asked him the meaning of the word *Musketicook,* the Indian name of Concord River. He pronounced it *Muskéeticook,* emphasizing the second syllable with a peculiar guttural sound, and said that it meant "Dead-water," which it is, and in this definition he agreed exactly with the St. Francis Indian with whom I talked in 1853.

On a point on the mainland some miles southwest of Sandbar Island, where we landed to stretch our legs and look at the vegetation, going inland a few steps, I discovered a fire still glowing beneath its ashes, where somebody had breakfasted, and a bed of twigs prepared for the following night. So I knew not only that they had just left, but that they designed to return, and by the breadth of the bed that there was more than one in the party. You might have gone within six feet of these signs without seeing them. There grew the beaked hazel, the only hazel which I saw on this journey, the *Diervilla,* rue seven feet high, which was very abundant on all the lake and river shores, and *Cornus stolonifera,* or red osier, whose bark, the Indian said, was good to smoke, and was called *maquoxigill,* "tobacco before white people came to this country, Indian tobacco."

The Indian was always very careful in approaching the shore, lest he should injure his canoe on the rocks, letting it swing round slowly sidewise, and was still more particular that we should not step into it on shore, nor till it floated free, and then should step gently lest we should open its seams, or make a hole in the bottom. He said that he would tell us when to jump.

Soon after leaving this point we passed the mouth of the Kennebec, and heard and saw the falls at the dam there, for even Moosehead Lake is dammed. After passing Deer Island, we saw the little steamer from Greenville, far east in the middle of the lake, she appeared nearly stationary. Sometimes we could hardly tell her from an island which had a few trees on it. Here we were exposed to the wind from over the whole breadth of the lake, and ran a little risk of being swamped. While I had my eye fixed on the spot where a large fish had leaped, we took in a gallon or two of water, which filled my lap; but we soon reached the shore and took the canoe over the bar, at Sand-bar Island, a few feet wide only, and so saved a considerable distance. One landed first at a more sheltered place, and walking round caught the canoe by the prow, to prevent it being injured against the shore.

Again we crossed a broad bay opposite the mouth of Moose River, before reaching the narrow strait at Mount Kineo, made what the voyageurs call a *traverse*, and found the water quite rough. A very little wind on these broad lakes raises a sea which will swamp a canoe. Looking off from a lee shore, the surface may appear to be very little agitated, almost smooth, a mile distant, or if you see a few white crests they appear nearly level with the rest of the lake; but when you get out so far, you may find quite a sea running, and erelong, before you think of it, a wave will gently creep up the side of the canoe and fill your lap, like a monster deliberately covering you with its slime before it swallows you, or it will strike the canoe violently, and break into it.

The same thing may happen when the wind rises suddenly, though it were perfectly calm and smooth there a few minutes before; so that nothing can save you, unless you can swim ashore, for it is impossible to get into a canoe again when it is upset. Since you sit flat on the bottom, though the danger should not be imminent, a little water is a great inconvenience, not to mention the wetting of your provisions. We rarely crossed even a bay directly, from point to point, when there was wind, but made a slight curve corresponding somewhat to the shore, that we might the sooner reach it if the wind increased. When the wind is aft, and not too strong, the Indian makes a sprit-sail of his blanket. He thus easily skims over the whole length of this lake in a day.

The Indian paddled on one side, and one of us on the other, to keep the canoe steady, and when he wanted to change hands he would say "t' other side." He asserted, in answer to our questions, that he had never upset a canoe himself, though he may have been upset by others. Think of our little eggshell of a canoe tossing across that great lake, a mere black speck to the eagle soaring above it.

My companion trailed for trout as we paddled along, but the Indian warning him that a big fish might upset us, for there are some very large ones there, he agreed to pass the line quickly to him in the stern if he had a bite. Beside trout, I heard of cusk, white-fish, etc., as found in this lake.[1]

While we were crossing this bay, where Mount Kineo rose

---

[1] In 1945 the Maine Department of Inland Fisheries and Game reported a collection of twenty-one species of fish from the waters and tributaries of Moosehead. The larger included togue or lake trout, brook or squaretail trout, two varieties of whitefish—common and Menominee—cusk, and common and fine-scaled suckers. The smaller varieties included smelt and three-spined stickleback. In addition there have been introduced into the Lake, which has been stocked since 1895, the ouananiche or landlocked salmon, and the Chinook salmon.

dark before us, within two or three miles, the Indian repeated the tradition respecting this mountain's having anciently been a cow moose,—how a mighty Indian hunter,

whose name I forget, succeeding in killing this queen of the
moose tribe with great difficulty, while her calf was killed
somewhere among the islands in Penobscot Bay, and, to his
eyes, this mountain had still the form of the moose in a re-
clining posture, its precipitous side presenting the outline of
her head. He told this at some length, though it did not
amount to much, and with apparent good faith, and asked
us how we supposed the hunter could have killed such a
mighty moose as that,—how we could do it. Whereupon a
man-of-war to fire broadsides into her was suggested, etc.
An Indian tells such a story as if he thought it deserved to
have a good deal said about it, only he has not got it to say,
and so he makes up for the deficiency by a drawling tone,
long-windedness, and a dumb wonder which he hopes will
be contagious.

We approached the land again through pretty rough
water, and then steered directly across the lake, at its narrowest part, to the eastern side, and were soon partly under
the lee of the mountain, about a mile north of the Kineo
House, having paddled about twenty miles. It was now about
noon. We designed to stop there that afternoon and night,
and spent half an hour looking along the shore northward for
a suitable place to camp. We took out all our baggage at one

place in vain, it being too rocky and uneven, and while engaged in this search we made our first acquaintance with the moose-fly.

At length, half a mile farther north, by going half a dozen rods into the dense spruce and fir wood on the side of the mountain, almost as dark as a cellar, we found a place sufficiently clear and level to lie down on, after cutting away a few bushes. We required a space only seven feet by six for our bed, the fire being four or five feet in front, though it made no odds how rough the hearth was; but it was not always easy to find this in those woods. The Indian first cleared a path to it from the shore with his axe, and we then carried up all our baggage, pitched our tent, and made our bed, in order to be ready for foul weather, which then threatened us, and for the night. He gathered a large armful of fir twigs, breaking them off, which he said were the best for our bed, partly, I thought, because they were the largest and could be most rapidly collected. It had been raining more or less for four or five days, and the wood was even damper than usual, but he got dry bark for the fire from the under side of a dead leaning hemlock, which, he said, he could always do.

This noon his mind was occupied with a law question, and I referred him to my companion, who was a lawyer. It appeared that he had been buying land lately (I think it was a hundred acres), but there was probably an incumbrance to it, somebody else claiming to have bought some grass on it for this year. He wished to know to whom the grass belonged, and was told that if the other man could prove that he bought the grass before he, Polis, bought the land, the former could take it, whether the latter knew it or not. To which he only answered, "Strange!" He went over this several times, fairly sat down to it, with his back to a tree, as if he meant to confine us to this topic henceforth; but as he made no headway, only reached the jumping-off place of his wonder at white men's institutions after each explanation, we let the subject die.

He said that he had fifty acres of grass, potatoes, etc., some-where above Oldtown, beside some about his house; that he hired a good deal of his work, hoeing, etc., and preferred white men to Indians, because "they keep steady, and know how."

After dinner we returned southward along the shore, in the canoe, on account of the difficulty of climbing over the rocks and fallen trees, and began to ascend the mountain along the edge of the precipice. But a smart shower coming up just then, the Indian crept under his canoe, while we, be-ing protected by our rubber coats, proceeded to botanize. So we sent him back to the camp for shelter, agreeing that he should come there for us with his canoe toward night. It had rained a little in the forenoon, and we trusted that this would be the clearing-up shower, which it proved; but our feet and legs were thoroughly wet by the bushes.

The clouds breaking away a little, we had a glorious wild view, as we ascended, of the broad lake with its fluctuating surface and numerous forest-clad islands, extending beyond our sight both north and south, and the boundless forest undulating away from its shores on every side, as densely packed as a rye-field, and enveloping nameless mountains in succession; but above all, looking westward over a large island was visible a very distant part of the lake, though we did not then suspect it to be Moosehead,—at first a mere broken white line seen through the tops of the island trees, like hay-caps, but spreading to a lake when we got higher. Beyond this we saw what appears to be called Bald Mountain on the map, some twenty-five miles distant, near the sources of the Penobscot. It was a perfect lake of the woods. But this was only a transient gleam, for the rain was not quite over.

Looking southward, the heavens were completely overcast, the mountains capped with clouds, and the lake generally wore a dark and stormy appearance, but from its surface just north of Sugar Island, six or eight miles distant, there was reflected upward to us through the misty air a bright blue tinge from the distant unseen sky of another latitude beyond. They probably had a clear sky then at Greenville, the south end of the lake. Standing on a mountain in the midst of a lake, where would you look for the first sign of approaching fair weather? Not into the heavens, it seems, but into the lake.

Again we mistook a little rocky inlet seen through the "drisk," [1] with some taller bare trunks or stumps on it, for the steamer with its smoke-pipes, but as it had not changed its position after half an hour, we were undeceived. So much do the works of man resemble the works of nature. A moose might mistake a steamer for a floating isle, and not be scared till he heard its puffing or its whistle.

If I wished to see a mountain or other scenery under the most favorable auspices, I would go to it in foul weather, so as to be there when it cleared up; we are then in the most suitable mood, and nature is most fresh and inspiring. There is no serenity so fair as that which is just established in a tearful eye.

Jackson, in his Report on the Geology of Maine, in 1838, says of this mountain: "Hornstone, which will answer for flints, occurs in various parts of the State, where trap-rocks have acted upon silicious slate. The largest mass of this stone known in the world is Mount Kineo, upon Moosehead Lake,

---

[1] Thoreau had come upon this interesting bit of dialect on his last excursion on Cape Cod a few weeks before. At Truro, on June 18, 1857, his Journal records:

A mizzling and rainy day with thick driving fog; a drizzling rain, or "drisk," as one called it.

which appears to be entirely composed of it, and rises seven hundred feet above the lake level. This variety of hornstone I have seen in every part of New England in the form of Indian arrow-heads, hatchets, chisels, etc., which were probably obtained from this mountain by the aboriginal inhabitants of the country."

I have myself found hundreds of arrow-heads made of the same material. It is generally slate-colored, with white specks, becoming a uniform white where exposed to the light and air, and it breaks with a conchoidal fracture, producing a ragged cutting edge. I noticed some conchoidal hollows more than a foot in diameter. I picked up a small thin piece which had so sharp an edge that I used it as a dull knife, and to see what I could do, fairly cut off an aspen one inch thick with it, by bending it and making many cuts; though I cut my fingers badly with the back of it in the mean while.

From the summit of the precipice which forms the southern and eastern sides of this mountain peninsula, and is its most remarkable feature, being described as five or six hundred feet high, we looked, and probably might have jumped down to the water, or to the seemingly dwarfish trees on the narrow neck of land which connects it with the main. It is a dangerous place to try the steadiness of your nerves. Hodge says that these cliffs descend "perpendicularly ninety feet" below the surface of the water.[1]

The plants which chiefly attracted our attention on this mountain were the mountain cinquefoil (*Potentilla tridentata*), abundant and in bloom still at the very base, by the water-side, though it is usually confined to the summits of mountains in our latitude; very beautiful hare-bells overhanging the precipice; bear-berry; the Canada blueberry (*Vaccinium Canadense*), similar to (the *V. Pennsylvanicum*) our

---

[1] Thoreau's description of Mount Kineo in 1853 will be found in the Appendix on page 322.

earliest one, but entire leaved and with a downy stem and leaf; I have not seen it in Massachusetts; *Diervilla trifida* [bush honeysuckle]; *Microstylis ophioglossoides* [adder's-mouth], an orchidaceous plant new to us; wild holly (*Nemopanthes Canadensis*); the great round-leaved orchis (*Platanthera orbiculata*), not long in bloom; *Spiranthes cernua* [ladies' tresses], at the top; bunch-berry, reddening as we ascended, green at the base of the mountain, red at the top; and the small fern, *Woodsia ilvensis,* growing in tufts, now in fruit. I have also received *Liparis liliifolia,* or tway-blade, from this spot.

Having explored the wonders of the mountain, and the weather being now entirely cleared up, we commenced the descent. We met the Indian, puffing and panting, about one third of the way up, but thinking that he must be near the top, and saying that it took his breath away. I thought that superstition had something to do with his fatigue. Perhaps he believed that he was climbing over the back of a tremendous moose. He said that he had never ascended Kineo. On reaching the canoe we found that he had caught a lake trout weighing about three pounds, at the depth of twenty-five or thirty feet, while we were on the mountain.

When we got to the camp, the canoe was taken out and turned over, and a log laid across it to prevent its being blown away. The Indian cut some large logs of damp and rotten hard wood to smoulder and keep fire through the night. The trout was fried for supper. Our tent was of thin cotton cloth and quite small, forming with the ground a triangular prism closed at the rear end, six feet long, seven wide, and four high, so that we could barely sit up in the middle. It required two forked stakes, a smooth ridge-pole, and a dozen or more pins to pitch it. It kept off dew and wind, and an ordinary rain, and answered our purpose well enough. We reclined within it till bedtime, each with his baggage at his head, or else sat about the fire, having hung our wet clothes on a pole before the fire for the night.

As we sat there, just before night, looking out through the dusky wood, the Indian heard a noise which he said was made by a snake. He imitated it at my request, making a low whistling note,—*pheet—pheet,*—two or three times repeated, somewhat like the peep of the hylodes, but not so loud. In answer to my inquiries, he said that he had never seen them while making it, but going to the spot he finds the snake. This, he said on another occasion, was a sign of rain. When I had selected this place for our camp, he had remarked that there were snakes there,—he saw them. But they won't do any hurt, I said. "Oh, no," he answered, "just as you say, it makes no difference to me."

He lay on the right side of the tent, because, as he said, he was partly deaf in one ear, and he wanted to lie with his good ear up. As we lay there, he inquired if I ever heard "Indian sing." I replied that I had not often, and asked him if he would not favor us with a song. He readily assented, and lying on his back, with his blanket wrapped around him, he commenced a slow, somewhat nasal, yet musical chant, in his own language, which probably was taught his tribe long ago by the Catholic missionaries. He translated it to us, sentence by sentence, afterward, wishing to see if we could remember it. It proved to be a very simple religious exercise or hymn, the burden of which was, that there was only one God who ruled all the world. This was hammered (or sung) out very thin, so that some stanzas wellnigh meant nothing at all, merely keeping up the idea. He then said that he would sing us a Latin song; but we did not detect any Latin, only one or two Greek words in it,—the rest may have been Latin with the Indian pronunciation.

His singing carried me back to the period of the discovery of America, to San Salvador and the Incas, when Europeans first encountered the simple faith of the Indian. There was, indeed, a beautiful simplicity about it; nothing of the dark and savage, only the mild and infantile. The sentiments of humility and reverence chiefly were expressed.

It was a dense and damp spruce and fir wood in which we lay, and, except for our fire, perfectly dark; and when I awoke in the night, I either heard an owl from deeper in the forest behind us, or a loon from a distance over the lake. Getting up some time after midnight to collect the scattered brands together, while my companions were sound asleep, I observed, partly in the fire, which had ceased to blaze, a perfectly regular elliptical ring of light, about five inches in its shortest diameter, six or seven in its longer, and from one eighth to one quarter of an inch wide. It was fully as bright as the fire, but not reddish or scarlet, like a coal, but a white and slumbering light, like the glowworm's. I could tell it from the fire only by its whiteness.

I saw at once that it must be phosphorescent wood, which I had so often heard of, but never chanced to see. Putting my finger on it, with a little hesitation, I found that it was a piece of dead moose-wood (*Acer striatum*) which the Indian had cut off in a slanting direction the evening before. Using my knife, I discovered that the light proceeded from that portion of the sap-wood immediately under the bark, and thus presented a regular ring at the end, which, indeed, appeared raised above the level of the wood, and when I pared off the bark and cut into the sap, it was all aglow along the log. I was surprised to find the wood quite hard and apparently sound, though probably decay had commenced in the sap, and I cut out some little triangular chips, and, placing them in the hollow of my hand, carried them into the camp, waked my companion, and showed them to him. They lit up the inside of my hand, revealing the lines and wrinkles, and appearing exactly like coals of fire raised to a white heat, and I saw at

once how, probably, the Indian jugglers had imposed on their people and on travelers, pretending to hold coals of fire in their mouths.

I also noticed that part of a decayed stump within four or five feet of the fire, an inch wide and six inches long, soft and shaking wood, shone with equal brightness. I neglected to ascertain whether our fire had anything to do with this, but the previous day's rain and long-continued wet weather undoubtedly had. I was exceedingly interested by this phenomenon, and already felt paid for my journey. It could hardly have thrilled me more if it had taken the form of letters, or of the human face. If I had met with this ring of light while groping in this forest alone, away from any fire, I should have been still more surprised. I little thought that there was such a light shining in the darkness of the wilderness for me.

The next day the Indian told me their name for this light, —*Artoosoqu'*,—and on my inquiring concerning the will-o'-the-wisp, and the like phenomena, he said that his "folks" sometimes saw fires passing along at various heights, even as high as the trees, and making a noise. I was prepared after this to hear of the most startling and unimagined phenomena, witnessed by "his folks;" they are abroad at all hours and seasons in scenes so unfrequented by white men. Nature must have made a thousand revelations to them which are still secrets to us.

I did not regret my not having seen this before, since I now saw it under circumstances so favorable. I was in just the frame of mind to see something wonderful, and this was a phenomenon adequate to my circumstances and expectation, and it put me on the alert to see more like it. I exulted like "a pagan suckled in a creed" that had never been worn at all, but was bran new, and adequate to the occasion. I let science slide, and rejoiced in that light as if it had been a fellow-creature. I saw that it was excellent, and was very glad to know that it was so cheap. A scientific *explanation,* as it is called, would have been altogether out of place there. That is for pale daylight. Science with its retorts would have put me to sleep; it was the opportunity to be ignorant that I improved. It suggested to me that there was something to be seen if one had eyes.

It made a believer of me more than before. I believed that the woods were not tenantless, but choke-full of honest spirits as good as myself any day,—not an empty chamber, in which chemistry was left to work alone, but an inhabited house,— and for a few moments I enjoyed fellowship with them. Your so-called wise man goes trying to persuade himself that there is no entity there but himself and his traps, but it is a great deal easier to believe the truth. It suggested, too, that the same experience always gives birth to the same sort of belief or religion. One revelation has been made to the Indian, another to the white man. I have much to learn of the Indian, nothing of the missionary. I am not sure but all that would tempt me to teach the Indian my religion would be his promise to teach me *his.* Long enough I had heard of irrelevant things; now at length I was glad to make acquaintance with the light that dwells in rotten wood. Where is all your knowledge gone to? It evaporates completely, for it has no depth.

I kept those little chips and wet them again the next night, but they emitted no light.

SATURDAY, *July* 25.

At breakfast this Saturday morning, the Indian, evidently curious to know what would be expected of him the next day, whether we should go along or not, asked me how I spent the Sunday when at home. I told him that I commonly sat in my chamber reading, etc., in the forenoon, and went to walk in the afternoon. At which he shook his head and said, "Er, that is ver bad." "How do you spend it?" I asked. He said that he did no work, that he went to church at Oldtown when he was at home; in short, he did as he had been taught by the whites. This led to a discussion in which I found myself in the minority. He stated that he was a Protestant, and asked me if I was. I did not at first know what to say, but I thought that I could answer with truth that I was.[1]

When we were washing the dishes in the lake, many fishes, apparently chivin, came close up to us to get the particles of grease. The weather seemed to be more settled this morning, and we set out early in order to finish our voyage up the lake before the wind arose. Soon after starting, the Indian directed our attention to the northeast carry, which we could plainly see, about thirteen miles distant in that direction as measured on the map, though it is called much farther. This carry is a rude wooden railroad, running north and south about two miles, perfectly straight, from the lake to the Penobscot, through a low tract, with a clearing three or four rods wide; but low as it is, it passes over the height of land there.

This opening appeared as a clear bright, or light point in the horizon, resting on the edge of the lake, whose breadth a hair could have covered at a considerable distance from the eye, and of no appreciable height. We should not have suspected it to be visible if the Indian had not drawn our attention to it. It was a remarkable kind of light to steer for,— daylight seen through a vista in the forest,—but visible as far as an ordinary beacon at night.

We crossed a deep and wide bay which makes eastward north of Kineo, leaving an island on our left, and keeping up the eastern side of the lake. This way or that led to some Tomhegan or *Socatarian* stream, up which the Indian had hunted, and whither I longed to go. The last name, however,

---

[1] Polis had more to say on this topic the next day on the West Branch. See Appendix, page 322.

had a bogus sound, too much like sectarian for me, as if a missionary had tampered with it; but I knew that the Indians were very liberal. I think I should have inclined to the Tomhegan first.[1]

We then crossed another broad bay, which, as we could no longer observe the shore particularly, afforded ample time for conversation. The Indian said that he had got his money by hunting, mostly high up the west branch of the Penobscot, and toward the head of the St. John; he had hunted there from a boy, and knew all about that region.[2] His game had been, beaver, otter, black cat (or fisher), sable, moose, etc. Loup cervier (or Canada lynx) were plenty yet in burnt grounds. For food in the woods, he uses partridges, ducks, dried moose meat, hedge-hog, etc. Loons, too, were good, only "bile 'em good." He told us at some length how he had suffered from starvation when a mere lad, being overtaken by winter when hunting with two grown Indians in the northern part of Maine, and obliged to leave their canoe on account of ice.

Pointing into the bay, he said that it was the way to various lakes which he knew. Only solemn bear-haunted mountains, with their great wooded slopes, were visible; where, as man is not, we suppose some other power to be. My imagination personified the slopes themselves, as if by their very length they would waylay you, and compel you to camp again on them before night. Some invisible glutton would seem to drop from the trees and gnaw at the heart of the solitary

---

[1] Two streams, the Tomhegan and the Socatean, empty into two bays to the westward of Farm Island.

[2] As the West Branch of the Penobscot passes the head of Moosehead up through Seboomook Deadwater, it forks. The South Branch comes in on the left. Swinging sharp right is the North Branch. At the junction of the latter with Dole Brook (the Middle Branch) it turns again to the right, becoming the Northeast Branch. This takes its rise in Abacotnetic Bog. From there a carry leads over into St. John Pond, from whence one may proceed down Baker Stream into Baker Lake and on down the St. John River.

hunter who threaded those woods; and yet I was tempted to walk there. The Indian said that he had been along there several times.

I asked him how he guided himself in the woods. "Oh," said he, "I can tell good many ways." When I pressed him further, he answered, "Sometimes I lookum side-hill," and he glanced toward a high hill or mountain on the eastern shore, "great difference between the north and south, see where the sun has shone most. So trees,—the large limbs bend toward south. Sometimes I lookum locks" (rocks). I asked what he saw on the rocks, but he did not describe anything in particular, answering vaguely, in a mysterious or drawling tone, "Bare locks on lake shore,—great difference between N.S. E.W. side,—can tell what the sun has shone on."

"Suppose," said I, "that I should take you in a dark night, right up here into the middle of the woods a hundred miles, set you down, and turn you round quickly twenty times, could you steer straight to Oldtown?" "Oh, yer," said he, "have done pretty much same thing. I will tell you. Some years ago I met an old white hunter at Millinocket; very good hunter. He said he could go anywhere in the woods. He wanted to hunt with me that day, so we start. We chase a moose all the forenoon, round and round, till middle of afternoon, when we kill him. Then I said to him, now you go straight to camp. Don't go round and round where we've been, but go straight. He said, I can't do that, I don't know where I am. Where you think camp? I asked. He pointed so. Then I laugh at him. I take the lead and go right off the other way, cross our tracks many times, straight camp." "How do you do that?" asked I. "Oh, I can't tell *you*," he replied. "Great difference between me and white man."

It appeared as if the sources of information were so various that he did not give a distinct, conscious attention to any one, and so could not readily refer to any when questioned about it, but he found his way very much as an animal does. Perhaps what is commonly called instinct in the animal, in this case is merely a sharpened and educated sense. Often, when an Indian says, "I don't know," in regard to the route he is to take, he does not mean what a white man would by those words, for his Indian instinct may tell him still as much as the most confident white man knows. He does not carry things in his head, nor remember the route exactly like a white man, but relies on himself at the moment. Not having experienced the need of the other sort of knowledge, all labeled and arranged, he has not acquired it.

The white hunter with whom I talked in the stage knew some of the resources of the Indian. He said that he steered by the wind, or by the limbs of the hemlocks, which were largest on the south side; also sometimes, when he knew that there was a lake near, by firing his gun and listening to hear the direction and distance of the echo from over it.

The course we took over this lake, and others afterward, was rarely direct, but a succession of curves from point to point, digressing considerably into each of the bays; and this was not merely on account of the wind, for the Indian, looking toward the middle of the lake, said it was hard to go there, easier to keep near the shore, because he thus got over it by successive reaches and saw by the shore how he got along.

The following will suffice for a common experience in crossing lakes in a canoe. As the forenoon advanced, the wind increased. The last bay which we crossed before reaching the desolate pier at the northeast carry was two or three miles over, and the wind was southwesterly. After going a third of the way, the waves had increased so as occasionally to wash into the canoe, and we saw that it was worse and worse ahead. At first we might have turned about, but were not willing to. It would have been of no use to follow the course of the shore, for not only the distance would have been much greater, but the waves ran still higher there on account of the greater sweep the wind had. At any rate it would have been dangerous now to alter our course, because the waves would have struck us at an advantage.

It will not do to meet them at right angles, for then they will wash in both sides, but you must take them quartering. So the Indian stood up in the canoe, and exerted all his skill and strength for a mile or two, while I paddled right along in order to give him more steerage-way. For more than a mile he did not allow a single wave to strike the canoe as it would, but turned it quickly from this side to that, so that it would always be on or near the crest of a wave when it broke, where all its force was spent, and we merely settled down with it. At length I jumped out on to the end of the pier, against which the waves were dashing violently, in order to lighten the canoe, and catch it at the landing, which was not much sheltered; but just as I jumped we took in two or three gallons of water. I remarked to the Indian, "You managed that well," to which he replied, "Ver few men do that. Great many waves; when I look out for one, another come quick."

While the Indian went to get cedar-bark, etc., to carry his canoe with, we cooked the dinner on the shore, at this end of the carry, in the midst of a sprinkling rain.

3. Down the West Branch

HE PREPARED his canoe for carrying in this wise. He took a cedar shingle or splint eighteen inches long and four or five wide, rounded at one end, that the corners might not be in the way, and tied it with cedar-bark by two holes made midway, near the edge on each side, to the middle cross-bar of the canoe. When the canoe was lifted upon his head bottom up, this shingle, with its rounded end uppermost, distributed the weight over his shoulders and head, while a band of cedar-bark, tied to the cross-bar on each side of the shingle, passed round his breast, and another longer one, outside of the last, round his forehead; also a hand on each side-rail served to steer the canoe and keep it from rocking. He thus carried it with his shoulders, head, breast, forehead, and both hands, as if the upper part of his body were all one hand to clasp and hold it. If you know of a better way, I should like to hear of it.

A cedar-tree furnished all the gear in this case, as it had the woodwork of the canoe. One of the paddles rested on the cross-bars in the bows. I took the canoe upon my head and found that I could carry it with ease, though the straps were not fitted to my shoulders; but I let him carry it, not caring to establish a different precedent, though he said that if I would carry the canoe, he would take all the rest of the baggage, except my companion's. This shingle remained tied to the cross-bar throughout the voyage, was always ready for the carries, and also served to protect the back of one passenger.

The Indian started off first with the canoe and was soon out of sight, going much faster than an ordinary walk. We could see him a mile or more ahead, when his canoe against the sky on the height of land between Moosehead and the Penobscot was all that was to be seen about him.

As we were returning over the track where I had passed but a few minutes before, we started a partridge with her young partly from beneath the wooden rails. While the young hastened away, she sat within seven feet of us and plumed herself, perfectly fearless, without making a noise or ruffling her feathers as they do in our neighborhood, and I thought it would be a good opportunity to observe whether she flew as quietly as other birds when not alarmed. We observed her till we were tired, and when we compelled her to get out of our way, though she took to wing as easily as if we had not been there and went only two or three rods into a tree, she flew with a considerable *whir*, as if this were not avoidable in a rapid motion of the wings.[1]

We were obliged to go over this carry twice, our load was so great. But the carries were an agreeable variety, and we improved the opportunity to gather the rare plants which we had seen, when we returned empty handed.

Northeast Carry comes out on the bank of the West Branch. And here there occurs a shift in the text. For Thoreau had

---

[1] This and the preceding paragraph are taken from Thoreau's Journal of July 25, 1857.

*been here four years before—"a-moose-hunting." This was
in 1853 in the early fall of the year in company with his relative, a Mr. Thatcher of Bangor. After the portage to the West
Branch, the account will follow the text of this second trip in
the Maine woods. Thoreau gave a memorable description of
their guide, Joe Aitteon, "a son of the Governor," who was
long remembered on the West Branch as an expert waterman
and river driver:*

*"He was a good-looking Indian, twenty-four years old,
apparently of unmixed blood, short and stout with a broad
face and reddish complexion, and eyes, methinks, narrower
and more turned up at the outer corners than ours, answering to the description of his race. Beside his underclothing, he
wore a red flannel shirt, woolen pants, and a black Kossuth
hat, the ordinary dress of the lumberman, and, to a considerable extent, of the Penobscot Indian. When, afterward, he
had occasion to take off his shoes and stockings, I was struck
with the smallness of his feet. He had worked a good deal as
a lumberman, and appeared to identify himself with that
class."* [1]

This was an interesting botanical locality for one coming
from the South to commence with; for many plants which are
rather rare, and one or two which are not found at all, in the
eastern part of Massachusetts, grew abundantly between the
rails,—as Labrador tea, Kalmia glauca [pale laurel], Canada
blueberry (which was still in fruit, and a second time in
bloom), Clintonia and Linnæa borealis [checkerberry], which
last a lumberer called *moxon,* creeping snowberry, painted
trillium, large-flowered bellwort, etc. I fancied that the Aster
radula [rough-leaved aster], Diplopappus umbellatus [double-

---

[1] It will be noticed that Thoreau never uses the term "lumberjack." The
terms then in current use were "logger," "lumberer," and "lumberman."
"Lumberjack" seems to have been the invention at a much later date of Hol-
man Day in his novels dealing with life in the north of Maine.

bristled aster], Solidago lanceolatus [bushy golden rod], red trumpet-weed, and many others which were conspicuously in bloom on the shore of the lake and on the carry, had a peculiarly wild and primitive look there.[1]

The spruce and fir trees crowded to the track on each side to welcome us, the arbor-vitæ, with its changing leaves, prompted us to make haste, and the sight of the canoe-birch gave us spirits to do so. Sometimes an evergreen just fallen lay across the track with its rich burden of cones, looking, still, fuller of life than our trees in the most favorable positions. You did not expect to find such *spruce* trees in the wild woods, but they evidently attend to their toilets each morning even there. Through such a front-yard did we enter that wilderness.

There was a very slight rise above the lake,—the country appearing like, and perhaps being partly a swamp,—and at length a gradual descent to the Penobscot, which I was surprised to find here a large stream, from twelve to fifteen rods wide, flowing from west to east, or at right angles with the lake, and not more than two and a half miles from it. The distance is nearly twice too great on the Map of the Public Lands, and on Colton's Map of Maine, and Russell Stream is placed too far down.[2] Jackson makes Moosehead Lake to be nine hundred and sixty feet above high water in Portland harbor. It is higher than Chesuncook, for the lumberers consider the Penobscot, where we struck it, twenty-five feet lower than Moosehead,—though eight miles above it is said to be the highest, so that the water can be made to flow either way,

---

[1] A further botanical discussion appears in the Appendix on page 323.

[2] Thoreau severely criticized the maps of Maine then available, declaring one of them to be "a labyrinth of errors." Two decades after his last trip, Lucius Lee Hubbard began the preparation of his map of Northern Maine— "Specially adapted to the uses of LUMBERMEN AND SPORTSMEN"—the accuracy and vitality of which is attested by its thirteen editions published between 1879 and 1929. On this map Thoreau's journeys may be traced with ease.

and the river falls a good deal between here and Chesuncook. The carry-man called this about one hundred and forty miles above Bangor by the river, or two hundred from the ocean, and fifty-five miles below Hilton's, on the Canada road, the first clearing above, which is four and a half miles from the source of the Penobscot.

At the north end of the carry, in the midst of a clearing of sixty acres or more, there was a log camp of the usual construction, with something more like a house adjoining, for the accommodation of the carry-man's family and passing lumberers. The bed of withered fir-twigs smelled very sweet, though really very dirty. There was also a store-house on the bank of the river, containing pork, flour, iron, batteaux, and birches, locked up.

We now proceeded to get our dinner, which always turned out to be tea, and to pitch canoes, for which purpose a large iron pot lay permanently on the bank. This we did in company with the explorers. Both Indians and whites use a mixture of rosin and grease for this purpose, that is, for the pitching, not the dinner. Joe took a small brand from the fire and blew the heat and flame against the pitch on his birch, and so melted and spread it. Sometimes he put his mouth over the suspected spot and sucked, to see if it admitted air; and at one place, where we stopped, he set his canoe high on crossed stakes, and poured water into it. I narrowly watched his motions, and listened attentively to his observations, for we had employed an Indian mainly that I might have an opportunity to study his ways. I heard him swear once, mildly, during this operation, about his knife being as dull as a hoe,— an accomplishment which he owed to his intercourse with the whites; and he remarked, "We ought to have some tea before we start; we shall be hungry before we kill that moose."

At mid-afternoon we embarked on the Penobscot. Our birch was nineteen and a half feet long by two and a half at

the widest part, and fourteen inches deep within, both ends alike, and painted green, which Joe thought affected the pitch and made it leak. This, I think, was a middling-sized one. That of the explorers [1] was much larger, though probably not much longer. This carried us three with our baggage, weighing in all between five hundred and fifty and six hundred pounds. We had two heavy, though slender, rock-maple paddles, one of them of bird's-eye maple. Joe placed birch-bark on the bottom for us to sit on, and slanted cedar splints against the cross-bars to protect our backs, while he himself sat upon a cross-bar in the stern. The baggage occupied the middle or widest part of the canoe. We also paddled by turns in the bows, now sitting with our legs extended, now sitting upon our legs, and now rising upon our knees; but I found none of these positions endurable, and was reminded of the complaints of the old Jesuit missionaries of the torture they endured from long confinement in constrained positions in canoes, in their long voyages from Quebec to the Huron country; but afterwards I sat on the cross-bars, or stood up, and experienced no inconvenience.

It was dead water for a couple of miles. The river had been raised about two feet by the rain, and lumberers were hoping for a flood sufficient to bring down the logs that were left in the spring. Its banks were seven or eight feet high, and densely covered with white and black spruce,—which, I think, must be the commonest trees thereabouts,—fir, arbor-vitæ, canoe, yellow, and black birch, rock, mountain, and a few red maples, beech, black and mountain ash, the large-

---

[1] These "two explorers for lumber" had been in company with them out of Greenville on the steamer crossing Moosehead. Thoreau had reported:

The explorers had a fine new birch on board, larger than ours, in which they had come up the Piscataquis from Howland, and they had had several messes of trout already. They were going to the neighborhood of Eagle and Chamberlain Lakes, or the head-waters of the St. John, and offered to keep us company as far as we went.

toothed aspen, many civil looking elms, now imbrowned, along the stream, and at first a few hemlocks also.[1]

We had not gone far before I was startled by seeing what I thought was an Indian encampment, covered with a red flag, on the bank, and exclaimed, "Camp!" to my comrades. I was slow to discover that it was a red maple changed by the frost. The immediate shores were also densely covered with the speckled alder, red osier, shrubby-willows or sallows, and the like. There were a few yellow lily pads still left, half-drowned, along the sides, and sometimes a white one. Many fresh tracks of moose were visible where the water was shallow, and on the shore, and the lily stems were freshly bitten off by them.

After paddling about two miles, we parted company with the explorers, and turned up Lobster Stream, which comes in on the right, from the southeast. This was six or eight rods wide, and appeared to run nearly parallel with the Penobscot. Joe said that it was so called from small fresh-water lobsters found in it. It is the Matahumkeag of the maps. My companion wished to look for moose signs, and intended, if it proved worth the while, to camp up that way, since the Indian advised it. On account of the rise of the Penobscot the water ran up this stream quite to the pond of the same name, one or two miles. The Spencer Mountains, east of the north end of Moosehead Lake, were now in plain sight in front of us.

The kingfisher flew before us, the pigeon woodpecker was seen and heard, and nuthatches and chickadees close at hand. Joe said that they called the chickadee *kecunnilessu* in his language. I will not vouch for the spelling of what possibly was never spelt before, but I pronounced after him till he said it would do. We passed close to a woodcock, which stood perfectly still on the shore, with feathers puffed up, as if sick.

---

[1] In the Appendix on page 324, there is a more detailed description of the trees then characterizing the Maine woods.

This Joe said they called *nipsquecohossus*. The kingfisher was
skuscumonsuck; bear was *wassus;* Indian Devil, *lunxus;* the
mountain-ash, *upahsis*. This was very abundant and beautiful. Moose tracks were not so fresh along this stream, except
in a small creek about a mile up it, where a large log had
lodged in the spring, marked "W-cross-girdle-crow-foot." We
saw a pair of moose horns on the shore, and I asked Joe if a
moose had shed them; but he said there was a head attached
to them, and I knew that they did not shed their heads more
than once in their lives.

After ascending about a mile and a half, to within a short
distance of Lobster Lake, we returned to the Penobscot. Just
below the mouth of the Lobster we found quick water, and
the river expanded to twenty or thirty rods in width. The
moose tracks were quite numerous and fresh here. We noticed
in a great many places narrow and well-trodden paths by
which they had come down to the river, and where they had
slid on the steep and clayey bank. Their tracks were either
close to the edge of the stream, those of the calves distinguishable from the others, or in shallow water; the holes made by
their feet in the soft bottom being visible for a long time.
They were particularly numerous where there was a small
bay, or pokelogan, as it is called, bordered by a strip of
meadow, or separated from the river by a low peninsula

covered with coarse grass, wool-grass, etc., wherein they had waded back and forth and eaten the pads. We detected the remains of one in such a spot.[1]

At one place, where we landed to pick up a summer duck, which my companion had shot, Joe peeled a canoe-birch for bark for his hunting-horn. He then asked if we were not going to get the other duck, for his sharp eyes had seen another fall in the bushes a little farther along, and my companion obtained it. I now began to notice the bright red berries of the tree-cranberry, which grows eight or ten feet high, mingled with the alders and cornel along the shore. There was less hard wood than at first. After proceeding a mile and three quarters below the mouth of the Lobster, we reached, about sundown, a small island at the head of what Joe called the Moosehorn Dead-water (the Moosehorn, in which he was going to hunt that night, coming in about three miles below), and on the upper end of this we decided to camp. On a point at the lower end lay the carcass of a moose killed a month or more before.

I will describe, once for all, the routine of camping at this season.[2] We generally told the Indian that we would stop at the first suitable place, so that he might be on the lookout for it. Having observed a clear, hard, and flat beach to land on, free from mud, and from stones which would injure the canoe, one would run up the bank to see if there were open and level space enough for the camp between the trees, or if it could be easily cleared, preferring at the same time a cool place, on account of insects. Sometimes we paddled a mile or more before finding one to our minds, for where the shore was suitable, the bank would often be too steep, or else too low and

---

[1] Pokelogan is an Indian word. The term "logan" is widely used in northern Maine to designate a marshy boglike pocket in a stream or pond.

[2] The description of making camp is taken from the account of the Allegash excursion near this spot in 1857.

grassy, and therefore mosquitoey. We then took out the baggage and drew up the canoe, sometimes turning it over on shore for safety. The Indian cut a path to the spot we had selected, which was usually within two or three rods of the water, and we carried up our baggage.

One, perhaps, takes canoe-birch bark, always at hand, and dead dry wood or bark, and kindles a fire five or six feet in front of where we intend to lie. It matters not, commonly, on which side this is, because there is little or no wind in so dense a wood at that season; and then he gets a kettle of water from the river, and takes out the pork, bread, coffee, etc., from their several packages. Another, meanwhile, having the axe, cuts down the nearest dead rock-maple or other dry hard wood, collecting several large logs to last through the night, also a green stake, with a notch or fork to it, which is slanted over the fire, perhaps resting on a rock or forked stake, to hang the kettle on, and two forked stakes and a pole for the tent.

The third man pitches the tent, cuts a dozen or more pins with his knife, usually of moose-wood, the common underwood, to fasten it down with, and then collects an armful or two of fir-twigs,[1] arbor-vitæ, spruce, or hemlock, whichever is at hand, and makes the bed, beginning at either end, and laying the twigs wrong side up, in regular rows, covering the stub ends of the last row; first, however, filling the hollows, if there are any, with coarser material. Wrangel says that his guides in Siberia first strewed a quantity of dry brushwood on the ground, and then cedar twigs on that.

Commonly, by the time the bed is made, or within fifteen or twenty minutes, the water boils, the pork is fried, and supper is ready. We eat this sitting on the ground, or a stump, if there is any, around a large piece of birch-bark for a table, each holding a dipper in one hand and a piece of ship-bread

---

[1] These twigs are called in Rasle's Dictionary, *Sediak*. [Thoreau]

or fried pork in the other, frequently making a pass with his hand, or thrusting his head into the smoke, to avoid the mosquitoes.

Next, pipes are lit by those who smoke, and veils are donned by those who have them, and we hastily examine and dry our plants, anoint our faces and hands, and go to bed,— and—the mosquitoes. Though you have nothing to do but see the country, there's rarely any time to spare, hardly enough to examine a plant, before the night or drowsiness is upon you.

Such was the ordinary experience.

4. The Moose Hunt

We concluded merely to prepare our camp, and leave our baggage here, that all might be ready when we returned from moose-hunting. Though I had not come a-hunting, and felt some compunctions about accompanying the hunters, I wished to see a moose near at hand, and was not sorry to learn how the Indian managed to kill one. I went as reporter or chaplain to the hunters,—and the chaplain has been known to carry a gun himself. After clearing a small space amid the dense spruce and fir trees, we covered the damp ground with a shingling of fir-twigs, and, while Joe was preparing his birch horn and pitching his canoe,—for this had to be done whenever we stopped long enough to build a fire, and was the principal labor which he took upon himself at such times,— we collected fuel for the night, large, wet, and rotting logs, which had lodged at the head of the island, for our hatchet was too small for effective chopping; but we did not kindle a fire, lest the moose should smell it. Joe set up a couple of forked stakes, and prepared half a dozen poles, ready to cast one of our blankets over in case it rained in the night, which precaution, however, was omitted the next night. We also plucked the ducks which had been killed for breakfast.

While we were thus engaged in the twilight, we heard faintly, from far down the stream, what sounded like two strokes of a wood-chopper's axe, echoing dully through the grim solitude. We are wont to liken many sounds, heard at a distance in the forest, to the stroke of an axe, because they resemble each other under those circumstances, and that is the one we commonly hear there. When we told Joe of this, he exclaimed, "By George, I'll bet that was a moose! They make a noise like that." These sounds affected us strangely, and by their very resemblance to a familiar one, where they probably had so different an origin, enhanced the impression of solitude and wildness.

At starlight we dropped down the stream, which was a dead-water for three miles, or as far as the Moosehorn; Joe telling us that we must be very silent, and he himself making no noise with his paddle, while he urged the canoe along with

effective impulses. It was a still night, and suitable for this purpose,—for if there is wind, the moose will smell you,— and Joe was very confident that he should get some. The harvest moon had just risen, and its level rays began to light up the forest on our right, while we glided downward in the shade on the same side, against the little breeze that was stirring. The lofty, spiring tops of the spruce and fir were very black against the sky, and more distinct than by day, close bordering this broad avenue on each side; and the beauty of the scene, as the moon rose above the forest, it would not be easy to describe.[1]

A bat flew over our heads, and we heard a few faint notes of birds from time to time, perhaps the myrtle-bird for one, or the sudden plunge of a musquash, or saw one crossing the stream before us, or heard the sound of a rill emptying in, swollen by the recent rain. About a mile below the island, when the solitude seemed to be growing more complete every moment, we suddenly saw the light and heard the crackling of a fire on the bank, and discovered the camp of the two explorers; they standing before it in their red shirts, and talking aloud of the adventures and profits of the day. They were just then speaking of a bargain, in which, as I understood, somebody had cleared twenty-five dollars. We glided by without speaking, close under the bank, within a couple of rods of them; and Joe, taking his horn, imitated the call of the moose, till we suggested that they might fire on us. This was the last we saw of them, and we never knew whether they detected or suspected us.

I have often wished since that I was with them. They search for timber over a given section, climbing hills and often high trees to look off,—explore the streams by which it is to be driven, and the like,—spend five or six weeks in the woods, they two alone, a hundred miles or more from any town,—roaming about, and sleeping on the ground where night overtakes them,—depending chiefly on the provisions

---

[1] In the accompanying illustration the ends of the birch do not follow the sweeping curve which is so distinctive a characteristic of the modern canoe. The fact is, the Indians' birch of this period did not do so. According to Lucius L. Hubbard, writing in 1884, "The ends curve more or less according to the fancy of the builder. . . ." *Woods and Lakes of Maine*, 115.

they carry with them, though they do not decline what game they come across,—and then in the fall they return and make report to their employers, determining the number of teams that will be required the following winter. Experienced men get three or four dollars a day for this work. It is a solitary and adventurous life, and comes nearest to that of the trapper of the West, perhaps. They work ever with a gun as well as an axe, let their beards grow, and live without neighbors, not on an open plain, but far within a wilderness.[1]

This discovery accounted for the sounds which we had heard, and destroyed the prospect of seeing moose yet awhile. At length, when we had left the explorers far behind, Joe laid down his paddle, drew forth his birch-horn,—a straight one, about fifteen inches long and three or four wide at the mouth, tied round with strips of the same bark,—and, standing up, imitated the call of the moose,—*ugh-ugh-ugh*, or *oo-oo-oo-oo*, and then a prolonged *oo-o-o-o-o-o-o-o*, and listened attentively for several minutes. We asked him what kind of noise he expected to hear. He said that if a moose heard it, he guessed we should find out; we should hear him coming half a mile off; he would come close to, perhaps into, the water, and my companion must wait till he got fair sight, and then aim just behind the shoulder.

The moose venture out to the river-side to feed and drink at night. Earlier in the season the hunters do not use a horn to call them out, but steal upon them as they are feeding along the sides of the stream, and often the first notice they have of one is the sound of the water dropping from its muzzle. An Indian whom I heard imitate the voice of the moose, and also that of the caribou and the deer, using a much longer horn than Joe's, told me that the first could be heard eight or ten

---

[1] Thoreau's sympathetic description of two timber cruisers whom he met a few days later on the steamer on Moosehead will be found in the Appendix on page 325.

miles, sometimes; it was a loud sort of bellowing sound, clearer and more sonorous than the lowing of cattle,—the caribou's a sort of snort,—and the small deer's like that of a lamb.

At length we turned up the Moosehorn, where the Indians at the carry had told us that they killed a moose the night before. This is a very meandering stream, only a rod or two in width, but comparatively deep, coming in on the right, fitly enough named Moosehorn, whether from its windings or its inhabitants. It was bordered here and there by narrow meadows between the stream and the endless forest, affording favorable places for the moose to feed, and to call them out on. We proceeded half a mile up this, as through a narrow, winding canal, where the tall, dark spruce and firs and arborvitæ towered on both sides in the moonlight, forming a perpendicular forest-edge of great height, like the spires of a Venice in the forest. In two places stood a small stack of hay on the bank, ready for the lumberer's use in the winter, looking strange enough there. We thought of the day when this might be a brook winding through smooth-shaven meadows on some gentleman's grounds; and seen by moonlight then, excepting the forest that now hems it in, how little changed it would appear!

Again and again Joe called the moose, placing the canoe by some favorable point of meadow for them to come out on, but listened in vain to hear one come rushing through the woods, and concluded that they had been hunted too much thereabouts. We saw, many times, what to our imaginations looked like a gigantic moose, with his horns peering from out the forest edge; but we saw the forest only, and not its inhabitants, that night. So at last we turned about. There was now a little fog on the water, though it was a fine, clear night above. There were very few sounds to break the stillness of the forest. Several times we heard the hooting of a great horned-owl, as at home, and told Joe that he would call out the moose for him, for he made a sound considerably like the horn,—but Joe answered, that the moose had heard that sound a thousand times, and knew better; and oftener still we were startled by the plunge of a musquash.

Once, when Joe had called again, and we were listening for moose, we heard, come faintly echoing, or creeping from far, through the moss-clad aisles, a dull, dry, rushing sound, with a solid core to it, yet as if half smothered under the grasp of the luxuriant and fungus-like forest, like the shutting of a door in some distant entry of the damp and shaggy wilderness. If we had not been there, no mortal had heard it. When we asked Joe in a whisper what it was, he answered, "Tree fall."

There is something singularly grand and impressive in the sound of a tree falling in a perfectly calm night like this, as if the agencies which overthrow it did not need to be excited, but worked with a subtle, deliberate, and conscious force, like a boa-constrictor, and more effectively then than even in a windy day. If there is any such difference, perhaps it is because trees with the dews of the night on them are heavier than by day.

Having reached the camp, about ten o'clock, we kindled our fire and went to bed. Each of us had a blanket, in which he lay on the fir-twigs, with his extremities toward the fire, but nothing over his head. It was worth the while to lie down in a country where you could afford such great fires; that was one whole side, and the bright side, of our world. We had first rolled up a large log some eighteen inches through and ten feet long, for a backlog, to last all night, and then piled on the trees to the height of three or four feet, no matter how green or damp. In fact, we burned as much wood that night as would, with economy and an air-tight stove, last a poor family in one of our cities all winter.

It was very agreeable, as well as independent, thus lying in the open air, and the fire kept our uncovered extremities warm enough. The Jesuit missionaries used to say, that, in their journeys with the Indians in Canada, they lay on a bed which had never been shaken up since the creation, unless by earthquakes. It is surprising with what impunity and comfort one who has always lain in a warm bed in a close apartment, and studiously avoided drafts of air, can lie down on the ground without a shelter, roll himself in a blanket, and sleep before a fire, in a frosty, autumn night just after a long rain-storm, and even come soon to enjoy and value the fresh air.

I lay awake awhile, watching the ascent of the sparks through the firs, and sometimes their descent in half-extinguished cinders on my blanket. They were as interesting as fireworks, going up in endless, successive crowds, each after an explosion, in an eager, serpentine course, some to five or six rods above the treetops before they went out. We do not suspect how much our chimneys have concealed; and now air-tight stoves have come to conceal all the rest. In the course of the night, I got up once or twice and put fresh logs on the fire, making my companions curl up their legs.

When we awoke in the morning (Saturday, September 17), there was considerable frost whitening the leaves. We heard the sound of the chickadee, and a few faintly lisping birds, and also of ducks in the water about the island. I took a botanical account of stock of our domains before the dew was off, and found that the ground hemlock, or American yew, was the prevailing under-shrub. We breakfasted on tea, hard bread, and ducks.

Before the fog had fairly cleared away we paddled down the stream again, and were soon past the mouth of the Moose-horn. These twenty miles of the Penobscot, between Moose-head and Chesuncook lakes, are comparatively smooth, and a great part dead-water; but from time to time it is shallow and rapid, with rocks or gravel beds, where you can wade across. There is no expanse of water, and no break in the forest, and the meadow is a mere edging here and there. There are no hills near the river nor within sight, except one or two distant mountains seen in a few places. The banks are from six to ten feet high, but once or twice rise gently to higher ground. In many places the forest on the bank was but a thin strip, letting the light through from some alder swamp or meadow behind.

The conspicuous berry-bearing bushes and trees along the shore were the red osier, with its whitish fruit, hobble-bush, mountain-ash, tree-cranberry, choke-cherry, now ripe, alternate cornel, and naked viburnum. Following Joe's example, I ate the fruit of the last, and also of the hobble-bush, but found them rather insipid and seedy. I looked very narrowly at the vegetation, as we glided along close to the shore, and frequently made Joe turn aside for me to pluck a plant, that I might see by comparison what was primitive about my native river. Horehound, horsemint, and the sensitive fern grew close to the edge, under the willows and alders, and woolgrass on the islands, as along the Assabet River in Concord. It was too late for flowers, except a few asters, goldenrods, etc. In several places we noticed the slight frame of a camp, such as we had prepared to set up, amid the forest by the river-side, where some lumberers or hunters had passed a night,—and sometimes steps cut in the muddy or clayey bank in front of it.

We stopped to fish for trout at the mouth of a small stream called Ragmuff, which came in from the west, about two miles below the Moosehorn. Here were the ruins of an old lumbering-camp, and a small space, which had formerly been cleared and burned over, was now densely overgrown with the red cherry and raspberries. While we were trying for trout, Joe, Indian-like, wandered off up the Ragmuff on his

own errands, and when we were ready to start was far beyond
call. So we were compelled to make a fire and get our dinner
here, not to lose time. Some dark reddish birds, with grayer
females (perhaps purple finches), and myrtle-birds in their
summer dress, hopped within six or eight feet of us and our
smoke. Perhaps they smelled the frying pork. The latter bird,
or both, made the lisping notes which I had heard in the forest. They suggested that the few small birds found in the
wilderness are on more familiar terms with the lumberman
and hunter than those of the orchard and clearing with the
farmer. I have since found the Canada jay, and partridges,
both the black and the common, equally tame there, as if they
had not yet learned to mistrust man entirely. The chickadee,
which is at home alike in the primitive woods and in our
wood-lots, still retains its confidence in the towns to a remarkable degree.

Joe at length returned, after an hour and a half, and said
that he had been two miles up the stream exploring, and had
seen a moose, but, not having the gun, he did not get him. We
made no complaint, but concluded to look out for Joe the
next time. However, this may have been a mere mistake, for
we had no reason to complain of him afterwards. As we continued down the stream, I was surprised to hear him whistling "O Susanna," and several other such airs, while his
paddle urged us along. Once he said, "Yes, sir-ee." His common word was "Sartain."

He paddled, as usual, on one side only, giving the birch an
impulse by using the side as a fulcrum. I asked him how the
ribs were fastened to the side rails. He answered, "I don't
know, I never noticed." Talking with him about subsisting
wholly on what the woods yielded, game, fish, berries, etc.,
I suggested that his ancestors did so; but he answered that he
had been brought up in such a way that he could not do it.
"Yes," said he, "that's the way they got a living, like wild fel-

lows, wild as bears. By George! I sha'n't go into the woods without provision,—hard bread, pork, etc." He had brought on a barrel of hard bread and stored it at the carry for his hunting. However, though he was a Governor's son, he had not learned to read.

At one place below this, on the east side, where the bank was higher and drier than usual, rising gently from the shore to a slight elevation, some one had felled the trees over twenty or thirty acres, and left them drying in order to burn. This was the only preparation for a house between the Moosehead carry and Chesuncook, but there was no hut nor inhabitants there yet. The pioneer thus selects a site for his house, which will, perhaps, prove the germ of a town.

My eyes were all the while on the trees, distinguishing between the black and white spruce and the fir. You paddle along in a narrow canal through an endless forest, and the vision I have in my mind's eye, still, is of the small, dark, and sharp tops of tall fir and spruce trees, and pagoda-like arbor-vitæs, crowded together on each side, with various hard woods inter-mixed. Some of the arbor-vitæs were at least sixty feet high. The hard woods, occasionally occurring exclusively, were less wild to my eye. I fancied them ornamental grounds, with farm-houses in the rear. The canoe and yellow birch, beech, maple, and elm are Saxon and Norman, but the spruce and fir, and pines generally, are Indian. The soft engravings which adorn the annuals give no idea of a stream in such a wilderness as this. The rough sketches in Jackson's Reports on the Geology of Maine answer much better.

At one place we saw a small grove of slender sapling white-pines, the only collection of pines that I saw on this voyage. Here and there, however, was a full-grown, tall, and slender, but defective one, what lumbermen call a *konchus* tree, which they ascertain with their axes, or by the knots. I did not learn whether this word was Indian or English. It reminded me of the Greek κόγχη, a conch or shell, and I amused myself with fancying that it might signify the dead sound which the trees yield when struck. All the rest of the pines had been driven off.

How far men go for the materials of their houses! The inhabitants of the most civilized cities, in all ages, send into far, primitive forests, beyond the bounds of their civilization, where the moose and bear and savage dwell, for their pine boards for ordinary use. And, on the other hand, the savage soon receives from cities iron arrow-points, hatchets, and guns, to point his savageness with.

The solid and well-defined fir-tops, like sharp and regular spear-heads, black against the sky, gave a peculiar, dark, and sombre look to the forest. The spruce-tops have a similar but more ragged outline,—their shafts also merely feathered below. The firs were somewhat oftener regular and dense pyramids. I was struck by this universal spiring upward of the forest evergreens. The tendency is to slender, spiring tops, while they are narrower below. Not only the spruce and fir, but even the arbor-vitæ and white-pine, unlike the soft, spreading, second-growth, of which I saw none; all spire upwards, lifting a dense spear-head of cones to the light and air, at any rate, while their branches straggle after as they may; as Indians lift the ball over the heads of the crowd in their desperate game. In this they resemble grasses, as also palms somewhat. The hemlock is commonly a tent-like pyramid from the ground to its summit.

After passing through some long rips, and by a large island, we reached an interesting part of the river called the Pine Stream Dead-Water, about six miles below Ragmuff, where the river expanded to thirty rods in width and had many islands in it, with elms and canoe-birches, now yellowing, along the shore, and we got our first sight of Ktaadn.

Here, about two o'clock, we turned up a small branch three or four rods wide, which comes in on the right from the south, called Pine Stream, to look for moose signs. We had gone but a few rods before we saw very recent signs along the water's edge, the mud lifted up by their feet being quite fresh, and Joe declared that they had gone along there but a short time before. We soon reached a small meadow on the east side, at an angle in the stream, which was, for the most part, densely covered with alders. As we were advancing along the edge of this, rather more quietly than usual, perhaps, on account of the freshness of the signs,—the design being to camp up this stream, if it promised well,—I heard a slight crackling of twigs deep in the alders, and turned Joe's attention to it; whereupon he began to push the canoe back rapidly; and we had receded thus half a dozen rods, when we suddenly spied two moose standing just on the edge of the open part of the meadow which we had passed, not more than six or seven rods distant, looking round the alders at us.

They made me think of great frightened rabbits, with their long ears and half-inquisitive, half-frightened looks; the true denizens of the forest (I saw at once), filling a vacuum which now first I discovered had not been filled for me,—*moose-*men, *wood-eaters*, the word is said to mean,—clad in a sort of Vermont gray, or homespun. Our Nimrod, owing to the retrograde movement, was now the farthest from the game; but being warned of its neighborhood, he hastily stood up, and, while we ducked, fired over our heads one barrel at the foremost, which alone he saw, though he did not know what kind of creature it was; whereupon this one dashed across the meadow and up a high bank on the northeast, so rapidly as to leave but an indistinct impression of its outlines on my mind.

At the same instant, the other, a young one, but as tall as a horse, leaped out into the stream, in full sight, and there stood cowering for a moment, or rather its disproportionate lowness behind gave it that appearance, and uttering two or three trumpeting squeaks. I have an indistinct recollection of seeing the old one pause an instant on the top of the bank in the woods, look toward its shivering young, and then dash away again. The second barrel was leveled at the calf, and when we expected to see it drop in the water, after a little hesitation, it, too, got out of the water, and dashed up the hill, though in a somewhat different direction.

All this was the work of a few seconds, and our hunter, having never seen a moose before, did not know but they were deer, for they stood partly in the water, nor whether he had fired at the same one twice or not. From the style in which they went off, and the fact that he was not used to standing up and firing from a canoe, I judged that we should not see anything more of them. The Indian said that they were a cow and her calf,—a yearling, or perhaps two years old, for they accompany their dams so long; but, for my part, I had not noticed much difference in their size. It was but two or three rods across the meadow to the foot of the bank, which, like all the world thereabouts, was densely wooded; but I was surprised to notice, that, as soon as the moose had passed behind the veil of the woods, there was no sound of footsteps to be heard from the soft, damp moss which carpets that forest, and long before we landed, perfect silence reigned. Joe said, "If you wound 'em moose, me sure get 'em."

We all landed at once. My companion reloaded; the Indian fastened his birch, threw off his hat, adjusted his waistband, seized the hatchet, and set out. He told me afterward, casually, that before we landed he had seen a drop of blood on the bank, when it was two or three rods off. He proceeded rapidly up the bank and through the woods, with a peculiar, elastic, noiseless, and stealthy tread, looking to right and left on the ground, and stepping in the faint tracks of the wounded moose, now and then pointing in silence to a single drop of blood on the handsome, shining leaves of the Clintonia borealis, which, on every side, covered the ground, or to a dry fern-stem freshly broken, all the while chewing some leaf or else the spruce gum. I followed, watching his motions more than the trail of the moose. After following the trail about forty rods in a pretty direct course, stepping over fallen trees and winding between standing ones, he at length lost it, for there were many other moose tracks there, and, returning once more to the last blood-stain, traced it a little way and lost it again, and, too soon, I thought, for a good hunter, gave it up entirely. He traced a few steps, also, the tracks of the calf; but, seeing no blood, soon relinquished the search.

I observed, while he was tracking the moose, a certain reticence or moderation in him. He did not communicate several observations of interest which he made, as a white man would have done, though they may have leaked out afterward. At another time, when we heard a slight crackling of twigs and he landed to reconnoitre, he stepped lightly and gracefully, stealing through the bushes with the least possible noise, in a way in which no white man does,—as it were, finding a place for his foot each time.

About half an hour after seeing the moose, we pursued our voyage up Pine Stream, and soon, coming to a part which was very shoal and also rapid, we took out the baggage, and proceeded to carry it round, while Joe got up with the canoe alone. We were just completing our portage and I was absorbed in the plants, admiring the leaves of the Aster macrophyllus, ten inches wide, and plucking the seeds of the great round-leaved orchis, when Joe exclaimed from the stream that he had killed a moose. He had found the cow-moose lying dead, but quite warm, in the middle of the stream, which was so shallow that it rested on the bottom, with hardly a third of its body above water. It was about an hour after it was shot, and it was swollen with water. It had run about a hundred rods and sought the stream again, cutting off a slight bend. No doubt a better hunter would have tracked it to this spot at once.

I was surprised at its great size, horse-like, but Joe said it was not a large cow-moose. My companion went in search of the calf again. I took hold of the ears of the moose, while Joe pushed his canoe down-stream toward a favorable shore, and so we made out, though with some difficulty, its long nose frequently sticking in the bottom, to drag it into still shallower water. It was a brownish black, or perhaps a dark iron-gray, on the back and sides, but lighter beneath and in front. I took the cord which served for the canoe's painter, and with Joe's assistance measured it carefully, the greatest distances first, making a knot each time. The painter being wanted, I reduced these measures that night with equal care to lengths and fractions of my umbrella, beginning with the smallest measures, and untying the knots as I proceeded; and when we arrived at Chesuncook the next day, finding a two-foot rule there, I reduced the last to feet and inches; and, moreover, I made myself a two-foot rule of a thin and narrow strip of black ash, which would fold up conveniently to six inches.

All this pains I took because I did not wish to be obliged to say merely that the moose was very large. Of the various dimensions which I obtained I will mention only two. The distance from the tips of the hoofs of the fore-feet, stretched out, to the top of the back between the shoulders, was seven feet and five inches. I can hardly believe my own measure, for this is about two feet greater than the height of a tall horse. (Indeed, I am now satisfied that this measurement was incorrect, but the other measures given here I can warrant to be correct, having proved them in a more recent visit to those woods.) The extreme length was eight feet and two inches. Another cow-moose, which I have since measured in those woods with a tape, was just six feet from the tip of the hoof to the shoulders, and eight feet long as she lay.

When afterward I asked an Indian at the carry how much taller the male was, he answered, "Eighteen inches," and made me observe the height of a cross-stake over the fire, more than four feet from the ground, to give me some idea of the depth of his chest. Another Indian, at Oldtown, told me that they were nine feet high to the top of the back, and that one which he tried weighed eight hundred pounds. The length of the spinal projections between the shoulders is very great. A white hunter, who was the best authority among hunters that I could have, told me that the male was *not* eighteen inches taller than the female; yet he agreed that he was sometimes nine feet high to the top of the back, and weighed a thousand pounds.

Only the male has horns, and they rise two feet or more above the shoulders,—spreading three or four, and sometimes six feet,—which would make him in all, sometimes, eleven feet high! According to this calculation, the moose is as tall, though it may not be as large, as the great Irish elk, Megaceros Hibernicus, of a former period, of which Mantell says that it "very far exceeded in magnitude any living species, the skeleton" being "upward of ten feet high from the ground to the highest point of the antlers." Joe said, that, though the moose shed the whole horn annually, each new horn has an additional prong; but I have noticed that they sometimes have more prongs on one side than on the other. I was struck with the delicacy and tenderness of the hoofs, which divide very far up, and the one half could be pressed very much behind the other, thus probably making the animal surer-footed on the uneven ground and slippery moss-covered logs of the primitive forest. They were very unlike the stiff and battered feet of our horses and oxen. The bare, horny part of the fore-foot was just six inches long, and the two portions could be separated four inches at the extremities.

The moose is singularly grotesque and awkward to look at. Why should it stand so high at the shoulders? Why have so long a head? Why have no tail to speak of? for in my examination I overlooked it entirely. Naturalists say it is an inch and a half long. It reminded me at once of the camelopard, high before and low behind,—and no wonder, for, like it, it is fitted to browse on trees. The upper lip projected two inches beyond the lower for this purpose. This was the kind of man that was at home there; for, as near as I can learn, that has never been the residence, but rather the hunting-ground of the Indian. The moose will, perhaps, one day become extinct; but how naturally then, when it exists only as a fossil relic, and unseen as that, may the poet or sculptor invent a fabulous animal with similar branching and leafy horns,—a sort of fucus or lichen in bone,—to be the inhabitant of such a forest as this!

Here, just at the head of the murmuring rapids, Joe now proceeded to skin the moose with a pocket-knife, while I looked on; and a tragical business it was,—to see that still warm and palpitating body pierced with a knife, to see the warm milk stream from the rent udder, and the ghastly naked red carcass appearing from within its seemly robe, which was made to hide it. The ball had passed through the shoulder-blade diagonally and lodged under the skin on the opposite side, and was partially flattened. My companion keeps it to show to his grandchildren. He has the shanks of another moose which he has since shot, skinned and stuffed, ready to be made into boots by putting in a thick leather sole. Joe said, if a moose stood fronting you, you must not fire, but advance toward him, for he will turn slowly and give you a fair shot.

In the bed of this narrow, wild, and rocky stream, between two lofty walls of spruce and firs, a mere cleft in the forest which the stream had made, this work went on. At length Joe had stripped off the hide and dragged it trailing to the shore, declaring that it weighed a hundred pounds, though probably fifty would have been nearer the truth. He cut off a large mass of the meat to carry along, and another, together with the tongue and nose, he put with the hide on the shore to lie there all night, or till we returned. I was surprised that he thought of leaving this meat thus exposed by the side of the carcass, as the simplest course, not fearing that any creature would touch it; but nothing did. This could hardly have happened on the bank of one of our rivers in the eastern part of Massachusetts; but I suspect that fewer small wild animals are prowling there than with us. Twice, however, in this excursion, I had a glimpse of a species of large mouse.

This stream was so withdrawn, and the moose tracks were so fresh, that my companions, still bent on hunting, concluded to go farther up it and camp, and then hunt up or down at night. Half a mile above this, at a place where I saw the Aster puniceus and the beaked hazel, as we paddled along, Joe, hearing a slight rustling amid the alders, and seeing something black about two rods off, jumped up and whispered, "Bear!" but before the hunter had discharged his piece, he corrected himself to "Beaver!"—"Hedgehog!" The bullet killed a large hedgehog more than two feet and eight inches long. The quills were rayed out and flattened on the hinder part of its back, even as if it had lain on that part, but were erect and long between this and the tail. Their

points, closely examined, were seen to be finely bearded or
barbed, and shaped like an awl, that is, a little concave, to

give the barbs effect. After about a mile of still water, we prepared our camp on the right side, just at the foot of a considerable fall. Little chopping was done that night, for fear
of scaring the moose. We had moose meat fried for supper. It
tasted like tender beef, with perhaps more flavor,—sometimes like veal.

After supper, the moon having risen, we proceeded to
hunt a mile up this stream, first "carrying" about the falls.
We made a picturesque sight, wending single file along the
shore, climbing over rocks and logs,—Joe, who brought up
the rear, twirling his canoe in his hands as if it were a feather,
in places where it was difficult to get along without a burden.
We launched the canoe again from the ledge over which
the stream fell, but after half a mile of still water, suitable for
hunting, it became rapid again, and we were compelled to
make our way along the shore, while Joe endeavored to get
up in the birch alone, though it was still very difficult for
him to pick his way amid the rocks in the night.

We on the shore found the worst of walking, a perfect
chaos of fallen and drifted trees, and of bushes projecting
far over the water, and now and then we made our way
across the mouth of a small tributary on a kind of network
of alders. So we went tumbling on in the dark, being on the
shady side, effectually scaring all the moose and bears that

might be thereabouts. At length we came to a standstill, and
Joe went forward to reconnoitre; but he reported that it was
still a continuous rapid as far as he went, or half a mile, with
no prospect of improvement, as if it were coming down from
a mountain. So we turned about, hunting back to the camp
through the still water.

It was a splendid moonlight night, and I, getting sleepy
as it grew late,—for I had nothing to do,—found it difficult
to realize where I was. This stream was much more unfrequented than the main one, lumbering operations being no
longer carried on in this quarter. It was only three or four
rods wide, but the firs and spruce through which it trickled
seemed yet taller by contrast. Being in this dreamy state,
which the moonlight enhanced, I did not clearly discern the
shore, but seemed, most of the time, to be floating through
ornamental grounds,—for I associated the fir-tops with such
scenes;—very high up some Broadway, and beneath or between their tops, I thought I saw an endless succession of
porticoes and columns, cornices and façades, verandas and
churches. I did not merely fancy this, but in my drowsy state
such was the illusion. I fairly lost myself in sleep several
times, still dreaming of that architecture and the nobility
that dwelt behind and might issue from it; but all at once I
would be aroused and brought back to a sense of my actual
position by the sound of Joe's birch-horn in the midst of all
this silence calling the moose, *ugh, ugh, oo-oo-oo-oo-oo-oo*,
and I prepared to hear a furious moose come rushing and
crashing through the forest, and see him burst out on to the
little strip of meadow by our side.

But, on more accounts than one, I had had enough of
moose-hunting. I had not come to the woods for this purpose,
nor had I foreseen it, though I had been willing to learn how
the Indian manœuvred: but one moose killed was as good,

if not as bad, as a dozen. The afternoon's tragedy, and my share in it, as it affected the innocence, destroyed the pleasure of my adventure. It is true, I came as near as is possible to come to being a hunter and miss it, myself; and as it is, I think that I could spend a year in the woods, fishing and hunting just enough to sustain myself, with satisfaction. This would be next to living like a philosopher on the fruits of the earth which you had raised, which also attracts me.

But this hunting of the moose merely for the satisfaction of killing him,—not even for the sake of his hide,—without making any extraordinary exertion or running any risk yourself, is too much like going out by night to some wood-side pasture and shooting your neighbor's horses. These are God's own horses, poor, timid creatures, that will run fast enough as soon as they smell you, though they *are* nine feet high. Joe told us of some hunters who a year or two before had shot down several oxen by night, somewhere in the Maine woods, mistaking them for moose. And so might any of the hunters; and what is the difference in the sport, but the name? In the former case, having killed one of God's and *your own* oxen, you strip off its hide,—because that is the common trophy, and, moreover, you have heard that it may be sold for moccasins,—cut a steak from its haunches, and leave the huge carcass to smell to heaven for you. It is no better, at least, than to assist at a slaughterhouse.

This afternoon's experience suggested to me how base or coarse are the motives which commonly carry men into the wilderness. The explorers and lumberers generally are all hirelings, paid so much a day for their labor, and as such they have no more love for wild nature than wood-sawyers have for forests. Other white men and Indians who come here are for the most part hunters, whose object is to slay as many moose and other wild animals as possible. But, pray, could not one spend some weeks or years in the solitude of this vast wilderness with other employments than these—employments perfectly sweet and innocent and ennobling? For one that comes with a pencil to sketch or sing, a thousand come with an axe or rifle. What a coarse and imperfect use Indians and hunters make of Nature! No wonder that their race is so soon exterminated. I already, and for weeks afterward, felt my nature the coarser for this part of my woodland experience, and was reminded that our life should be lived as tenderly and daintily as one would pluck a flower.

With these thoughts, when we reached our camping-ground, I decided to leave my companions to continue moose-hunting down the stream, while I prepared the camp, though they requested me not to chop much nor make a large fire, for fear I should scare their game. In the midst of the damp fir-wood, high on the mossy bank, about nine o'clock of this bright moonlight night, I kindled a fire, when they were gone, and, sitting on the fir-twigs, within sound of the falls, examined by its light the botanical specimens which I had collected that afternoon, and wrote down some of the reflections which I have here expanded; or I walked along the shore and gazed up the stream, where the whole space above the falls was filled with mellow light. As I sat before the fire on my fir-twig seat, without walls above or around me, I remembered how far on every hand that wilderness stretched, before you came to cleared or cultivated fields, and wondered if any bear or moose was watching the light of my fire; for Nature looked sternly upon me on account of the murder of the moose.

Strange that so few ever came to the woods to see how the pine lives and grows and spires, lifting its evergreen arms to the light,—to see its perfect success; but most are content to behold it in the shape of many broad boards brought to market, and deem *that* its true success! But the pine is no more lumber than man is, and to be made into boards and

houses is no more its true and highest use than the truest use
of a man is to be cut down and made into manure. There is
a higher law affecting our relation to pines as well as to men.

A pine cut down, a dead pine, is no more a pine than a
dead human carcass is a man. Can he who has discovered
only some of the values of whalebone and whale oil be said
to have discovered the true use of the whale? Can he who
slays the elephant for his ivory be said to have "seen the
elephant"? These are petty and accidental uses; just as if a
stronger race were to kill us in order to make buttons and
flageolets of our bones; for everything may serve a lower as
well as a higher use. Every creature is better alive than dead,
men and moose and pine-trees, and he who understands it
aright will rather preserve its life than destroy it.

Is it the lumberman, then, who is the friend and lover of
the pine, stands nearest to it, and understands its nature best?
Is it the tanner who has barked it, or he who has boxed it
for turpentine, whom posterity will fable to have been
changed into a pine at last? No! no! it is the poet; he it is
who makes the truest use of the pine,—who does not fondle
it with an axe, nor tickle it with a saw, nor stroke it with a
plane,—who knows whether its heart is false without cutting into it,—who has not bought the stumpage of the township on which it stands. All the pines shudder and heave a
sigh when *that* man steps on the forest floor. No, it is the
poet, who loves them as his own shadow in the air, and lets
them stand.

I have been into the lumber-yard, and the carpenter's shop,
and the tannery, and the lampblack factory, and the turpentine clearing; but when at length I saw the tops of the
pines waving and reflecting the light at a distance high over
all the rest of the forest, I realized that the former were not
the highest uses of the pine. It is not their bones or hide or
tallow that I love most. It is the living spirit of the tree, not

its spirit of turpentine, with which I sympathize, and which heals my cuts. It is as immortal as I am, and perchance will go to as high a heaven, there to tower above me still.

Erelong, the hunters returned, not having seen a moose, but, in consequence of my suggestions, bringing a quarter of the dead one, which, with ourselves, made quite a load for the canoe.

5. Ansell Smith's

AFTER breakfasting on moose meat, we returned down Pine Stream on our way to Chesuncook Lake, which was about five miles distant. We could see the red carcass of the moose lying in Pine Stream when nearly half a mile off. Just below the mouth of this stream were the most considerable rapids between the two lakes, called Pine Stream Falls, where were large flat rocks washed smooth, and at this time you could easily wade across above them.[1]

Joe ran down alone while we walked over the portage, my companion collecting spruce gum for his friends at home, and I looking for flowers. Near the lake, which we were ap-

---

[1] Four years later when passing this spot Thoreau recalled:

"A Bangor merchant had told us that two men in his employ were drowned some time ago while passing these falls in a batteau, and a third clung to a rock all night, and was taken off in the morning."

Pine Stream Falls have long since disappeared—"flowed out," in the vernacular—by the raising of the level of Chesuncook Lake by Ripogenus Dam. They are visible only when the water is occasionally pulled down to a very low level.

proaching with as much expectation as if it had been a university,—for it is not often that the stream of our life opens into such expansions,—were islands, and a low and meadowy shore with scattered trees, birches, white and yellow, slanted over the water, and maples,—many of the white birches killed, apparently by inundations. There was considerable native grass; and even a few cattle—whose movements we heard, though we did not see them, mistaking them at first for moose—were pastured there.

On entering the lake, where the stream runs southeasterly, and for some time before, we had a view of the mountains about Ktaadn (*Katahdinauquoh* one says they are called), like a cluster of blue fungi of rank growth, apparently twenty-five or thirty miles distant, in a southeast direction, their summits concealed by clouds. Joe called some of them the *Souadneunk* mountains. This is the name of a stream there, which another Indian told us meant "Running between mountains." Though some lower summits were afterward uncovered, we got no more complete view of Ktaadn while we were in the woods.

The clearing to which we were bound was on the right of the mouth of the river, and was reached by going round a low point, where the water was shallow to a great distance from the shore. Chesuncook Lake extends northwest and southeast, and is called eighteen miles long and three wide, without an island.[1] We had entered the northwest corner of it, and when near the shore could see only part way down it. The principal mountains visible from the land here were those already mentioned, between southeast and east, and a few summits a little west of north, but generally the north and northwest horizon about the St. John and the British boundary was comparatively level.

---

[1] This is no longer the fact. In the upper end of the Lake, Gero Island has been formed by the backed-up flowage.

Ansell Smith's, the oldest and principal clearing about this lake, appeared to be quite a harbor for batteaux and canoes; seven or eight of the former were lying about, and there was a small scow for hay, and a capstan on a platform, now high and dry, ready to be floated and anchored to tow rafts with. It was a very primitive kind of harbor, where boats were drawn up amid the stumps,—such a one, methought, as the Argo might have been launched in. There were five other huts with small clearings on the opposite side of the lake, all at this end and visible from this point. One of the Smiths told me that it was so far cleared that they came here to live and built the present house four years before, though the family had been here but a few months.

I was interested to see how a pioneer lived on this side of the country. His life is in some respects more adventurous than that of his brother in the West; for he contends with winter as well as the wilderness, and there is a greater interval of time at least between him and the army which is to follow. Here immigration is a tide which may ebb when it has swept away the pines; there it is not a tide, but an inundation, and roads and other improvements come steadily rushing after.

As we approached the log-house, a dozen rods from the lake, and considerably elevated above it, the projecting ends of the logs lapping over each other irregularly several feet at the corners gave it a very rich and picturesque look, far removed from the meanness of weather-boards. It was a very spacious, low building, about eighty feet long, with many large apartments. The walls were well clayed between the logs, which were large and round, except on the upper and under sides, and as visible inside as out, successive bulging cheeks gradually lessening upwards and tuned to each other with the axe, like Pandean pipes.

Probably the musical forest gods had not yet cast them

HENRY
BUGBEE
KANE

aside; they never do till they are split or the bark is gone. It was a style of architecture not described by Vitruvius, I suspect, though possibly hinted at in the biography of Orpheus; none of your frilled or fluted columns, which have cut such a false swell, and support nothing but a gable end and their builder's pretensions,—that is, with the multitude; and as for "ornamentation," one of those words with a dead tail which architects very properly use to describe their flourishes, there were the lichens and mosses and fringes of bark, which nobody troubled himself about. We certainly leave the handsomest paint and clapboards behind in the woods, when we strip off the bark and poison ourselves with white-lead in the towns. We get but half the spoils of the forest. For beauty, give me trees with the fur on.

This house was designed and constructed with the free-dom of stroke of a forester's axe, without other compass and square than Nature uses. Wherever the logs were cut off by a window or door, that is, were not kept in place by alternate overlapping, they were held one upon another by very large pins, driven in diagonally on each side, where branches might have been, and then cut off so close up and down as not to project beyond the bulge of the log, as if the logs clasped each other in their arms. These logs were posts, studs, boards, clap-boards, laths, plaster, and nails, all in one. Where the citizen uses a mere sliver or board, the pioneer uses the whole trunk of a tree. The house had large stone chimneys, and was roofed with spruce-bark. The windows were imported, all but the casings. One end was a regular logger's camp, for the board-ers, with the usual fir floor and log benches. Thus this house was but a slight departure from the hollow tree, which the bear still inhabits,—being a hollow made with trees piled up, with a coating of bark like its original.

The cellar was a separate building, like an ice-house, and it answered for a refrigerator at this season, our moose meat being kept there. It was a potato hole with a permanent roof. Each structure and institution here was so primitive that you could at once refer it to its source; but our buildings commonly suggest neither their origin nor their purpose. There was a large, and what farmers would call handsome, barn, part of whose boards had been sawed by a whip-saw; and the saw-pit, with its great pile of dust, remained before the house. The long split shingles on a portion of the barn were laid a foot to the weather, suggesting what kind of weather they have there. Grant's barn at Caribou Lake was said to be still larger, the biggest ox-nest in the woods, fifty feet by a hundred. Think of a monster barn in that primitive forest lifting its gray back above the tree-tops! Man makes very much such a nest for his domestic animals, of withered grass and fodder, as the squirrels and many other wild creatures do for themselves.

There was also a blacksmith's shop, where plainly a good deal of work was done. The oxen and horses used in lumbering operations were shod, and all the iron-work of sleds, etc., was repaired or made here. I saw them load a batteau at the Moosehead carry, the next Tuesday, with about thirteen hundredweight of bar iron for this shop. This reminded me how primitive and honorable a trade was Vulcan's. I do not hear that there was any carpenter or tailor among the gods. The smith seems to have preceded these and every other mechanic at Chesuncook as well as on Olympus, and his family is the most widely dispersed, whether he be christened John or Ansell.

Smith owned two miles down the lake by half a mile in width. There were about one hundred acres cleared here. He cut seventy tons of English hay this year on this ground, and twenty more on another clearing, and he uses it all himself in lumbering operations. The barn was crowded with pressed hay, and a machine to press it. There was a large gar-

den full of roots,—turnips, beets, carrots, potatoes, etc., all
of great size. They said that they were worth as much here
as in New York. I suggested some currants for sauce, especially as they had no apple-trees set out, and showed how
they could be easily obtained.

There was the usual long-handled axe of the primitive
woods by the door, three and a half feet long,—for my new
black-ash rule was in constant use,—and a large, shaggy dog,
whose nose, report said, was full of porcupine quills. I can
testify that he looked very sober. This is the usual fortune of
pioneer dogs, for they have to face the brunt of the battle for
their race, and act the part of Arnold Winkelried without intending it. If he should invite one of his town friends up this
way, suggesting moose meat and unlimited freedom, the latter might pertinently inquire, "What is that sticking in your
nose?" When a generation or two have used up all the ene-
mies' darts, their successors lead a comparatively easy life.
We owe to our fathers analogous blessings. Many old people
receive pensions for no other reason, it seems to me, but as a
compensation for having lived a long time ago. No doubt our
town dogs still talk, in a snuffling way, about the days that
tried dogs' noses. How they got a cat up there I do not know,
for they are as shy as my aunt about entering a canoe. I wondered that she did not run up a tree on the way; but perhaps
she was bewildered by the very crowd of opportunities.

Twenty or thirty lumberers, Yankee and Canadian, were
coming and going,—Aleck among the rest,—and from time
to time an Indian touched here. In the winter there are
sometimes a hundred men lodged here at once. The most interesting piece of news that circulated among them appeared
to be, that four horses belonging to Smith, worth seven hundred dollars, had passed by farther into the woods a week
before.

The white-pine-tree was at the bottom or farther end of

all this. It is a war against the pines, the only real Aroostook or Penobscot war.[1] I have no doubt that they lived pretty much the same sort of life in the Homeric age, for men have always thought more of eating than of fighting; then, as now, their minds ran chiefly on the "hot bread and sweet cakes;" and the fur and lumber trade is an old story to Asia and Europe. I doubt if men ever made a trade of heroism. In the days of Achilles, even, they delighted in big barns, and perchance in pressed hay, and he who possessed the most valuable team was the best fellow.

We had designed to go on at evening up the Caucomgomoc, whose mouth was a mile or two distant, to the lake of the same name, about ten miles off; but some Indians of Joe's acquaintance, who were making canoes on the Caucomgomoc, came over from that side, and gave so poor an account of the moose-hunting, so many had been killed there lately, that my companions concluded not to go there. Joe spent this Sunday and the night with his acquaintances. The lumberers told me that there were many moose hereabouts, but no caribou or deer. A man from Oldtown had killed ten or twelve moose, within a year, so near the house that they heard all his guns. His name may have been Hercules, for aught I know, though I should rather have expected to hear the rattling of his club; but, no doubt, he keeps pace with

---

[1] Early in 1839 a state of war had actually threatened between Maine and the Province of New Brunswick. The quest for white pine in the country which now forms Aroostook County had been its cause, owing to the unsettled state of the northeastern boundary. In addition to private warfare among the lumberers, it led to the building of forts and the marching of militia, but there was no bloodshed. By cleverly conducted mediation General Winfield Scott averted actual hostilities and the troops were disbanded. The line was settled by the Webster-Ashburton Treaty in 1842. Thoreau makes several references to this affair, known as the Aroostook War. It appears that Joe Polis had assisted one of the surveying parties.

"He had been consulted at Augusta, and gave advice, which he said was followed, respecting the eastern boundary of Maine, as determined by highlands and streams, at the time of the difficulties on that side. He was employed with the surveyors on the line."

the improvements of the age, and uses a Sharps' rifle now; probably he gets all his armor made and repaired at Smith's shop. One moose had been killed and another shot at within the sight of the house within two years. I do not know whether Smith has yet got a poet to look after the cattle, which, on account of the early breaking up of the ice, are compelled to summer in the woods, but I would suggest this office to such of my acquaintances as love to write verses and go a-gunning.

After a dinner, at which apple-sauce was the greatest luxury to me, but our moose meat was oftenest called for by the lumberers, I walked across the clearing into the forest, southward, returning along the shore. For my dessert, I helped myself to a large slice of the Chesuncook woods, and took a hearty draught of its waters with all my senses. The woods were as fresh and full of vegetable life as a lichen in wet weather, and contained many interesting plants; but unless they are of white-pine, they are treated with as little respect here as a mildew, and in the other case they are only the more quickly cut down. The shore was of coarse, flat, slate rocks, often in slabs, with the surf beating on it. The rocks and bleached drift-logs, extending some way into the shaggy woods, showed a rise and fall of six or eight feet, caused partly by the dam at the outlet. They said that in winter the snow was three feet deep on a level here, and sometimes

four or five,—that the ice on the lake was two feet thick, clear, and four feet including the snow-ice. Ice had already formed in vessels.

We lodged here this Sunday night in a comfortable bed-room, apparently the best one; and all that I noticed unusual in the night—for I still kept taking notes, like a spy in the camp—was the creaking of the thin split boards, when any of our neighbors stirred.

Such were the first rude beginnings of a town.[1] They spoke of the practicability of a winter road to the Moosehead carry, which would not cost much, and would connect them with steam and staging and all the busy world. I almost doubted if the lake would be there,—the self-same lake,—preserve its form and identity, when the shores should be cleared and settled; as if these lakes and streams which explorers report never awaited the advent of the citizen.

The sight of one of these frontier houses, built of these great logs, whose inhabitants have unflinchingly maintained

[1] This little community of Chesuncook today numbers about fifty houses and is known in the Maine woods as Suncook, or sometimes as Suncook Village. It was founded, as noted by Thoreau, in 1849, by Ansell Smith. A few years later he brought his family and women and children were there in Thoreau's time. In 1916, as a result of the construction of the modern dam at Ripogenus at the foot of Chesuncook Lake, the site of the old cemetery was "flowed out." Seventy bodies were removed to higher ground. As in the 1850's, its prosperity depends upon lumbering operations and to this day no road leads in to it.

their ground many summers and winters in the wilderness, reminds me of famous forts, like Ticonderoga or Crown Point, which have sustained memorable sieges. They are especially winter-quarters, and at this season this one had a partially deserted look, as if the siege were raised a little, the snow-banks being melted from before it, and its garrison accordingly reduced. I think of their daily food as rations,—it is called "supplies;" a Bible and a great-coat are munitions of war, and a single man seen about the premises is a sentinel on duty. You expect that he will require the countersign, and will perchance take you for Ethan Allen, come to demand the surrender of his fort in the name of the Continental Congress. It is a sort of ranger service. Arnold's expedition is a daily experience with these settlers.[1] They can prove that they were out at almost any time; and I think that all the first generation of them deserve a pension more than any that went to the Mexican war.

---

[1] The reference is to Benedict Arnold's march up the Kennebec, across the Dead River region and over the Height-of-Land to Quebec, in the fall of 1775.

6. The Indian Camp

EARLY the next morning we started on our return up the Penobscot, my companion wishing to go about twenty-five miles above the Moosehead carry to a camp near the junction of the two forks, and look for moose there. Our host allowed us something for the quarter of the moose which we had brought, and which he was glad to get. Two explorers from Chamberlain Lake started at the same time that we did. Red flannel shirts should be worn in the woods, if only for the fine contrast which this color makes with the evergreens and the water.

Thus I thought when I saw the forms of the explorers in their birch, poling up the rapids before us, far off against the forest. It is the surveyor's color also, most distinctly seen under all circumstances. We stopped to dine at Ragmuff, as

before. My companion it was who wandered up the stream
to look for moose this time, while Joe went to sleep on the
bank, so that we felt sure of him; and I improved the opportunity to botanize and bathe. Soon after starting again, while
Joe was gone back in the canoe for the frying-pan, which had
been left, we picked a couple of quarts of tree-cranberries for
a sauce.

I was surprised by Joe's asking me how far it was to the
Moosehorn. He was pretty well acquainted with this stream,
but he had noticed that I was curious about distances, and
had several maps. He and Indians generally, with whom I
have talked, are not able to describe dimensions or distances
in our measures with any accuracy. He could tell, perhaps,
at what time we should arrive, but not how far it was.

We saw a few wood-ducks, sheldrakes, and black ducks,
but they were not so numerous there at that season as on our
river at home. We scared the same family of wood-ducks before us, going and returning. We also heard the note of one
fish-hawk, somewhat like that of a pigeon-woodpecker, and
soon after we saw him perched near the top of a dead white-
pine against the island where we had first camped, while a
company of peetweets were twittering and teetering about
over the carcass of a moose on a low sandy spit just beneath.
We drove the fish-hawk from perch to perch, each time elicit-
ing a scream or whistle, for many miles before us. Our course
being up-stream, we were obliged to work much harder than
before, and had frequent use for a pole. Sometimes all three
of us paddled together, standing up, small and heavily laden
as the canoe was. About six miles from Moosehead, we began to see the mountains east of the north end of the lake,
and at four o'clock we reached the carry.

The Indians were still encamped here.[1] There were three,

---

[1] On the way down, curiously enough, Thoreau's "Chesuncook" account
does not mention this Indian camp. The reason indubitably is that in his

including the St. Francis Indian who had come in the steamer
with us. One of the others was called Sabattis. Joe and the
St. Francis Indian were plainly clear Indian, the other two
apparently mixed Indian and white; but the difference was
confined to their features and complexion, for all that I could
see. We here cooked the tongue of the moose for supper,—
having left the nose, which is esteemed the choicest part, at
Chesuncook, boiling, it being a good deal of trouble to pre-

pare it. We also stewed our tree-cranberries (Viburnum
opulus), sweetening them with sugar. The lumberers sometimes cook them with molasses. They were used in Arnold's
expedition. This sauce was very grateful to us who had been
confined to hard bread, pork, and moose meat, and, not with-
standing their seeds, we all three pronounced them equal to
the common cranberry; but perhaps some allowance is to
be made for our forest appetites. It would be worth the while
to cultivate them, both for beauty and for food. I afterward

Journal he described at some length the technical detail of the building of
a canoe there. This was omitted in the preparation of "Chesuncook," and
with it went all reference to the Indian camp. This camp was still there in
1857. See Appendix, page 326. For the description of the construction of the
canoe see pp. 300 ff.

saw them in a garden in Bangor. Joe said that they were called *ebeemenar*.

While we were getting supper, Joe commenced curing the moose-hide, on which I had sat a good part of the voyage, he having already cut most of the hair off with his knife at the Caucomgomoc. He set up two stout forked poles on the bank, seven or eight feet high, and as much asunder east and west, and having cut slits eight or ten inches long, and the same distance apart, close to the edge, on the sides of the hide, he threaded poles through them, and then, placing one of the poles on the forked stakes, tied the other down tightly at the bottom. The two ends also were tied with cedar-bark, their usual string, to the upright poles, through small holes at short intervals. The hide, thus stretched, and slanted a little to the north, to expose its flesh side to the sun, measured, in the extreme, eight feet long by six high. Where any flesh still adhered, Joe boldly scored it with his knife to lay it open to the sun. It now appeared somewhat spotted and injured by the duck shot. You may see the old frames on which hides have been stretched at many camping-places in these woods.

For some reason or other, the going to the forks of the Penobscot was given up, and we decided to stop here, my companion intending to hunt down the stream at night. The Indians invited us to lodge with them, but my companion inclined to go to the log-camp on the carry. This camp was close and dirty, and had an ill smell, and I preferred to accept the Indians' offer, if we did not make a camp for ourselves; for, though they were dirty, too, they were more in the open air, and were much more agreeable, and even refined company, than the lumberers. The most interesting question entertained at the lumberers' camp was, which man could "handle" any other on the carry; and, for the most part, they possessed no qualities which you could not lay hands on. So we went to the Indians' camp or wigwam.

It was rather windy, and therefore Joe concluded to hunt after midnight, if the wind went down, which the other Indians thought it would not do, because it was from the south. The two mixed-bloods, however, went off up the river for moose at dark, before we arrived at their camp. This Indian camp was a slight, patched-up affair, which had stood there several weeks, built shed-fashion, open to the fire on the west. If the wind changed, they could turn it round. It was formed by two forked stakes and a cross-bar, with rafters slanted from this to the ground. The covering was partly an old sail, partly birch-bark, quite imperfect, but securely tied on, and coming down to the ground on the sides. A large log was rolled up at the back side for a headboard, and two or three moose-hides were spread on the ground with the hair up. Various articles of their wardrobe were tucked around the sides and corners, or under the roof.

They were smoking moose meat on just such a crate as is represented by With, in De Bry's "Collectio Peregrinationum," published in 1588, and which the natives of Brazil called *boucan* (whence buccaneer), on which were frequently shown pieces of human flesh drying along with the rest. It was erected in front of the camp over the usual large fire, in the form of an oblong square. Two stout forked stakes, four or five feet apart and five feet high, were driven into the ground at each end, and then two poles ten feet long were stretched across over the fire, and smaller ones laid transversely on these a foot apart. On the last hung large, thin slices of moose meat smoking and drying, a space being left open over the centre of the fire. There was the whole heart, black as a thirty-two pound ball, hanging at one corner.

They said that it took three or four days to cure this meat, and it would keep a year or more. Refuse pieces lay about on the ground in different stages of decay, and some pieces also in the fire, half buried and sizzling in the ashes, as black and

dirty as an old shoe. These last I at first thought were thrown away, but afterwards found that they were being cooked. Also a tremendous rib-piece was roasting before the fire, being impaled on an upright stake forced in and out between the ribs. There was a moose-hide stretched and curing on poles like ours, and quite a pile of cured skins close by. They had killed twenty-two moose within two months, but, as they could use but very little of the meat, they left the carcasses on the ground. Altogether it was about as savage a sight as was ever witnessed, and I was carried back at once three hundred years. There were many torches of birch-bark, shaped like straight tin horns, lying ready for use on a stump outside.

For fear of dirt, we spread our blankets over their hides, so as not to touch them anywhere. The St. Francis Indian and Joe alone were there at first, and we lay on our backs talking with them till midnight. They were very sociable, and, when they did not talk with us, kept up a steady chatting in their own language. We heard a small bird just after dark, which, Joe said, sang at a certain hour in the night,—at ten o'clock, he believed. We also heard the hylodes and tree-toads, and the lumberers singing in their camp a quarter of a mile off. I told them that I had seen pictured in old books pieces of human flesh drying on these crates; whereupon they repeated some tradition about the Mohawks eating human flesh, what parts they preferred, etc., and also of a battle with the Mohawks near Moosehead, in which many of the latter were killed; but I found that they knew but little of the history of their race, and could be entertained by stories about their ancestors as readily as any way.

At first I was nearly roasted out, for I lay against one side of the camp, and felt the heat reflected not only from the birch-bark above, but from the side; and again I remembered the sufferings of the Jesuit missionaries, and what extremes of heat and cold the Indians were said to endure. I struggled long between my desire to remain and talk with them and my impulse to rush out and stretch myself on the cool grass; and when I was about to take the last step, Joe, hearing my murmurs, or else being uncomfortable himself, got up and partially dispersed the fire. I suppose that that is Indian manners, —to defend yourself.

While lying there listening to the Indians, I amused myself with trying to guess at their subject by their gestures, or some proper name introduced. There can be no more startling evidence of their being a distinct and comparatively aboriginal race than to hear this unaltered Indian language, which the white man cannot speak nor understand. We may suspect change and deterioration in almost every other particular but the language which is so wholly unintelligible to us. It took me by surprise, though I had found so many arrow-heads, and convinced me that the Indian was not the invention of historians and poets. It was a purely wild and primitive American sound, as much as the barking of a *chickaree*, and I could not understand a syllable of it; but Paugus, had he been there, would have understood it. These Abenakis gossiped, laughed, and jested, in the language in which Eliot's Indian Bible is written, the language which has been spoken in New England who shall say how long? These were the sounds that issued from the wigwams of this country before Columbus was born; they have not yet died away; and, with remarkably few exceptions, the language of their forefathers is still copious enough for them. I felt that I stood, or rather lay, as near to the primitive man of America, that night, as any of its discoverers ever did.[1]

In the midst of their conversation, Joe suddenly appealed to me to know how long Moosehead Lake was.

Meanwhile, as we lay there, Joe was making and trying his

---

[1] A list of Indian words compiled by Thoreau will be found in the Appendix on page 336.

horn, to be ready for hunting after midnight. The St. Francis Indian also amused himself with sounding it, or rather calling through it; for the sound is made with the voice, and not by blowing through the horn. The latter appeared to be a speculator in moose-hides. He bought my companion's for two dollars and a quarter, green. Joe said that it was worth two and a half at Oldtown. Its chief use is for moccasins. One or two of these Indians wore them. I was told that, by a recent law of Maine, foreigners are not allowed to kill moose there at any season; white Americans can kill them only at a particular season, but the Indians of Maine at all seasons.[1] The St. Francis Indian accordingly asked my companion for a *wighiggin*, or bill, to show, since he was a foreigner. He lived near Sorel. I found that he could write his name very well, Tahmunt Swasen.

One Ellis, an old white man of Guilford, a town through which we passed, not far from the south end of Moosehead, was the most celebrated moose-hunter of those parts. Indians and whites spoke with equal respect of him. Tahmunt said that there were more moose here than in the Adirondack country in New York, where he had hunted; that three years before there were a great many about, and there were a great many now in the woods, but they did not come out to the water. It was of no use to hunt them at midnight,—they would not come out then. I asked Sabattis, after he came home, if the moose never attacked him. He answered that you must not fire many times, so as to mad him. "I fire once and hit him in the right place, and in the morning I find him. He won't go far. But if you keep firing, you mad him. I fired once five bullets, every one through the heart, and he did not mind 'em at all; it only made him more mad." I asked him if

---

[1] A statute containing the provisions described by Thoreau had passed the Maine Legislature and was approved on March 29, 1853 (*Chapter 27 of the Acts and Resolves of the State of Maine, 1853*).

they did not hunt them with dogs. He said that they did so in winter, but never in the summer, for then it was of no use; they would run right off straight and swiftly a hundred miles.

Another Indian said that the moose, once scared, would run all day. A dog will hang to their lips, and be carried along till he is swung against a tree and drops off. They cannot run on a "glaze," though they can run in snow four feet deep; but the caribou can run on ice. They commonly find two or three moose together. They cover themselves with water, all but their noses, to escape flies. He had the horns of what he called "the black moose that goes in low lands." These spread three or four feet. The "red moose" was another kind, "running on mountains," and had horns which spread six feet. Such were his distinctions. Both can move their horns. The broad flat blades are covered with hair, and are so soft, when the animal is alive, that you can run a knife through them. They regard it as a good or bad sign, if the horns turn this way or that. His caribou horns had been gnawed by mice in his wigwam, but he thought that the horns neither of the moose nor of the caribou were ever gnawed while the creature was alive, as some have asserted.

An Indian, whom I met after this at Oldtown, who had carried about a bear and other animals of Maine to exhibit, told me that thirty years ago there were not so many moose in Maine as now; also, that the moose were very easily tamed, and would come back when once fed, and so would deer, but not caribou. The Indians of this neighborhood are about as familiar with the moose as we are with the ox, having associated with them for so many generations. Father Rasles, in his Dictionary of the Abenaki Language, gives not only a word for the male moose (*aianbé*), and another for the female (*hèrar*), but for the bone which is in the middle of the heart of the moose (!), and for his left hind-leg.

There were none of the small deer up there; they are more

common about the settlements. One ran into the city of Bangor two years before, and jumped through a window of costly plate glass, and then into a mirror, where it thought it recognized one of its kind, and out again, and so on, leaping over the heads of the crowd, until it was captured. This the inhabitants speak of as the deer that went a-shopping. The last-mentioned Indian spoke of the *lunxus* or Indian devil (which I take to be the cougar, and not the *Gulo luscus*) as the only animal in Maine which man need fear; it would follow a man, and did not mind a fire. He also said that beavers were getting to be pretty numerous again, where we went, but their skins brought so little now that it was not profitable to hunt them.

I had put the ears of our moose, which were ten inches long, to dry along with the moose meat over the fire, wishing to preserve them; but Sabattis told me that I must skin and cure them, else the hair would all come off. He observed that they made tobacco pouches of the skins of their ears, putting the two together inside to inside. I asked him how he got fire; and he produced a little cylindrical box of friction matches. He also had flints and steel, and some punk, which was not dry; I think it was from the yellow birch. "But suppose you upset, and all these and your powder get wet." "Then," said he, "we wait till we get to where there is some fire." I produced from my pocket a little vial, containing matches, stoppled watertight, and told him, that, though we were upset, we should still have some dry matches; at which he stared without saying a word.

We lay awake thus a long while talking, and they gave us the meaning of many Indian names of lakes and streams in the vicinity,—especially Tahmunt. I asked the Indian name of Moosehead Lake. Joe answered *Sebamook;* Tahmunt pronounced it *Sebemook.* When I asked what it meant, they answered, Moosehead Lake. At length, getting my meaning, they alternately repeated the word over to themselves, as a philologist might,—*Sebamook*,—*Sebamook*,—now and then comparing notes in Indian; for there was a slight difference in their dialects; and finally Tahmunt said, "Ugh! I know,"— and he rose up partly on the moose-hide,—"like as here is a place, and there is a place," pointing to different parts of the hide, "and you take water from there and fill this, and it stays here; that is *Sebamook*."

I understood him to mean that it was a reservoir of water which did not run away, the river coming in on one side and passing out again near the same place, leaving a permanent bay. Another Indian said, that it meant Large Bay Lake, and that *Sebago* and *Sebec*, the names of other lakes, were kindred words, meaning large open water. Joe said that *Seboois* meant Little River. I observed their inability, often described, to convey an abstract idea. Having got the idea, though indistinctly, they groped about in vain for words with which to express it. Tahmunt thought that the whites called it Moose-head Lake, because Mount Kineo, which commands it, is shaped like a moose's head, and that Moose River was so called "because the mountain points right across the lake to its mouth." John Josselyn, writing about 1673, says, "Twelve miles from Casco Bay, and passable for men and horses, is a lake, called by the Indians Sebug. On the brink thereof, at one end, is the famous rock, shaped like a moose deer or helk, diaphanous, and called the Moose Rock." He appears to have confounded Sebamook with Sebago, which is nearer, but has no "diaphanous" rock on its shore.

I give more of their definitions, for what they are worth,— partly *because* they differ sometimes from the commonly received ones. They never analyzed these words before. After long deliberation and repeating of the word, for it gave much trouble, Tahmunt said that *Chesuncook* meant a place where many streams emptied in (?), and he enumerated them,— Penobscot, Umbazookskus, Cusabesex, Red Brook, etc.—

"*Caucomgomoc,*—what does that mean?" "What are those large white birds?" he asked. "Gulls," said I. "Ugh! Gull Lake."— *Pammadumcook,* Joe thought, meant the Lake with Gravelly Bottom or Bed.—*Kenduskeag,* Tahmunt concluded at last, after asking if birches went up it, for he said that he was not much acquainted with it, meant something like this: "You go up Penobscot till you come to *Kenduskeag,* and you go by, you don't turn up there. That is *Kenduskeag.*" (?) Another Indian, however, who knew the river better, told us afterward that it meant Little Eel River.—*Mattawamkeag* was a place where two rivers meet. (?)—*Penobscot* was Rocky River. One writer says that this was "originally the name of only a section of the main channel, from the head of the tide-water to a short distance above Oldtown."

A very intelligent Indian, whom we afterward met, son-in-law of Neptune, gave us also these other definitions: *Umbazookskus,* Meadow Stream; *Millinoket,* Place of Islands; *Aboljacarmegus,* Smooth-Ledge Falls (and Dead-Water); *Aboljacarmeguscook,* the stream emptying in (the last was the word he gave when I asked about *Aboljacknagesic,* which he did not recognize); *Mattahumkeag,* Sand-Creek Pond; *Piscataquis,* Branch of a River.

I asked our hosts what *Musketaquid,* the Indian name of Concord, Massachusetts, meant; but they changed it to *Musketicook,* and repeated that, and Tahmunt said that it meant Dead Stream, which is probably true. *Cook* appears to mean stream, and perhaps *quid* signifies the place or ground. When I asked the meaning of the names of two of our hills, they answered that they were another language. As Tahmunt said that he traded at Quebec, my companion inquired the meaning of the word *Quebec,* about which there has been so much question. He did not know, but began to conjecture. He asked what those great ships were called that carried soldiers. "Men-of-war," we answered. "Well," he said, "when the English ships came up the river, they could not go any farther, it was so narrow there; they must go back,—go-back,—that's Quebec." I mention this to show the value of his authority in the other cases.

Late at night the other two Indians came home from moose-hunting, not having been successful, aroused the fire again, lighted their pipes, smoked awhile, took something strong to drink, and ate some moose meat, and, finding what room they could, lay down on the moose-hides; and thus we passed the night, two white men and four Indians, side by side.

When I awoke in the morning the weather was drizzling. One of the Indians was lying outside, rolled in his blanket, on the opposite side of the fire, for want of room. Joe had neglected to awake my companion, and he had done no hunting that night. Tahmunt was making a cross-bar for his canoe with a singularly shaped knife, such as I have since seen other Indians using. The blade was thin, about three quarters of an

inch wide, and eight or nine inches long, but curved out of its plane into a hook, which he said made it more convenient to shave with. As the Indians very far north and northwest use the same kind of knife, I suspect that it was made according to an aboriginal pattern, though some white artisans may use a similar one.[1]

---

[1] The "singularly shaped knife" was what the Maine woodsman calls his crooked knife. The cutting edge is reversed from the position in a jackknife and fitted without a joint and at an obtuse angle into a wooden handle. To use it a man turning his right hand upward grasps the handle and draws the knife toward him as if the tool were a draw shave. Thus equipped, a good

The Indians baked a loaf of flour bread in a spider on its edge before the fire for their breakfast; and while my companion was making tea, I caught a dozen sizable fishes in the Penobscot, two kinds of sucker and one trout. After we had breakfasted by ourselves, one of our bed-fellows, who had also breakfasted, came along, and, being invited, took a cup of tea, and finally, taking up the common platter, licked it clean. But he was nothing to a white fellow, a lumberer, who was continually stuffing himself with the Indians' moose meat, and was the butt of his companions accordingly. He seems to have thought that it was a feast "to eat all." It is commonly said that the white man finally surpasses the Indian on his own ground, and it was proved true in this case. I cannot swear to his employment during the hours of darkness, but I saw him at it again as soon as it was light, though he came a quarter of a mile to his work.

The rain prevented our continuing any longer in the woods; so giving some of our provisions and utensils to the Indians, we took leave of them. This being the steamer's day, I set out for the lake at once. I walked over the carry alone and waited at the head of the lake. An eagle, or some other large bird, flew screaming away from its perch by the shore at my approach. For an hour after I reached the shore there was not a human being to be seen, and I had all that wide prospect to myself.

---

woodsman will fashion handily from a log of birch, maple, ash, or cedar, with the aid of his axe, his paddle, axe, and tool handles, thwart, and so forth. Those inexpert in the use of a crooked knife had best beware. With one slip it is mighty easy to slit your left arm from wrist to elbow.

7. Chesuncook and Umbazookskus

Alone on the shore of Moosehead, Thoreau had awaited the arrival of the little steamer that was to take him to Greenville. Three days after his return by stage to Bangor, he noted on September 24, 1853: "I got my first clear view of Ktaadn on this excursion from a hill about two miles northwest of Bangor whither I went for this purpose. After this I was ready to return to Massachusetts."

From that hill Ktaadn bore just west of north. From Chesuncook Deadwater, its bearing is southeast. Thus, four years later when Thoreau reached this latter point at the head of Chesuncook Lake in company with Edward Hoar and Joe Polis, he had completed nearly half of his circuit. It is at this point that the text returns to and continues with the account of the last trip on Sunday, July 26, 1857.

From this dead water the outlines of the mountains about Ktaadn were visible. The top of Ktaadn was concealed by a cloud, but the Souneunk Mountains were nearer, and quite visible. We steered across the northwest end of the lake, from which we looked down south-southeast, the whole length to Joe Merry Mountain, seen over its extremity. It is an agreeable change to cross a lake, after you have been shut up in the woods, not only on account of the greater expanse of water, but also of sky. It is one of the surprises which Nature has in store for the traveler in the forest. To look down, in this case, over eighteen miles of water, was liberating and civilizing even. No doubt, the short distance to which you can see in the woods, and the general twilight, would at length react on the inhabitants, and make them *salvages*.

The lakes also reveal the mountains, and give ample scope and range to our thought. The very gulls which we saw sitting on the rocks, like white specks, or circling about, reminded me of custom-house officers. Already there were half a dozen log-huts about this end of the lake, though so far from a road.[1] I perceive that in these woods the earliest settlements are, for various reasons, clustering about the lakes, but partly, I think, for the sake of the neighborhood as the oldest clearings. They are forest schools already established,—great centres of light. Water is a pioneer which the settler follows, taking advantage of its improvements.

Thus far only I had been before. About noon we turned northward, up a broad kind of estuary, and at its northeast corner found the Caucomgomoc River, and after going about a mile from the lake, reached the Umbazookskus, which comes in on the right at a point where the former river, coming from the west, turns short to the south. Our course was up the Umbazookskus, but as the Indian knew of a good camping-place, that is, a cool place where there were few

---

[1] This was the camp where Thoreau had spent a day and night in 1853.

mosquitoes about half a mile farther up the Caucomgomoc, we went thither. The latter river, judging from the map, is the longer and principal stream, and, therefore, its name must prevail below the junction. So quickly we changed the civilizing sky of Chesuncook for the dark wood of the Caucomgomoc.

On reaching the Indian's camping-ground, on the south side, where the bank was about a dozen feet high, I read on the trunk of a fir-tree, blazed by an axe, an inscription in charcoal which had been left by him. It was surmounted by a drawing of a bear paddling a canoe, which he said was the sign which had been used by his family always. The drawing, though rude, could not be mistaken for anything but a bear, and he doubted my ability to copy it. The inscription ran thus, *verbatim et literatim*. I interline the English of his Indian as he gave it to me.[1]

(The figure of a bear in a boat.)
July 26,
1853.

———

Niasoseb.
We alone Joseph.
   Polis   *clioi*
   Polis   start
   sia   *olta*
   for   Oldtown
   ouke   *ni*
   right   away.
   quambi

———

July 15,
1855.
Niasoseb.

---

[1] In this respect the Maine woodsman today follows the path of the Indian. Every camp ground bears a record of his successive visits, usually written on the yellow sign of the Maine Forestry Service.

He added now below:—

1857,
July 26.
Io. Polis.

This was one of his homes. I saw where he had sometimes stretched his moose-hides on the opposite or sunny north side of the river, where there was a narrow meadow.

After we had selected a place for our camp, and kindled our fire, almost exactly on the site of the Indian's last camp here, he, looking up, observed, "That tree danger." It was a dead part, more than a foot in diameter, of a large canoe-birch, which branched at the ground. This branch, rising thirty feet or more, slanted directly over the spot which we had chosen for our bed. I told him to try it with his axe; but he could not shake it perceptibly, and therefore seemed inclined to disregard it, and my companion expressed his willingness to run the risk. But it seemed to me that we should be fools to lie under it, for though the lower part was firm, the top, for aught we knew, might be just ready to fall, and we should at any rate be very uneasy if the wind arose in the night. It is a common accident for men camping in the woods to be killed by a falling tree. So the camp was moved to the other side of the fire.

It was, as usual, a damp and shaggy forest, that Caucomgomoc one, and the most you knew about it was, that on this side it stretched toward the settlements, and on that to still more unfrequented regions. You carried so much topography in your mind always,—and sometimes it seemed to make a considerable difference whether you sat or lay nearer the settlements, or farther off, than your companions,—were the rear or frontier man of the camp. But there is really the same difference between our positions wherever we may be camped, and some are nearer the frontiers on feather-beds in the towns than others on fir-twigs in the backwoods.

The Indian said that the Umbazookskus, being a dead stream with broad meadows, was a good place for Moose, and he frequently came a-hunting here, being out alone three weeks or more from Oldtown. He sometimes, also, went a-hunting to the Seboois Lakes, taking the stage, with his gun and ammunition, axe and blankets, hard bread and pork, perhaps for a hundred miles of the way, and jumped off at the wildest place on the road, where he was at once at home, and every rod was a tavern-site for him. Then, after a short journey through the woods, he would build a spruce-bark canoe in one day, putting but few ribs into it, that it might be light, and, after doing his hunting with it on the lakes, would return with his furs the same way he had come. Thus you have an Indian availing himself cunningly of the advantages of civilization, without losing any of his woodcraft, but proving himself the more successful hunter for it.

This man was very clever and quick to learn anything in his line. Our tent was of a kind new to him; but when he had once seen it pitched, it was surprising how quickly he would find and prepare the pole and forked stakes to pitch it with, cutting and placing them right the first time, though I am sure that the majority of white men would have blundered several times.

This river came from Caucomgomoc Lake, about ten miles farther up. Though it was sluggish here, there were falls not far above us, and we saw the foam from them go by from time to time. The Indian said that *Caucomgomoc* meant Big-gull Lake (*i. e.*, Herring-gull, I suppose), *gomoc* meaning lake. Hence this was *Caucomgomoctook,* or the river from that lake. This was the Penobscot *Caucomgomoctook!* there was another St. John, one not far north. He finds the eggs of this gull, sometimes twenty together, as big as hen's eggs, on rocky ledges on the west side of Millinocket River, for instance, and eats them.

Now I thought I would observe how he spent his Sunday. While I and my companion were looking about at the trees and river, he went to sleep. Indeed, he improved every opportunity to get a nap, whatever the day.

Rambling about the woods at this camp, I noticed that they consisted chiefly of firs, black spruce, and some white, red maple, canoe-birch, and, along the river, the hoary alder, *Alnus incana*. I name them in the order of their abundance. The *Viburnum nudum* [withe-rod] was a common shrub, and of smaller plants, there were the dwarf-cornel, great round-leaved orchis, abundant and in bloom (a greenish-white flower growing in little communities), *Uvularia grandiflora* [large-flowered benwort], whose stem tasted like a cucumber, *Pyrola secunda* [one-sided Pyrola], apparently the commonest Pyrola in those woods, now out of bloom, *Pyrola elliptica* [shinleaf], and *Chiogenes hispidula* [creeping snowberry]. The *Clintonia borealis* [checkerberry], with ripe berries, was very abundant, and perfectly at home there. Its leaves, disposed commonly in triangles about its stem, were just as handsomely formed and green, and its berries as blue and glossy, as if it grew by some botanist's favorite path.

I could trace the outlines of large birches that had fallen long ago, collapsed and rotted and turned to soil, by faint yellowish-green lines of feather-like moss, eighteen inches wide and twenty or thirty feet long, crossed by other similar lines.

I heard a Maryland yellow-throat's midnight strain, wood-thrush, kingfisher (tweezer bird), or parti-colored warbler, and a night-hawk. I also heard and saw red squirrels, and heard a bullfrog. The Indian said that he heard a snake.

Wild as it was, it was hard for me to get rid of the associations of the settlements. Any steady and monotonous sound, to which I did not distinctly attend, passed for a sound of human industry. The waterfalls which I heard were not without

their dams and mills to my imagination,—and several times I
found that I had been regarding the steady rushing sound of
the wind from over the woods beyond the rivers as that of a
train of cars,—the cars at Quebec. Our minds anywhere,
when left to themselves, are always thus busily drawing con-
clusions from false premises.

I asked the Indian to make us a sugar-bowl of birch-bark,
which he did, using the great knife which dangled in a sheath
from his belt; but the bark broke at the corners when he bent
it up, and he said it was not good; that there was a great difference in this respect between the bark of one canoe-birch and
that of another, *i. e.*, one cracked more easily than another. I
used some thin and delicate sheets of this bark which he split
and cut, in my flower-book; thinking it would be good to
separate the dried specimens from the green.

My companion, wishing to distinguish between the black
and white spruce, asked Polis to show him a twig of the latter,
which he did at once, together with the black; indeed, he

could distinguish them about as far as he could see them; but
as the two twigs appeared very much alike, my companion
asked the Indian to point out the difference; whereupon the
latter, taking the twigs, instantly remarked, as he passed his
hand over them successively in a stroking manner, that the
white was rough (*i. e.*, the needles stood up nearly perpendic-

ular), but the black smooth (*i. e.*, as if bent or combed down). This was an obvious difference, both to sight and touch. However, if I remember rightly, this would not serve to distinguish the white spruce from the light-colored variety of the black.

I asked him to let me see him get some black spruce root, and make some thread. Whereupon, without looking up at the trees overhead, he began to grub in the ground, instantly distinguishing the black spruce roots, and cutting off a slender one, three or four feet long, and as big as a pipe-stem, he split the end with his knife, and, taking a half between the thumb and forefinger of each hand, rapidly separated its whole length into two equal semi-cylindrical halves; then giving me another root, he said, "You try." But in my hands it immediately ran off one side, and I got only a very short piece. In short, though it looked very easy, I found that there was a great art in splitting these roots. The split is skillfully humored by bending short with this hand or that, and so kept in the middle. He then took off the bark from each half, pressing a short piece of cedar bark against the convex side with both hands, while he drew the root upward with his teeth. An Indian's teeth are strong, and I noticed that he used his often where we should have used a hand. They amounted to a third hand. He thus obtained, in a moment, a very neat, tough, and flexible string, which he could tie into a knot, or make into a fish-line even.

It is said that in Norway and Sweden the roots of the Norway spruce (*Abies excelsa*) are used in the same way for the same purpose. He said that you would be obliged to give half a dollar for spruce root enough for a canoe, thus prepared. He had hired the sewing of his own canoe, though he made all the rest. The root in his canoe was of a pale slate color, probably acquired by exposure to the weather, or perhaps from being boiled in water first.

He had discovered the day before that his canoe leaked a

little, and said that it was owing to stepping into it violently, which forced the water under the edge of the horizontal seams on the side. I asked him where he would get pitch to mend it with, for they commonly use hard pitch, obtained of the whites at Oldtown. He said that he could make something very similar, and equally good, not of spruce gum, or the like, but of material which we had with us; and he wished me to guess what. But I could not, and he would not tell me, though he showed me a ball of it when made, as big as a pea, and like black pitch, saying, at last, that there were some things which a man did not tell even his wife. It may have been his own discovery. In Arnold's expedition the pioneers used for their canoe "the turpentine of the pine, and the scrapings of the pork-bag."

Being curious to see what kind of fishes there were in this dark, deep, sluggish river, I cast in my line just before night, and caught several small somewhat yellowish sucker-like fishes, which the Indian at once rejected, saying that they were *Michigan* fish (*i. e., soft* and *stinking* fish) and good for nothing. Also, he would not touch a pout, which I caught, and said that neither Indians nor whites thereabouts ever ate them, which I thought was singular, since they are esteemed in Massachusetts, and he had told me that he ate hedgehogs, loons, etc. But he said that some small silvery fishes, which I called white chivin, which were similar in size and form to the first, were the best fish in the Penobscot waters, and if I would toss them up the bank to him, he would cook them for me. After cleaning them, not very carefully, leaving the heads on, he laid them on the coals and so broiled them.

Returning from a short walk, he brought a vine in his hand, and asked me if I knew what it was, saying that it made the best tea of anything in the woods. It was the Creeping Snowberry (*Chiogenes hispidula*), which was quite common there, its berries just grown. He called it *cowosnebagosar*, which name implies that it grows where old prostrate trunks have collapsed and rotted. So we determined to have some tea made of this to-night. It had a slight checkerberry flavor, and we both agreed that it was really better than the black tea which we had brought. We thought it quite a discovery, and that it might well be dried, and sold in the shops. I, for one, however, am not an old tea-drinker, and cannot speak with authority to others. It would have been particularly good to carry along for a cold drink during the day, the water thereabouts being invariably warm. The Indian said that they also used for tea a certain herb which grew in low ground, which he did not find there, and *Ledum,* or Labrador tea, which I have since found and tried in Concord; also hemlock leaves, the last especially in the winter, when the other plants were covered with snow; and various other things; but he did not approve of *arbor vitæ,* which I said I had drunk in those woods. We could have had a new kind of tea every night.

Just before night we saw a *musquash* (he did not say musk-rat), the only one we saw in this voyage, swimming downward on the opposite side of the stream. The Indian, wishing to get one to eat, hushed us, saying, "Stop, me call 'em;" and, sitting flat on the bank, he began to make a curious squeaking, wiry sound with his lips, exerting himself considerably. I was greatly surprised,—thought that I had at last got into the wilderness, and that he was a wild man indeed, to be talking to a musquash!

I did not know which of the two was the strangest to me. He seemed suddenly to have quite forsaken humanity, and gone over to the musquash side. The musquash, however, as near as I could see, did not turn aside, though he may have hesitated a little, and the Indian said that he saw our fire; but it was evident that he was in the habit of calling the musquash to him, as he said. An acquaintance of mine who was hunting moose in those woods a month after this, tells me that his Indian in this way repeatedly called the musquash within reach of his paddle in the moonlight, and struck at them.

The Indian said a particularly long prayer this Sunday evening, as if to atone for working in the morning.

MONDAY, July 27.

Having rapidly loaded the canoe, which the Indian always carefully attended to, that it might be well trimmed, and each having taken a look, as usual, to see that nothing was left, we set out again, descending the Caucomgomoc, and turning northeasterly up the *Umbazookskus*. This name, the Indian said, meant *Much Meadow River*. We found it a very meadowy stream, and dead water, and now very wide on account of the rains, though, he said, it was sometimes quite narrow. The space between the woods, chiefly bare meadow, was from fifty to two hundred rods in breadth, and is a rare place for moose. It reminded me of the Concord; and what increased the resemblance was one old musquash house almost afloat.

In the water on the meadows grew sedges, wool-grass, the common blue-flag abundantly, its flower just showing itself above the high water, as if it were a blue water-lily, and higher in the meadows a great many clumps of a peculiar narrow-leaved willow (*Salix petiolaris*), which is common in our river meadows. It was the prevailing one here, and the Indian said that the musquash ate much of it; and here also grew the red osier (*Cornus stolonifera*), its large fruit now whitish.

Though it was still early in the morning, we saw nighthawks circling over the meadow, and as usual heard the *Pepe* (*Muscicapa Cooperi*) [olive-sided flycatcher), which is one of the prevailing birds in these woods, and the robin. It was unusual for the woods to be so distant from the shore, and there was quite an echo from them, but when I was shouting in order to awake it, the Indian reminded me that I should scare the moose, which he was looking out for, and which we all wanted to see. The word for echo was *Pockadunkquaywayle.*

A broad belt of dead larch-trees along the distant edge of
the meadow, against the forest on each side, increased the
usual wildness of the scenery.[1] The Indian called these juniper, and said that they had been killed by the back-water
caused by the dam at the outlet of Chesuncook Lake, some
twenty miles distant. I plucked at the water's edge the
Asclepias incarnata [swamp milkweed], with quite handsome flowers, a brighter red than our variety (the *pulchra*).
It was the only form of it which I saw there.

Having paddled several miles up the Umbazookskus, it
suddenly contracted to a mere brook, narrow and swift, the
larches and other trees approaching the bank and leaving no
open meadow, and we landed to get a black-spruce pole for
pushing against the stream. This was the first occasion for one.
The one selected was quite slender, cut about ten feet long,
merely whittled to a point, and the bark shaved off. The
stream, though narrow and swift, was still deep, with a muddy
bottom, as I proved by diving to it. Beside the plants which
I have mentioned, I observed on the bank here the *Salix cor-
data* and *rostrata* [long-beaked willow], *Ranunculus recurvatus* [hooked crowfoot], and *Rubus triflorus* [dwarf raspberry]
with ripe fruit.

While we were thus employed, two Indians in a canoe hove
in sight round the bushes, coming down stream. Our Indian
knew one of them, an old man, and fell into conversation
with him in Indian. He belonged at the foot of Moosehead.
The other was of another tribe. They were returning from
hunting. I asked the younger if they had seen any moose, to
which he said no; but I, seeing the moose-hides sticking out
from a great bundle made with their blankets in the middle
of the canoe, added, "Only their hides." As he was a foreigner,

---

[1] This standing dead timber is commonly called dry-ki. Today a further
rise in the waters of Chesuncook has obliterated the fantastic scene that was
Umbazookskus Meadow, together with the confluence of this stream with the
Caucomgomoc.

he may have wished to deceive me, for it is against the law for
white men and foreigners to kill moose in Maine at this season.

But, perhaps, he need not have been alarmed, for the
moose-wardens are not very particular. I heard quite directly
of one who being asked by a white man going into the woods
what he would say if he killed a moose, answered, "If you
bring me a quarter of it, I guess you won't be troubled." His
duty being, as he said, only to prevent the "indiscriminate"
slaughter of them for their hides. I suppose that he would
consider it an *indiscriminate* slaughter when a quarter was
not reserved for himself. Such are the perquisites of this office.

We continued along through the most extensive larch
wood which I had seen,—tall and slender trees with fantastic
branches. But though this was the prevailing tree here, I do
not remember that we saw any afterward. You do not find
straggling trees of this species here and there throughout the
wood, but rather a little forest of them. The same is the case
with the white and red pines, and some other trees, greatly
to the convenience of the lumberer. They are of a social habit,
growing in "veins," "clumps," "groups," or "communities," as
the explorers call them, distinguishing them far away, from
the top of a hill or a tree, the white-pines towering above the
surrounding forest, or else they form extensive forests by
themselves. I would have liked to come across a large community of pines, which had never been invaded by the lumbering army.

We saw some fresh moose tracks along the shore, but the
Indian said that the moose were not driven out of the woods
by the flies, as usual at this season, on account of the abundance of water everywhere. The stream was only from one
and one half to three rods wide, quite winding, with occasional small islands, meadows, and some very swift and shallow places. When we came to an island, the Indian never
hesitated which side to take, as if the current told him which

was the shortest and deepest.[1] It was lucky for us that the water was so high. We had to walk but once on this stream, carrying a part of the load, at a swift and shallow reach, while he got up with the canoe, not being obliged to take out, though he said it was very strong water. Once or twice we passed the red wreck of a batteau which had been stove some spring.

While making this portage I saw many splendid specimens of the great purple-fringed orchis, three feet high. It is remarkable that such delicate flowers should here adorn these wilderness paths. Having resumed our seats in the canoe, I felt the Indian wiping my back, which he had accidentally spat upon. He said it was a sign that I was going to be married.

The Umbazookskus River is called ten miles long. Having poled up the narrowest point some three or four miles, the next opening in the sky was over Umbazookskus Lake, which we suddenly entered about eleven o'clock in the forenoon. It stretches northwesterly four or five miles, with what the Indian called the Caucomgomoc Mountain seen far beyond it. It was an agreeable change.

This lake was very shallow a long distance from the shore, and I saw stone heaps on the bottom, like those in the Assabet at home. The canoe ran into one. The Indian thought that they were made by an eel. Joe Aitteon in 1853 thought that they were made by chub. We crossed the southeast end of the lake to the carry into Mud Pond.

---

[1] An experienced canoeman is always aware of the set of the current in a stream and, as Thoreau points out, follows unerringly the deeper side.

8. Mud Pond Carry

UMBAZOOKSKUS LAKE is the head of the Penobscot in this direction, and Mud Pond is the nearest bend of the Allegash, one of the chief sources of the St. John. Hodge, who went through this way to the St. Lawrence in the service of the State, calls the portage here a mile and three quarters long, and states that Mud Pond has been found to be fourteen feet higher than Umbazookskus Lake. As the west branch of the Penobscot at the Moosehead carry [1] is considered about twenty-five feet lower than Moosehead Lake, it appears that the Penobscot in the upper part of its course runs in a broad and shallow valley, between the Kennebec and St. John, and lower than either of them, though, judging from the map, you might expect it to be the highest.

Mud Pond is about halfway from Umbazookskus to Chamberlain Lake, into which it empties, and to which we were bound. The Indian said that this was the wettest carry in the

---

[1] Nowadays known as Northeast Carry.

State, and as the season was a very wet one, we anticipated an unpleasant walk. As usual he made one large bundle of the pork-keg, cooking utensils, and other loose traps, by tying them up in his blanket. We should be obliged to go over the carry twice, and our method was to carry one half part way, and then go back for the rest.

Our path ran close by the door of a log-hut in a clearing at this end of the carry, which the Indian, who alone entered it, found to be occupied by a Canadian and his family, and that the man had been blind for a year. He seemed peculiarly unfortunate to be taken blind there, where there were so few eyes to see for him. He could not even be led out of that country by a dog, but must be taken down the rapids as passively as a barrel of flour.[1] This was the first house above Chesuncook, and the last on the Penobscot waters, and was built here, no doubt, because it was the route of the lumberers in the winter and spring.

After a slight ascent from the lake through the springy soil of the Canadian's clearing, we entered on a level and very wet and rocky path through the universal dense evergreen forest, a loosely paved gutter merely, where we went leaping from rock to rock and from side to side, in the vain attempt to keep out of the water and mud. We concluded that it was yet Penobscot water, though there was no flow to it. It was on this carry that the white hunter whom I met in the stage, as he told me, had shot two bears a few months before. They stood directly in the path, and did not turn out for him. They might be excused for not turning out there, or only taking the right as the law directs. He said that at this season bears were found on the mountains and hillsides, in search of berries, and were apt to be saucy,—that we might come across them up Trout

---

[1] Further tragedy was in store for this man—Jules Thurlotte. In the following year his wife disappeared with another Frenchman, one Joe Goodblood. Left alone on the carry, the blind man was found and cared for by passing woodsmen.

Stream; and he added, what I hardly credited, that many Indians slept in their canoes, not daring to sleep on land, on account of them.

Here commences what was called, twenty years ago, the best timber land in the State. This very spot was described as "covered with the greatest abundance of pine," but now this appeared to me, comparatively, an uncommon tree there, —and yet you did not see where any more could have stood, amid the dense growth of cedar, fir, etc. It was then proposed to cut a canal from lake to lake here, but the outlet was finally made further east, at Telos Lake, as we shall see.

The Indian with his canoe soon disappeared before us; but erelong he came back and told us to take a path which turned off westward, it being better walking, and, at my suggestion, he agreed to leave a bough in the regular carry at that place, that we might not pass it by mistake. Thereafter, he said, we were to keep the main path, and he added, "You see 'em my tracks." But I had not much faith that we could distinguish his tracks, since others had passed over the carry within a few days.

We turned off at the right place, but were soon confused by numerous logging-paths, coming into the one we were on, by which lumberers had been to pick out those pines which I have mentioned. However, we kept what we considered the main path, though it was a winding one, and in this, at long intervals, we distinguished a faint trace of a footstep. This, though comparatively unworn, was at first a better, or, at least, a drier road than the regular carry which we had left. It led through an arbor-vitæ wilderness of the grimmest character. The great fallen and rotting trees had been cut through and rolled aside, and their huge trunks abutted on the path on each side, while others still lay across it two or three feet high.

It was impossible for us to discern the Indian's trail in the elastic moss, which, like a thick carpet, covered every rock and fallen tree, as well as the earth. Nevertheless, I did occasionally detect the track of a man, and I gave myself some credit for it. I carried my whole load at once, a heavy knapsack, and a large India-rubber bag, containing our bread and a blanket, swung on a paddle; in all, about sixty pounds; but my companion preferred to make two journeys, by short stages, while I waited for him. We could not be sure that we were not depositing our loads each time farther off from the true path.

As I sat waiting for my companion, he would seem to be gone a long time, and I had ample opportunity to make observations on the forest. I now first began to be seriously molested by the black-fly, a very small but perfectly formed fly of that color, about one tenth of an inch long, which I first felt, and then saw, in swarms about me, as I sat by a wider and more than usually doubtful fork in this dark forest path. The hunters tell bloody stories about them,—how they settle in a ring about your neck, before you know it, and are wiped off in great numbers with your blood. But remembering that I had a wash in my knapsack, prepared by a thoughtful hand in Bangor, I made haste to apply it to my face and hands, and was glad to find it effectual, as long as it was fresh, or for twenty minutes, not only against black-flies, but all the insects that molested us. They would not alight on the part thus defended. It was composed of sweet-oil and oil of turpentine, with a little oil of spearmint, and camphor. However, I finally concluded that the remedy was worse than the disease. It was so disagreeable and inconvenient to have your face and hands covered with such a mixture.

Three large slate-colored birds of the jay genus (*Garrulus Canadensis*), the Canada jay, moose-bird, meat-bird, or what not, came flitting silently and by degrees toward me, and hopped down the limbs inquisitively to within seven or eight

feet. They were more clumsy and not nearly so handsome as the blue-jay. Fish-hawks, from the lake, uttered their sharp whistling notes low over the top of the forest near me, as if they were anxious about a nest there.

After I had sat there some time, I noticed at this fork in the path a tree which had been blazed, and the letters "Chamb. L." written on it with red chalk. This I knew to mean Chamberlain Lake. So I concluded that on the whole we were on the right course, though as we had come nearly two miles, and saw no signs of Mud Pond, I did harbor the suspicion that we might be on a direct course to Chamberlain Lake, leaving out Mud Pond. This I found by my map would be about five miles northeasterly, and I then took the bearing by my compass.

My companion having returned with his bag, and also defended his face and hands with the insect wash, we set forward again. The walking rapidly grew worse, and the path more indistinct, and at length, after passing through a patch of *Calla palustris* [water arum], still abundantly in bloom, we found ourselves in a more open and regular swamp, made less passable than ordinary by the unusual wetness of the season. We sank a foot deep in water and mud at every step, and sometimes up to our knees, and the trail was almost obliterated, being no more than that a musquash leaves in similar places, when he parts the floating sedge. In fact, it probably was a musquash trail in some places. We concluded that if Mud Pond was as muddy as the approach to it was wet, it certainly deserved its name.

It would have been amusing to behold the dogged and deliberate pace at which we entered that swamp, without interchanging a word, as if determined to go through it, though it should come up to our necks. Having penetrated a considerable distance into this, and found a tussock on which we could deposit our loads, though there was no place to sit, my companion went back for the rest of his pack. I had thought to observe on this carry when we crossed the dividing line between the Penobscot and St. John, but as my feet had hardly been out of the water the whole distance, and it was all level and stagnant, I began to despair of finding it.

I remembered hearing a good deal about the "highlands" dividing the waters of the Penobscot from those of the St. John, as well as the St. Lawrence, at the time of the northeast boundary dispute, and I observed by my map, that the line claimed by Great Britain as the boundary prior to 1842 passed between Umbazookskus Lake and Mud Pond, so that we had either crossed or were then on it. These, then, according to *her* interpretation of the treaty of '83, were the "highlands which divide those rivers that empty themselves into the St. Lawrence from those which fall into the Atlantic Ocean." Truly an interesting spot to stand on,—if that were it,—though you could not sit down there. I thought that if the commissioners themselves, and the king of Holland with

them, had spent a few days here, with their packs upon their
backs, looking for that "highland," they would have had an
interesting time, and perhaps it would have modified their
views of the question somewhat. The king of Holland would
have been in his element. Such were my meditations while
my companion was gone back for his bag.

It was a cedar swamp, through which the peculiar note
of the white-throated sparrow rang loud and clear. There
grew the side-saddle flower, Labrador tea, *Kalmia glauca*
[pale laurel], and, what was new to me, the Low Birch
(*Betula pumila*), a little round-leafed shrub, two or three feet
high only. We thought to name this swamp after the latter.

After a long while my companion came back, and the Indian with him. We had taken the wrong road, and the Indian
had lost us. He had very wisely gone back to the Canadian's
camp, and asked him which way we had probably gone, since
he could better understand the ways of white men, and he
told him correctly that we had undoubtedly taken the supply
road to Chamberlain Lake (slender supplies they would get
over such a road at this season). The Indian was greatly surprised that we should have taken what he called a "tow"
(*i. e.*, tote or toting or supply) road, instead of a carry path,
—that we had not followed his tracks,—said it was "strange,"
and evidently thought little of our woodcraft.[1]

Having held a consultation, and eaten a mouthful of bread,
we concluded that it would perhaps be nearer for us two now
to keep on to Chamberlain Lake, omitting Mud Pond, than
to go back and start anew for the last place, though the Indian had never been through this way, and knew nothing
about it. In the meanwhile he would go back and finish

---

[1] When following an unfamiliar tote road, the woodsman takes careful
note of how its branches come in to it. If they debouch in the general direction in which he is traveling, all is well, for then he is going down the road.
But if they open up in front of him, he knows that he is penetrating deeper
into the woods.

carrying over his canoe and bundle to Mud Pond, cross that, and go down its outlet and up Chamberlain Lake, and trust to meet us there before night. It was now a little after noon. He supposed that the water in which we stood had flowed back from Mud Pond which could not be far off eastward, but was unapproachable through the dense cedar swamp.

Keeping on, we were erelong agreeably disappointed by reaching firmer ground, and we crossed a ridge where the path was more distinct, but there was never any outlook over the forest. While descending the last, I saw many specimens of the great round-leaved orchis, of large size; one which I measured had leaves, as usual, flat on the ground, nine and a half inches long, and nine wide, and was two feet high. The dark, damp wilderness is favorable to some of these orchidaceous plants, though they are too delicate for cultivation. I also saw the swamp gooseberry (*Ribes lacustre*), with green fruit, and in all the low ground, where it was not too wet, the *Rubus triflorus* [dwarf raspberry] in fruit. At one place I heard a very clear and piercing note from a small hawk, like a single note from a white-throated sparrow, only very much louder, as he dashed through the tree-tops over my head. I wondered that he allowed himself to be disturbed by our presence, since it seemed as if he could not easily find his nest again himself in that wilderness.

We also saw and heard several times the red squirrel, and often, as before observed, the bluish scales of the fir cones which it had left on a rock or fallen tree. This, according to the Indian, is the only squirrel found in those woods, except a very few striped ones. It must have a solitary time in that dark evergreen forest, where there is so little life, seventy-five miles from a road as we had come. I wondered how he could call any particular tree there his home; and yet he would run up the stem of one out of the myriads, as if it were an old road to him. How can a hawk ever find him

there? I fancied that he must be glad to see us, though he did
seem to chide us. One of those sombre fir and spruce woods
is not complete unless you hear from out its cavernous mossy
and twiggy recesses his fine alarum,—his spruce voice, like the
working of the sap through some crack in a tree,—the working of the spruce-beer. Such an impertinent fellow would
occasionally try to alarm the wood about me. "Oh," said I,
"I am well acquainted with your family, I know your cousins
in Concord very well. Guess the mail's irregular in these
parts, and you'd like to hear from 'em." But my overtures
were vain, for he would withdraw by his aerial turnpikes
into a more distant cedar-top, and spring his rattle again.

We then entered another swamp, at a necessarily slow
pace, where the walking was worse than ever, not only on
account of the water, but the fallen timber, which often
obliterated the indistinct trail entirely. The fallen trees were
so numerous, that for long distances the route was through
a succession of small yards, where we climbed over fences
as high as our heads, down into water often up to our knees,
and then over another fence into a second yard, and so on;
and going back for his bag my companion once lost his way
and came back without it. In many places the canoe would
have run if it had not been for fallen timber. Again it would
be more open, but equally wet, too wet for trees to grow,
and no place to sit down.

It was a mossy swamp, which it required the long legs of
a moose to traverse, and it is very likely that we scared some
of them in our transit, though we saw none. It was ready
to echo the growl of a bear, the howl of a wolf, or the scream
of a panther; but when you get fairly into the middle of one
of these grim forests, you are surprised to find that the larger
inhabitants are not at home commonly, but have left only
a puny red squirrel to bark at you. Generally speaking, a
howling wilderness does not howl: it is the imagination of

the traveler that does the howling. I did, however, see one
dead porcupine; perhaps he had succumbed to the difficulties of the way. These bristly fellows are a very suitable small
fruit of such unkempt wildernesses.

Making a logging-road in the Maine woods is called
"swamping it," and they who do the work are called "swampers." I now perceived the fitness of the term. This was the
most perfectly swamped of all the roads I ever saw. Nature
must have coöperated with art here. However, I suppose
they would tell you that this name took its origin from the
fact that the chief work of road-makers in those woods is
to make the swamps passable. We came to a stream where
the bridge, which had been made of logs tied together with
cedar bark, had been broken up, and we got over as we could.
This probably emptied into Mud Pond, and perhaps the
Indian might have come up it and taken us in there if he had
known it. Such as it was, this ruined bridge was the chief
evidence that we were on a path of any kind.

We then crossed another low rising ground, and I, who
wore shoes, had an opportunity to wring out my stockings,
but my companion, who used boots, had found that this was
not a safe experiment for him, for he might not be able to
get his wet boots on again. He went over the whole ground,
or water, three times, for which reason our progress was very
slow; beside that the water softened our feet, and to some
extent unfitted them for walking. As I sat waiting for him,
it would naturally seem an unaccountable time that he was
gone. Therefore, as I could see through the woods that the
sun was getting low, and it was uncertain how far the lake
might be, even if we were on the right course, and in what
part of the world we should find ourselves at nightfall, I
proposed that I should push through with what speed I
could, leaving boughs to mark my path, and find the lake and

the Indian, if possible, before night, and send the latter back to carry my companion's bag.

Having gone about a mile, and got into low ground again, I heard a noise like the note of an owl, which I soon discovered to be made by the Indian, and, answering him, we soon came together. He had reached the lake, after crossing Mud Pond, and running some rapids below it, and had come up about a mile and a half on our path. If he had not come back to meet us, we probably should not have found him that night, for the path branched once or twice before reaching this particular part of the lake. So he went back for my companion and his bag, while I kept on.

Having waded through another stream, where the bridge of logs had been broken up and half floated away,—and this was not altogether worse than our ordinary walking, since it was less muddy,—we continued on, through alternate mud and water, to the shore of Apmoojenegamook Lake, which we reached in season for a late supper, instead of dining there, as we had expected, having gone without our dinner. It was at least five miles by the way we had come, and as my companion had gone over most of it three times, he had walked full a dozen miles, bad as it was. In the winter, when the water is frozen, and the snow is four feet deep, it is no doubt a tolerable path to a footman. As it was, I would not have missed that walk for a good deal.

If you want an exact recipe for making such a road, take one part Mud Pond, and dilute it with equal parts of Umbazookskus and Apmoojenegamook; then send a family of musquash through to locate it, look after the grades and culverts, and finish it to their minds, and let a hurricane follow to do the fencing.

9. The Headwaters of the Allegash

WE HAD come out on a point extending into Apmoojenegamook, or Chamberlain Lake, west of the outlet of Mud Pond,
where there was a broad, gravelly, and rocky shore, encumbered with bleached logs and trees. We were rejoiced to see
such dry things in that part of the world. But at first we
did not attend to dryness so much as to mud and wetness.
We all three walked into the lake up to our middle to wash
our clothes.

This was another noble lake, called twelve miles long,
east and west; if you add Telos Lake, which, since the dam
was built, has been connected with it by dead water, it will
be twenty; and it is apparently from a mile and a half to two
miles wide. We were about midway its length, on the south
side. We could see the only clearing in these parts, called the
"Chamberlain Farm," with two or three log buildings close
together, on the opposite shore, some two and a half miles
distant.[1] The smoke of our fire on the shore brought over two

<hr />

[1] The Chamberlain Farm had been cleared in 1846 by Eben S. Coe of
Bangor as a supply base for the lumbering operations on the East Branch and

men in a canoe from the farm, that being a common signal
agreed on when one wishes to cross. It took them about
half an hour to come over, and they had their labor for their
pains this time. Even the English name of the lake had a
wild, woodland sound, reminding me of that Chamberlain
who killed Paugus at Lovewell's fight.

After putting on such dry clothes as we had, and hanging
the others to dry on the pole which the Indian arranged over
the fire, we ate our supper, and lay down on the pebbly shore
with our feet to the fire, without pitching our tent, making a
thin bed of grass to cover the stones. Here first I was molested
by the little midge called the No-see-em (*Simulium nocivum*,
the latter word is not the Latin for no-see-em), especially
over the sand at the water's edge, for it is a kind of sand-fly.
You would not observe them but for their light-colored
wings. They are said to get under your clothes, and produce a feverish heat, which I suppose was what I felt that
night.

Our insect foes in this excursion, to sum them up, were first,
mosquitoes, the chief ones, but only troublesome at night, or
when we sat still on shore by day; second, black flies (*Simulium molestum*), which molested us more or less on the carries by day, as I have before described, and sometimes in
narrower parts of the stream. Harris mistakes when he says
they are not seen after June. Third, moose-flies. The big ones,
Polis said, were called *Bososquasis.* It is a stout, brown fly,
much like a horse-fly, about eleven sixteenths of an inch long,
commonly rusty colored beneath, with unspotted wings.
They can bite smartly, according to Polis, but are easily
avoided or killed. Fourth, the No-see-ems above mentioned.
Of all these, the mosquitoes are the only ones that troubled

---

at the head of Telos Lake. For over eighty years it served this purpose and
at its peak it comprised six hundred acres. The site is clearly visible today from
the south shore of Chamberlain.

me seriously; but, as I was provided with a wash and a veil, they have not made any deep impression.

The Indian would not use our wash to protect his face and hands, for fear that it would hurt his skin, nor had he any veil; he, therefore, suffered from insects now, and throughout this journey, more than either of us. I think that he suffered more than I did, when neither of us was protected. He regularly tied up his face in his handkerchief, and buried it in his blanket, and he now finally lay down on the sand between us and the fire for the sake of the smoke, which he tried to make enter his blanket about his face, and for the same purpose he lit his pipe and breathed the smoke into his blanket.

As we lay thus on the shore, with nothing between us and the stars, I inquired what stars he was acquainted with, or had names for. They were the Great Bear, which he called by this name, the Seven Stars, which he had no English name for, "the morning star," and "the north star."

In the middle of the night, as indeed each time we lay on the shore of a lake, we heard the voice of the loon, loud and distinct, from far over the lake. It is a very wild sound, quite in keeping with the place and the circumstances of the traveler, and very unlike the voice of a bird. I could lie awake for hours listening to it, it is so thrilling. When camping in such a wilderness as this, you are prepared to hear sounds from some of its inhabitants which will give voice to its wildness. Some idea of bears, wolves, or panthers runs in your head naturally, and when this note is first heard very far off at midnight, as you lie with your ear to the ground,—the forest being perfectly still about you, you take it for granted that it is the voice of a wolf or some other wild beast, for only the last part is heard when at a distance,—you conclude that it is a pack of wolves baying the moon, or, perchance, cantering after a moose. Strange as it may seem, the "mooing" of a cow on a mountain-side comes nearest to my idea of the voice of a bear; and this bird's note resembled that. It was the unfailing and characteristic sound of those lakes.

We were not so lucky as to hear wolves howl, though that is an occasional serenade. Some friends of mine, who two years ago went up the Caucomgomoc River, were serenaded by wolves while moose-hunting by moonlight. It was a sudden burst, as if a hundred demons had broken loose,—a startling sound enough, which, if any, would make your hair stand on end, and all was still again. It lasted but a moment, and you'd have thought there were twenty of them, when probably there were only two or three. They heard it twice only, and they said it gave expression to the wilderness which it had lacked before. I heard of some men who, while skinning a moose lately in those woods, were driven off from the carcass by a pack of wolves, which ate it up.

This of the loon—I do not mean its laugh, but its looning, —is a long-drawn call, as it were sometimes singularly human to my ear,—*hoo-hoo-ooooo,* like the hallooing of a man on a very high key, having thrown his voice into his head. I have heard a sound exactly like it when breathing heavily through my own nostrils, half awake at ten at night, suggesting my affinity to the loon; as if its language were but a dialect of my own, after all. Formerly, when lying awake at midnight in those woods, I had listened to hear some words or syllables of their language, but it chanced that I listened in vain until I heard the cry of the loon. I have heard it occasionally on the ponds of my native town, but there its wildness is not enhanced by the surrounding scenery.

I was awakened at midnight by some heavy, low-flying bird, probably a loon, flapping by close over my head, along the shore. So, turning the other side of my half-clad body to the fire, I sought slumber again.

When we awoke, we found a heavy dew on our blankets. I lay awake very early, and listened to the clear, shrill *ah-tette-tette-te,* of the white-throated sparrow, repeated at

short intervals, without the least variation, for half an hour, as if it could not enough express its happiness. Whether my companions heard it or not, I know not, but it was a kind of matins to me, and the event of that forenoon.[1]

It was a pleasant sunrise, and we had a view of the mountains in the southeast. Ktaadn appeared about southeast by south. A double-topped mountain, about southeast by east, and another portion of the same, east-southeast. The last the Indian called Nerlumskeechticook, and said that it was at the head of the East Branch, and we should pass near it on our return that way.

---

[1] The call of the white-throated sparrow to which Thoreau gave the Latin tag, *fringilla albicollis,* had evoked another memorable passage up on the West Branch. See Appendix, page 326.

We did some more washing in the lake this morning, and with our clothes hung about on the dead trees and rocks, the shore looked like washing-day at home. The Indian, taking the hint, borrowed the soap, and, walking into the lake, washed his only cotton shirt on his person, then put on his pants and let it dry on him.

I observed that he wore a cotton shirt, originally white, a greenish flannel one over it, but no waistcoat, flannel drawers, and strong linen or duck pants, which also had been white, blue woolen stockings, cowhide boots, and a Kossuth hat. He carried no change of clothing, but putting on a stout, thick jacket, which he laid aside in the canoe, and seizing a full-sized axe, his gun and ammunition, and a blanket, which would do for a sail or knapsack, if wanted, and strapping on his belt, which contained a large sheath-knife, he walked off at once, ready to be gone all summer.[1]

This looked very independent; a few simple and effective tools, and no India-rubber clothing. He was always the first ready to start in the morning, and if it had not held some of our property, would not have been obliged to roll up his blanket. Instead of carrying a large bundle of his own extra clothing, etc., he brought back the great-coats of moose tied up in his blanket. I found that his outfit was the result of a long experience, and in the main hardly to be improved on, unless by washing and an extra shirt. Wanting a button here, he walked off to a place where some Indians had recently encamped, and searched for one, but I believe in vain.

Having softened our stiffened boots and shoes with the

---

[1] The black hat traditionally worn by lumbermen had been in use prior to Thoreau's trips. It was a slouch hat of soft felt with a rolled brim, and an advertisement in the *Bangor Daily Whig & Courier* in 1844 described it as "a new article for lumbermen, warranted to shed water." Thoreau apparently used the name of the similar article popularized by the Hungarian patriot, Louis Kossuth, in his visits to America in 1852 and 1853. It is significant that this term "Kossuth" does not appear in the Ktaadn and the Maine Woods account published in 1848.

pork fat, the usual disposition of what was left at breakfast,
we crossed the lake early, steering in a diagonal direction,
northeasterly about four miles, to the outlet, which was not
to be discovered till we were close to it. The Indian name,
Apmoojenegamook, means lake that is crossed, because the
usual course lies across, and not along it. This is the largest
of the Allegash lakes, and was the first St. John's water that
we floated on. It is shaped in the main like Chesuncook.
There are no mountains or high hills very near it. At Bangor
we had been told of a township many miles farther northwest; it was indicated to us as containing the highest land
thereabouts, where, by climbing a particular tree in the
forest, we could get a general idea of the country. I have no
doubt that the last was good advice, but we did not go there.
We did not intend to go far down the Allegash, but merely
to get a view of the great lakes which are its source, and
then return this way to the East Branch of the Penobscot. The
water now, by good rights, flowed northward, if it could be
said to flow at all.

After reaching the middle of the lake, we found the waves
as usual pretty high, and the Indian warned my companion,
who was nodding, that he must not allow himself to fall
asleep in the canoe lest he should upset us; adding, that when
Indians want to sleep in a canoe, they lie down straight on
the bottom. But in this crowded one that was impossible.
However, he said that he would nudge him if he saw him
nodding.

A belt of dead trees stood all around the lake, some far out
in the water, with others prostrate behind them, and they
made the shore, for the most part, almost inaccessible. This
is the effect of the dam at the outlet. Thus the natural sandy
or rocky shore, with its green fringe, was concealed and destroyed. We coasted westward along the north side, searching for the outlet, about one quarter of a mile distant from

this savage-looking shore, on which the waves were breaking violently, knowing that it might easily be concealed amid
this rubbish, or by the over-lapping of the shore. It is remarkable how little these important gates to a lake are blazoned.
There is no triumphal arch over the modest inlet or outlet,
but at some undistinguished point it trickles in or out through
the uninterrupted forest, almost as through a sponge.

We reached the outlet in about an hour, and carried over
the dam there, which is quite a solid structure, and about
one quarter of a mile farther there was a second dam. The
reader will perceive that the result of this particular damming about Chamberlain Lake is, that the head-waters of
the St. John are made to flow by Bangor. They have thus
dammed all the larger lakes, raising their broad surfaces
many feet; Moosehead, for instance, some forty miles long,
with its steamer on it; thus turning the forces of nature
against herself, that they might float their spoils out of the
country. They rapidly run out of these immense forests all
the finer, and more accessible pine timber, and then leave
the bears to watch the decaying dams, not clearing nor cul-
tivating the land, nor making roads, nor building houses,
but leaving it a wilderness as they found it. In many parts,
only these dams remain, like deserted beaver-dams. Think
how much land they have flowed, without asking Nature's
leave! When the State wishes to endow an academy or university, it grants it a tract of forest land: one saw represents
an academy; a gang, a university.

The wilderness experiences a sudden rise of all her streams
and lakes, she feels ten thousand vermin gnawing at the
base of her noblest trees, many combining, drag them off,
jarring over the roots of the survivors, and tumble them into
the nearest stream, till, the fairest having fallen, they scam-
per off to ransack some new wilderness, and all is still again.
It is as when a migrating army of mice girdles a forest of

pines. The chopper fells trees from the same motive that the mouse gnaws them,—to get his living. You tell me that he has a more interesting family than the mouse. That is as it happens. He speaks of a "berth" of timber, a good place for him to get into, just as a worm might. When the chopper would praise a pine, he will commonly tell you that the one he cut was so big that a yoke of oxen stood on its stump; as if that were what the pine had grown for, to become the foot-stool of oxen.

In my mind's eye, I can see these unwieldy tame deer, with a yoke binding them together, and brazen-tipped horns be-traying their servitude, taking their stand on the stump of each giant pine in succession throughout this whole forest, and chewing their cud there, until it is nothing but an ox-pasture, and run out at that. As if it were good for the oxen, and some terebinthine or other medicinal quality ascended into their nostrils. Or is their elevated position intended merely as a symbol of the fact that the pastoral comes next in order to the sylvan or hunter life?

The character of the logger's admiration is betrayed by his very mode of expressing it. If he told all that was in his mind, he would say, it was so big that I cut it down and then a yoke of oxen could stand on its stump. He admires the log, the carcass or corpse, more than the tree. Why, my dear sir, the tree might have stood on its own stump, and a great deal more comfortably and firmly than a yoke of oxen can, if you had not cut it down. What right have you to celebrate the virtues of the man you murdered?

The Anglo-American can indeed cut down, and grub up all this waving forest, and make a stump speech, and vote for Buchanan on its ruins, but he cannot converse with the spirit of the tree he fells, he cannot read the poetry and mythology which retire as he advances. He ignorantly erases mythological tablets in order to print his handbills and town-meeting warrants on them. Before he has learned his a b c in the beautiful but mystic lore of the wilderness which Spenser and Dante had just begun to read, he cuts it down, coins a *pine-tree* shilling (as if to signify the pine's value to him), puts up a *dee*strict school-house, and introduces Webster's spelling-book.

Below the last dam, the river being swift and shallow, though broad enough, we two walked about half a mile to lighten the canoe. I made it a rule to carry my knapsack when I walked, and also to keep it tied to a cross-bar when in the canoe, that it might be found with the canoe if we should upset. I heard the dog-day locust here, and afterward on

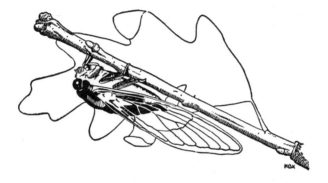

the carries, a sound which I had associated only with more open, if not settled countries. The area for locusts must be small in the Maine woods.

We were now fairly on the Allegash River, which name our Indian said meant hemlock bark. These waters flow northward about one hundred miles, at first very feebly, then southeasterly two hundred and fifty more to the Bay of Fundy. After perhaps two miles of river, we entered Heron Lake,[1]

---

[1] This is an error, which is clear from Thoreau's description of his route and the locality, as well as his references elsewhere to Eagle Lake. It probably arose from reliance on Colton's Railroad and Township Map of Maine, the 1856 edition of which erroneously calls Pongobawahean (?), Lake "Heron." On the Hubbard maps the spelling is Pongokwahemook, or Eagle Lake.

called on the map *Pongokwahem,* scaring up forty or fifty young *shecorways,* sheldrakes, at the entrance, which ran over the water with great rapidity, as usual in a long line.

This was the fourth great lake, lying northwest and south-east, like Chesuncook, and most of the long lakes in that neighborhood, and, judging from the map, it is about ten miles long. We had entered it on the southwest side, and saw a dark mountain northeast over the lake, not very far off nor high, which the Indian said was called *Peaked Mountain,* and used by explorers to look for timber from. There was also some other high land more easterly. The shores were in the same ragged and unsightly condition, encumbered with dead timber, both fallen and standing, as in the last lake, owing to the dam on the Allegash below.[1] Some low points or islands were almost drowned.

I saw something white a mile off on the water, which turned out to be a great gull on a rock in the middle, which the Indian would have been glad to kill and eat, but it flew away long before we were near; and also a flock of summer ducks that were about the rock with it. I asking him about herons, since this was Heron Lake, he said that he found the blue heron's nests in the hard-wood trees. I thought that I saw a light-colored object move along the opposite or northern shore, four or five miles distant. He did not know what it could be, unless it were a moose, though he had never seen a white one; but he said that he could distinguish a moose "anywhere on shore, clear across the lake."

Rounding a point, we stood across a bay for a mile and a

[1] The references to the dry-ki are significant. At this time recently constructed dams had flowed out the shores of Churchill, Eagle, Chamberlain, Telos, and Chesuncook Lakes. The same condition prevails in our time. In 1923 the shores of Eagle Lake were unmarred and unmatched in their beauty. Seventeen years later the dry-ki caused by raising the Lake to drive pulp was so thick that one could not get ashore save on a high bank. The Maine lake has ever been in a state of flux. Before the day of the lumberman, the beaver dams had in lesser degree the same effect.

half or two miles, toward a large island, three or four miles down the lake. We met with ephemeræ (shad-fly) midway, about a mile from the shore, and they evidently fly over the whole lake. On Moosehead I had seen a large devil's-needle half a mile from the shore, coming from the middle of the lake, where it was three or four miles wide at least. It had probably crossed. But at last, of course, you come to lakes so large that an insect cannot fly across them; and this, perhaps, will serve to distinguish a large lake from a small one.

We landed on the southeast side of the island,[1] which was rather elevated and densely wooded, with a rocky shore, in season for an early dinner. Somebody had camped there not long before, and left the frame on which they stretched a moose-hide, which our Indian criticised severely, thinking it showed but little woodcraft. Here were plenty of the shells of crayfish, or fresh-water lobsters, which had been washed ashore, such as have given a name to some ponds and streams. They are commonly four or five inches long. The Indian proceeded at once to cut a canoe-birch, slanted it up against another tree on the shore, tying it with a withe, and lay down to sleep in its shade.

When we were on the Caucomgomoc, he recommended to us a new way home, the very one which we had first thought of, by the St. John. He even said that it was easier, and would take but little more time than the other, by the East Branch of the Penobscot, though very much farther round; and, taking the map, he showed where we should be each night, for he was familiar with the route.[2] According to his calculation, we should reach the French settlements the next night after this, by keeping northward down the Allegash,

---

[1] Pillsbury Island.

[2] This was the route later to become famous by the name of the Allegash Trip, that is, as far as the French settlements.

and when we got into the main St. John the banks would be more or less settled all the way; as if that were a recommendation. There would be but one or two falls, with short carrying-places, and we should go down the stream very fast, even a hundred miles a day, if the wind allowed; and he indicated where we should carry over into Eel River to save a bend below Woodstock in New Brunswick, and so into the Schoodic Lake, and thence to the Mattawamkeag.

It would be about three hundred and sixty miles to Bangor this way, though only about one hundred and sixty by the other; but in the former case we should explore the St. John from its source through two thirds of its course, as well as the Schoodic Lake and Mattawamkeag,—and we were again tempted to go that way. I feared, however, that the banks of the St. John were too much settled. When I asked him which course would take us through the wildest country, he said the route by the East Branch. Partly from this consideration, as also from its shortness, we resolved to adhere to the latter route, and perhaps ascend Ktaadn on the way. We made this island the limit of our excursion in this direction.

We had now seen the largest of the Allegash lakes. The next dam "was about fifteen miles" farther north, down the Allegash, and it was dead water so far. We had been told in Bangor of a man who lived alone, a sort of hermit, at that dam, to take care of it, who spent his time tossing a bullet from one hand to the other, for want of employment,—as if we might want to call on him. This sort of tit-for-tat intercourse between his two hands, bandying to and fro a leaden subject, seems to have been his symbol for society.[1]

This island, according to the map, was about a hundred

---

[1] In the north of Maine, people who act this way are known as "woods queer." It is said that when a man hears voices talking to him, it is time he got out of the woods and into the clear.

and ten miles in a straight line north-northwest from Bangor, and about ninety-nine miles east-southeast from Quebec. There was another island visible toward the north end of the lake, with an elevated clearing on it; but we learned afterward that it was not inhabited, had only been used as a pasture for cattle which summered in these woods, though our informant said that there was a hut on the mainland near the outlet of the lake. This unnaturally smooth-shaven, squarish spot, in the midst of the otherwise uninterrupted forest, only reminded us how uninhabited the country was. You would sooner expect to meet a bear than an ox in such a clearing. At any rate, it must have been a surprise to the bears when they came across it. Such, seen far or near, you know at once to be man's work, for Nature never does it. In order to let in the light to the earth as on a lake, he clears off the forest on the hillsides and plains, and sprinkles fine grass-seed, like an enchanter, and so carpets the earth with a firm sward.

Polis had evidently more curiosity respecting the few settlers in those woods than we. If nothing was said, he took it for granted that we wanted to go straight to the next log-hut. Having observed that we came by the log-huts at Chesuncook, and the blind Canadian's at the Mud Pond carry, without stopping to communicate with the inhabitants, he took occasion now to suggest that the usual way was, when you came near a house, to go to it, and tell the inhabitants what you had seen or heard, and then they tell you what they had seen; but we laughed, and said that we had had enough of houses for the present, and had come here partly to avoid them.

In the mean while, the wind, increasing, blew down the Indian's birch, and created such a sea that we found ourselves prisoners on the island, the nearest shore, which was the western, being perhaps a mile distant, and we took the canoe out to prevent its drifting away. We did not know but we should be compelled to spend the rest of the day and the night there. At any rate, the Indian went to sleep again in the shade of his birch, my companion busied himself drying his plants, and I rambled along the shore westward, which was quite stony, and obstructed with fallen, bleached, or drifted trees for four or five rods in width. I found growing on this broad, rocky, and gravelly shore the *Salix rostrata* [long-beaked willow], *discolor* [glaucous willow], and *lucida* [shining willow], *Ranunculus recurvatus* [hooked crowfoot], *Potentilla Norvegica* [cinquefoil], *Scutellaria lateriflora* [mad-dog skullcap], *Eupatorium purpureum* [Joe-Pye-weed], *Aster Tradescanti* [Tradescant's aster], *Mentha Canadensis* [wild mint], *Epilobium angustifolium* [great willow-herb], abundant. *Lycopus minatus* [bugle weed], *Solidago lanceolata* [bushy goldenrod], *Spiræa salicifolia* [common meadow-sweet], *Antennaria margaraticea* [pearly everlasting], *Prunella* [self-heal], *Rumex acetosella* [sheep sorrel], Raspberries, Wool-grass, *Onoclea* [fern], etc. The nearest trees were *Betula papyracea* [canoe birch] and *excelsa* [yellow birch], and *Populus tremuloides* [American aspen]. I give these names because it was my farthest northern point.[1]

Our Indian said that he was a doctor, and could tell me some medicinal use for every plant I could show him. I immediately tried him. He said that the inner bark of the aspen (*Populus tremuloides*) was good for sore eyes; and so with various other plants, proving himself as good as his word. According to his account, he had acquired such knowledge in his youth from a wise old Indian with whom he associated,

---

[1] For Thoreau's meticulously detailed report on the flora of the Maine woods, see the Appendix, page 331.

and he lamented that the present generation of Indians "had lost a great deal."

He said that the caribou was a "very great runner," that there was none about this lake now, though there used to be many, and pointing to the belt of dead trees caused by the dams, he added, "No likum stump,—when he sees that he scared." [1]

Pointing southeasterly over the lake and distant forest, he observed, "Me go Oldtown in three days." I asked how he would get over the swamps and fallen trees. "Oh," said he, "in winter all covered, go anywhere on snowshoes, right across lakes." When I asked how he went, he said, "First I go Ktaadn, west side, then I go Millinocket, then Pamadum-cook, then Nicketow, then Lincoln, then Oldtown," or else he went a shorter way by the Piscataquis. What a wilderness walk for a man to take alone! None of your half-mile swamps, none of your mile-wide woods merely, as on the skirts of our towns, without hotels, only a dark mountain or a lake for guide-board and station, over ground much of it impassable in summer!

It reminded me of Prometheus Bound. Here was travel-ing of the old heroic kind over the unaltered face of nature. From the Allegash, or Hemlock River, and Pongoquahem Lake, across great Apmoojenegamook, and leaving the Ner-lumskeechticook Mountain on his left, he takes his way un-der the bear-haunted slopes of Souneunk and Ktaadn Moun-tains to Pamadumcook and Millinocket's inland seas (where

---

[1] Caribou were once plentiful in the State of Maine. In his Journal on this trip Thoreau had recorded that in the previous winter a single hunter had killed fifteen of them around Moosehead. The last record known to the writer of this note was a penciled legend scrawled on a beam in the barn formerly at Chamberlain Farm: "Saw a cariboux this day." The date was 1900 and the spelling bespeaks a Frenchman, *i. e.*, French-Canadian. This is in accord with the recollection of the last caribou seen by old timers around Green-ville.

often gulls'-eggs may increase his store), and so on to the
forks of the Nicketow (*nia soseb* "we alone Joseph" seeing
what our folks see), ever pushing the boughs of the fir and
spruce aside, with his load of furs, contending day and night,
night and day, with the shaggy demon vegetation, traveling through the mossy graveyard of trees. Or he could go
by "that rough tooth of the sea," Kineo, great source of ar-
rows and of spears to the ancients, when weapons of stone
were used. Seeing and hearing moose, caribou, bears, porcu-
pines, lynxes, wolves, and panthers. Places where he might
live and die and never hear of the United States, which make
such a noise in the world,—never hear of America, so called
from the name of a European gentleman.

There is a lumberer's road called the Eagle Lake road,
from the Seboois to the east side of this lake. It may seem
strange that any road through such a wilderness should be
passable, even in winter, when the snow is three or four feet
deep, but at that season, wherever lumbering operations are
actively carried on, teams are continually passing on the
single track, and it becomes as smooth almost as a railway. I
am told that in the Aroostook country the sleds are required
by law to be of one width (four feet), and sleighs must be
altered to fit the track, so that one runner may go in one rut
and the other follow the horse. Yet it is very bad turning out.

We had for some time seen a thunder-shower coming up
from the west over the woods of the island, and heard the
muttering of the thunder, though we were in doubt whether
it would reach us; but now the darkness rapidly increasing,
and a fresh breeze rustling the forest, we hastily put up the
plants which we had been drying, and with one consent
made a rush for the tent material and set about pitching it.
A place was selected and stakes and pins cut in the shortest
possible time, and we were pinning it down lest it should be
blown away, when the storm suddenly burst over us.

As we lay huddled together under the tent, which leaked considerably about the sides, with our baggage at our feet, we listened to some of the grandest thunder which I ever heard,—rapid peals, round and plump, bang, bang, bang, in succession, like artillery from some fortress in the sky; and the lightning was proportionally brilliant. The Indian said, "It must be good powder." All for the benefit of the moose and us, echoing far over the concealed lakes. I thought it must be a place which the thunder loved, where the lightning practised to keep its hand in, and it would do no harm to shatter a few pines. What had become of the ephemeræ and devil's-needles then? Were they prudent enough to seek harbor before the storm? Perhaps their motions might guide the voyageur.

Looking out I perceived that the violent shower falling on the lake had almost instantaneously flattened the waves,— the commander of that fortress had smoothed it for us so, —and, it clearing off, we resolved to start immediately, before the wind raised them again. Going outside, I said that I saw clouds still in the southwest, and heard thunder there. The Indian asked if the thunder went "lound" (round), saying that if it did we should have more rain. I thought that it did. We embarked, nevertheless, and paddled rapidly back toward the dams. The white-throated sparrows on the shore were about, singing, *Ah te, e, e, te, e, e, te,* or else *ah te, e, e, te, e, e, te, e, e, te, e, e.*

At the outlet of Chamberlain Lake we were overtaken by another gusty rain-storm, which compelled us to take shelter, the Indian under his canoe on the bank, and we ran under the edge of the dam. However, we were more scared than wet. From my covert I could see the Indian peeping out from beneath his canoe to see what had become of the rain. When we had taken our respective places thus once or twice, the rain not coming down in earnest, we commenced rambling about the neighborhood, for the wind had by this time raised such waves on the lake that we could not stir, and we feared that we should be obliged to camp there. We got an early supper on the dam and tried for fish there, while waiting for the tumult to subside. The fishes were not only few, but small and worthless, and the Indian declared that there were no good fishes in the St. John's waters; that we must wait till we got to the Penobscot waters.

At length, just before sunset, we set out again. It was a wild evening when we coasted up the north side of this Apmoojenegamook Lake. One thunder-storm was just over, and the waves which it had raised still running with violence, and another storm was now seen coming up in the southwest, far over the lake; but it might be worse in the morning, and we wished to get as far as possible on our way up the lake while we might. It blowed hard against the northern shore about an eighth of a mile distant on our left, and there was just as much sea as our shallow canoe would bear, without our taking unusual care. That which we kept off, and toward which the waves were driving, was as dreary and harborless a shore as you can conceive. For half a dozen rods in width it was a perfect maze of submerged trees, all dead and bare and bleaching, some standing half their original height, others prostrate, and criss-across, above or beneath the surface, and mingled with them were loose trees and limbs and stumps, beating about.

Imagine the wharves of the largest city in the world, decayed, and the earth and planking washed away, leaving the spiles standing in loose order, but often of twice the ordinary height, and mingled with and beating against them the wreck of ten thousand navies, all their spars and timbers, while there rises from the water's edge the densest and grimmest wilderness, ready to supply more material when the former fails, and you may get a faint idea of that coast. We could not have landed if we would, without the greatest danger of being swamped; so blow as it might, we must depend on coasting by it. It was twilight, too, and that stormy cloud was advancing rapidly in our rear. It was a pleasant excitement,

yet we were glad to reach, at length, in the dusk, the cleared shore of the Chamberlain Farm.

We landed on a low and thinly wooded point there, and while my companions were pitching the tent, I ran up to the house to get some sugar, our six pounds being gone;—it was no wonder they were, for Polis had a sweet tooth. He would first fill his dipper nearly a third full of sugar, and then add the coffee to it. Here was a clearing extending back from the lake to a hill-top, with some dark-colored log buildings and a storehouse in it, and half a dozen men standing in front of the principal hut, greedy for news. Among them was the man who tended the dam on the Allegash and tossed the bullet. He having charge of the dams, and learning that we were going to Webster Stream the next day, told me that some of their men, who were haying at Telos Lake, had shut the dam at the canal there in order to catch trout, and if we wanted more water to take us through the canal, we might raise the gate, for he would like to have it raised.

The Chamberlain Farm is no doubt a cheerful opening in the woods, but such was the lateness of the hour that it has left but a dusky impression on my mind. As I have said, the influx of light merely is civilizing, yet I fancied that they walked about on Sundays in their clearing somewhat as in a prison-yard. They were unwilling to spare more than four pounds of brown sugar,—unlocking the storehouse to get it, —since they only kept a little for such cases as this, and they charged twenty cents a pound for it, which certainly it was worth to get it up there.

When I returned to the shore it was quite dark, but we had a rousing fire to warm and dry us by, and a snug apartment behind it. The Indian went up to the house to inquire after a brother who had been absent hunting a year or two, and while another shower was beginning, I groped about cutting spruce and arbor-vitæ twigs for a bed. I preferred the arbor-vitæ on account of its fragrance, and spread it particularly thick about the shoulders. It is remarkable with what pure satisfaction the traveler in these woods will reach his camping-ground on the eve of a tempestuous night like this, as if he had got to his inn, and, rolling himself in his blanket, stretch himself on his six feet by two bed of dripping fir-twigs, with a thin sheet of cotton for roof, snug as a meadow-mouse in its nest. Invariably our best nights were those when it rained, for then we were not troubled with mosquitoes.

You soon come to disregard rain on such excursions, at least in the summer, it is so easy to dry yourself, supposing a dry change of clothing is not to be had. You can much sooner dry you by such a fire as you can make in the woods than in anybody's kitchen, the fireplace is so much larger, and wood so much more abundant. A shed-shaped tent will catch and reflect the heat like a Yankee-baker, and you may be drying while you are sleeping.[1]

Some who have leaky roofs in the towns may have been kept awake, but we were soon lulled asleep by a steady, soaking rain, which lasted all night. To-night, the rain not coming at once with violence, the twigs were soon dried by the reflected heat.

WEDNESDAY, *July* 29

When we awoke it had done raining, though it was still cloudy. The fire was put out, and the Indian's boots, which stood under the eaves of the tent, were half full of water. He was much more improvident in such respects than either of us, and he had to thank us for keeping his powder dry. We decided to cross the lake at once, before breakfast, or while we could; and before starting I took the bearing of the shore which we wished to strike, S.S.E. about three miles distant, lest a sudden misty rain should conceal it when we were midway. Though the bay in which we were was perfectly quiet and smooth, we found the lake already wide awake outside, but not dangerously or unpleasantly so; nevertheless, when you get out on one of those lakes in a canoe like this, you do not forget that you are completely at the mercy of the wind, and a fickle power it is. The playful waves may at any time become too rude for you in their sport, and play right on over you. We saw a few *she-cor-ways* and a *fish-hawk* thus early, and after much steady paddling and dancing over the dark waves of Apmoojenegamook, we found ourselves in the neighborhood of the southern land, heard the waves breaking on it, and turned our thoughts wholly to that side. After coast-

---

[1] The lumberman's phrase for this is "to turn in wet and turn out smoking." A contemporary description of a river drive in 1868 reads, "We didn't get two hours sleep a night on the average; and we slept in our wet clothes, anywhere we could catch a moment."

ing eastward along this shore a mile or two, we breakfasted
on a rocky point, the first convenient place that offered.

It was well enough that we crossed thus early, for the
waves now ran quite high, and we should have been obliged
to go round somewhat, but beyond this point we had comparatively smooth water. You can commonly go along one
side or the other of a lake, when you cannot cross it. The Indian was looking at the hard-wood ridges from time to time,
and said that he would like to buy a few hundred acres somewhere about this lake, asking our advice. It was to buy as near
the crossing-place as possible.

My companion and I, having a minute's discussion on some
point of ancient history, were amused by the attitude which
the Indian, who could not tell what we were talking about,
assumed. He constituted himself umpire, and, judging by our
air and gesture, he very seriously remarked from time to time,
"you beat," or "he beat."

Leaving a spacious bay,[1] a northeasterly prolongation of
Chamberlain Lake, on our left, we entered through a short
strait into a small lake a couple of miles over, called on the
map *Telasinis,* but the Indian had no distinct name for it, and
thence into *Telos* Lake, which he called *Paytaywecomgomoc,*
or Burnt-Ground Lake. This curved round toward the northeast, and may have been three or four miles long as we paddled. He had not been here since 1825. He did not know what
Telos meant; thought it was not Indian. He used the word
"*Spokelogan*" (for an inlet in the shore which led nowhere),
and when I asked its meaning said that there was "no Indian
in 'em." There was a clearing, with a house and barn, on the
southwest shore, temporarily occupied by some men who
were getting the hay, as we had been told; also a clearing for
a pasture on a hill on the west side of the lake. We landed on
a rocky point on the northeast side, to look at some Red Pines

---

[1] This bay is known to Maine woodsmen as the arm of Chamberlain.

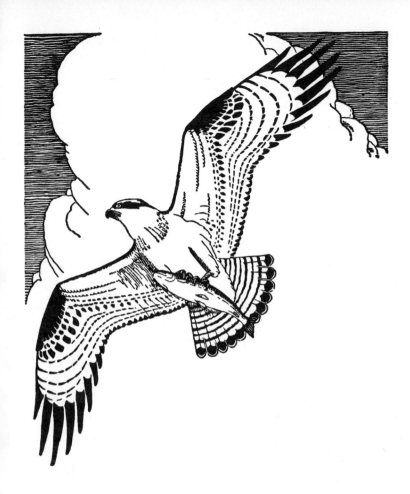

(*Pinus resinosa*), the first we had noticed, and get some cones, for our few which grow in Concord do not bear any.

The outlet from the lake into the East Branch of the Penobscot is an artificial one, and it was not very apparent where it was exactly, but the lake ran curving far up northeasterly into two narrow valleys or ravines, as if it had for a long time been groping its way toward the Penobscot waters, or remembered when it anciently flowed there; by observing where the horizon was lowest, and following the longest of these, we at length reached the dam, having come about a dozen miles from the last camp. Somebody had left a line set for trout, and the jackknife with which the bait had been cut on the dam beside it, an evidence that man was near, and on a deserted log close by a loaf of bread baked in a Yankee-baker.

These proved the property of a solitary hunter, whom we soon met, and canoe and gun and traps were not far off. He told us that it was twenty miles farther on our route to the foot of Grand Lake, where you could catch as many trout as you wanted, and that the first house below the foot of the lake, on the East Branch, was Hunt's, about forty-five miles farther; though there was one about a mile and a half up Trout Stream, some fifteen miles ahead, but it was rather a blind route to it. It turned out that, though the stream was in our favor, we did not reach the next house till the morning of the third day after this. The nearest permanently inhabited house behind us was now a dozen miles distant, so that the interval between the two nearest houses on our route was about sixty miles.

This hunter, who was a quite small, sunburnt man, having already carried his canoe over, and baked his loaf, had nothing so interesting and pressing to do as to observe our transit. He had been out a month or more alone. How much more wild and adventurous his life than that of the hunter in Concord woods, who gets back to his house and the mill-dam every night! Yet they in the towns who have wild oats to sow commonly sow them on cultivated and comparatively exhausted ground. And as for the rowdy world in the large cities, so little enterprise has it that it never adventures in this direction, but like vermin clubs together in alleys and drinking-saloons, its highest accomplishment, perchance, to run beside a fire-engine and throw brickbats. But the former is comparatively an independent and successful man, getting his living in a way that he likes, without disturbing his human neighbors. How much more respectable also is the life of the solitary pioneer or settler in these, or any woods,—having real difficulties, not of his own creation, drawing his subsistence directly from nature,—than that of the helpless multitudes in the towns who depend on gratifying the extremely artificial wants of society and are thrown out of employment by hard times!

Here for the first time we found the raspberries really plenty,—that is, on passing the height of land between the Allegash and the East Branch of the Penobscot; the same was true of the blueberries.

10. Lost in the Maine Woods

Telos Lake, the head of the St. John on this side, and Webster Pond, the head of the East Branch of the Penobscot, are only about a mile apart, and they are connected by a ravine, in which but little digging was required to make the water of the former, which is the highest, flow into the latter. This canal, which is something less than a mile long and about four rods wide, was made a few years before my first visit to Maine. Since then the lumber of the upper Allegash and its lakes has been run down the Penobscot, that is, up the Allegash, which here consists principally of a chain of large and stagnant lakes, whose thoroughfares, or river-links, have been made nearly equally stagnant by damming, and then down the Penobscot. The rush of the water has produced such changes in the canal that it has now the appearance of a very rapid mountain stream flowing through a ravine, and you would not suspect that any digging had been required to persuade the waters of the St. John to flow into the Penobscot here. It was so winding that one could see but little way down.

It is stated by Springer, in his "Forest Life," that the cause of this canal being dug was this: according to the treaty of 1842 with Great Britain, it was agreed that all the timber run down the St. John, which rises in Maine, "when within the Province of New Brunswick . . . shall be dealt with as if it were the produce of the said Province," which was thought by our side to mean that it should be free from taxation. Immediately, the Province, wishing to get something out of the Yankees, levied a duty on all the timber that passed down the St. John; but to satisfy its own subjects "made a corresponding discount on the stumpage charged those hauling timber from the crown lands." The result was that the Yankees made the St. John run the other way, or down the Penobscot, so that the Province lost both its duty and its water, while the Yankees, being greatly enriched, had reason to thank it for the suggestion.[1]

It is wonderful how well watered this country is. As you paddle across a lake, bays will be pointed out to you, by following up which, and perhaps the tributary stream which empties in, you may, after a short portage, or possibly, at some seasons, none at all, get into another river, which empties far away from the one you are on. Generally, you may go in any direction in a canoe, by making frequent but not very long portages.

You are only realizing once more what all nature distinctly

---

[1] There was another outcome of the cutting of this sluice. A Bangor lumberman, one Rufus Dwinel, gained control of it and levied a stiff toll on all logs sluiced through it. There was uproar in the lumber camps and a descent in force. Dwinel countered in kind and the sluice was guarded by a hundred rugged loggers armed with knives, picks, handspikes, and axes. Ultimately the affair was settled in the legislature. It is known to local history as the "Telos War."

remembers here, for no doubt the waters flowed thus in a
former geological period, and, instead of being a lake country,
it was an archipelago. It seems as if the more youthful and
impressible streams can hardly resist the numerous invita-
tions and temptations to leave their native beds and run
down their neighbors' channels. Your carries are often over
half-submerged ground, on the dry channels of a former
period. In carrying from one river to another, I did not go
over such high and rocky ground as in going about the falls
of the same river. For in the former case I was once lost in a
swamp, as I have related, and, again, found an artificial canal
which appeared to be natural.

I remember once dreaming of pushing a canoe up the
rivers of Maine, and that, when I had got so high that the
channels were dry, I kept on through the ravines and gorges,
nearly as well as before, by pushing a little harder, and now
it seemed to me that my dream was partially realized.

Wherever there is a channel for water, there is a road for
the canoe. The pilot of the steamer which ran from Oldtown
up the Penobscot in 1854 told me that she drew only fourteen
inches, and would run easily in two feet of water, though
they did not like to. It is said that some Western steamers can
run on a heavy dew, whence we can imagine what a canoe
may do. Montresor, who was sent from Quebec by the
English about 1760 to explore the route to the Kennebec,
over which Arnold afterward passed, supplied the Penobscot
near its source with water by opening the beaver-dams, and
he says, "This is often done." He afterward states that the
Governor of Canada had forbidden to molest the beaver
about the outlet of the Kennebec from Moosehead Lake, on
account of the service which their dams did by raising the
water for navigation.

This canal, so called, was a considerable and extremely
rapid and rocky river. The Indian decided that there was

water enough in it without raising the dam, which would only make it more violent, and that he would run down it alone, while we carried the greater part of the baggage. Our provision being about half consumed, there was the less left in the canoe. We had thrown away the pork-keg, and wrapt its contents in birch bark, which is the unequaled wrapping-paper of the woods.

Following a moist trail through the forest, we reached the head of Webster Pond about the same time with the Indian, notwithstanding the velocity with which he moved, our route being the most direct. The Indian name of Webster Stream, of which this pond is the source, is, according to him, *Madunkchunk i. e.,* Height of Land, and of the pond, *Madunkchunk-gamooc,* or Height of Land Pond. The latter was two or three miles long. We passed near a pine on its

shore which had been splintered by lightning, perhaps the day before. This was the first proper East Branch Penobscot water that we came to.

At the outlet of Webster Lake was another dam, at which we stopped and picked raspberries, while the Indian went down the stream a half-mile through the forest, to see what he had got to contend with. There was a deserted log camp here, apparently used the previous winter, with its "hovel" or barn for cattle. In the hut was a large fir-twig bed, raised two feet from the floor occupying a large part of the single apartment, a long narrow table against the wall, with a stout log bench before it, and above the table a small window, the only one there was, which admitted a feeble light. It was a simple and strong fort erected against the cold, and suggested what valiant trencher work had been done there. I discovered one or two curious wooden traps, which had not been used for a long time, in the woods near by. The principal part consisted of a long and slender pole.

We got our dinner on the shore, on the upper side of the dam. As we were sitting by our fire, concealed by the earth bank of the dam, a long line of sheldrake, half-grown, came waddling over it from the water below, passing within about a rod of us, so that we could almost have caught them in our hands. They were very abundant on all the streams and lakes which we visited, and every two or three hours they would rush away in a long string over the water before us, twenty to fifty of them at once, rarely ever flying, but running with great rapidity up or down the stream, even in the midst of the most violent rapids, and apparently as fast up as down, or else crossing diagonally, the old, as it appeared, behind, and driving them, and flying to the front from time to time, as if to direct them. We also saw many small black dippers, which behaved in a similar manner, and, once or twice, a few black ducks.

An Indian at Oldtown had told us that we should be obliged to carry ten miles between Telos Lake on the St. John and Second Lake on the East Branch of the Penobscot; but the lumberers whom we met assured us that there would not be more than a mile of carry. It turned out that the Indian, who had lately been over this route, was nearest right, as far

as we were concerned. However, if one of us could have assisted the Indian in managing the canoe in the rapids, we
might have run the greater part of the way; but as he was
alone in the management of the canoe in such places, we
were obliged to walk the greater part. I did not feel quite
ready to try such an experiment on Webster Stream, which
had so bad a reputation. According to my observation, a batteau, properly manned, shoots rapids as a matter of course,
which a single Indian with a canoe carries round.

My companion and I carried a good part of the baggage on
our shoulders, while the Indian took that which would be
least injured by wet in the canoe. We did not know when we
should see him again, for he had not been this way since the
canal was cut, nor for more than thirty years. He agreed to
stop when he got to smooth water, come up and find our path
if he could, and halloo for us, and after waiting a reasonable
time go on and try again,—and we were to look out in like
manner for him.

He commenced by running through the sluiceway and
over the dam, as usual, standing up in his tossing canoe, and
was soon out of sight behind a point in a wild gorge. This
Webster Stream is well known to lumbermen as a difficult
one. It is exceedingly rapid and rocky, and also shallow, and
can hardly be considered navigable, unless that may mean
that what is launched in it is sure to be carried swiftly down
it, though it may be dashed to pieces by the way. It is somewhat like navigating a thunder-spout. With commonly an ir-
resistible force urging you on, you have got to choose your
own course each moment, between the rocks and shallows,
and to get into it, moving forward always with the utmost
possible moderation, and often holding on, if you can, that
you may inspect the rapids before you.

By the Indian's direction we took an old path on the south
side, which appeared to keep down the stream, though at a

considerable distance from it, cutting off bends, perhaps to Second Lake, having first taken the course from the map with a compass, which was northeasterly, for safety. It was a wild wood-path, with a few tracks of oxen which had been driven over it, probably to some old camp clearing, for pasturage, mingled with the tracks of moose which had lately used it. We kept on steadily for about an hour without putting down our packs, occasionally winding around or climbing over a fallen tree, for the most part far out of sight and hearing of the river; till, after walking about three miles, we were glad to find that the path came to the river again at an old camp ground, where there was a small opening in the forest, at which we paused.

Swiftly as the shallow and rocky river ran here, a continuous rapid with dancing waves, I saw, as I sat on the shore, a long string of sheldrakes, which something scared, run up the opposite side of the stream by me, with the same ease that they commonly did down it, just touching the surface of the waves, and getting an impulse from them as they flowed from under them; but they soon came back, driven by the Indian, who had fallen a little behind us on account of the windings. He shot round a point just above, and came to land by us with considerable water in his canoe.

He had found it, as he said, "very strong water," and had been obliged to land once before to empty out what he had taken in. He complained that it strained him to paddle so hard in order to keep his canoe straight in its course, having no one in the bows to aid him, and, shallow as it was, said that it would be no joke to upset there, for the force of the water was such that he had as lief I would strike him over the head with a paddle as have that water strike him. Seeing him come out of that gap was as if you should pour water down

an inclined and zigzag trough, then drop a nutshell into it, and, taking a short cut to the bottom, get there in time to see it come out, notwithstanding the rush and tumult, right side up, and only partly full of water. After a moment's breathing-space, while I held his canoe, he was soon out of sight again around another bend, and we, shouldering our packs, resumed our course.

We did not at once fall into our paths again, but made our way with difficulty along the edge of the river, till at length, striking inland through the forest, we recovered it. Before going a mile we heard the Indian calling to us. He had come up through the woods and along the path to find us, having reached sufficiently smooth water to warrant his taking us in. The shore was about one fourth of a mile distant, through a dense, dark forest, and as he led us back to it, winding rapidly about to the right and left, I had the curiosity to look down carefully, and found that he was following his steps backward. I could only occasionally perceive his trail in the moss, and yet he did not appear to look down nor hesitate an instant, but led us out exactly to his canoe. This surprised me, for without a compass, or the sight or noise of the river to guide us, we could not have kept our course many minutes, and could have retraced our steps but a short distance, with a great deal of pains and very slowly, using a laborious circumspection. But it was evident that he could go back through the forest wherever he had been during the day.

After this rough walking in the dark woods it was an agreeable change to glide down the rapid river in the canoe once more. This river, which was about the size of our Assabet (in Concord), though still very swift, was almost perfectly smooth here, and showed a very visible declivity, a regularly inclined plane, for several miles, like a mirror set a little aslant, on which we coasted down. This very obvious regular descent, particularly plain when I regarded the water-line against the shores, made a singular impression on me, which the swiftness of our motion probably enhanced, so that we seemed to be gliding down a much steeper declivity than we were, and that we could not save ourselves from rapids and falls if we should suddenly come to them. My companion did not perceive this slope, but I have a surveyor's eyes, and I satisfied myself that it was no ocular illusion. You could tell at a glance on approaching such a river, which way the water flowed, though you might perceive no motion. I observed the angle at which a level line would strike the surface, and calculated the amount of fall in a rod, which did not need to be remarkably great to produce this effect.

It was very exhilarating, and the perfection of traveling, quite unlike floating on our dead Concord River, the coasting down this inclined mirror, which was now and then gently winding, down a mountain, indeed, between two evergreen forests, edged with lofty dead white-pines, sometimes slanted halfway over the stream, and destined soon to bridge it. I saw some monsters there, nearly destitute of branches, and scarcely diminishing in diameter for eighty or ninety feet.[1]

As we thus swept along, our Indian repeated in a deliberate and drawling tone the words "Daniel Webster, great lawyer," apparently reminded of him by the name of the stream, and he described his calling on him once in Boston, at what he supposed was his boarding-house. He had no business with him, but merely went to pay his respects, as we should say. In answer to our questions, he described his person well enough. It was on the day after Webster delivered his Bunker Hill oration, which I believe Polis heard. The first time he called he waited till he was tired without seeing him, and then went away. The next time, he saw him go by the door of the room in which he was waiting several times, in his shirt-sleeves, without noticing him. He thought that if he had come

---

[1] See also Appendix, page 327.

to see Indians, they would not have treated him so. At length, after very long delay, he came in, walked toward him, and asked in a loud voice, gruffly, "What do you want?" and he, thinking at first, by the motion of his hand, that he was going to strike him, said to himself, "You'd better take care, if you try that I shall know what to do." He did not like him, and declared that all he said "was not worth talk about a musquash." We suggested that probably Mr. Webster was very busy, and had a great many visitors just then.

Coming to falls and rapids, our easy progress was suddenly terminated. The Indian went along shore to inspect the water, while we climbed over the rocks, picking berries. The peculiar growth of blueberries on the tops of large rocks here made the impression of high land, and indeed this was the Height-of-land Stream. When the Indian came back, he remarked, "You got to walk; ver strong water." So, taking out his canoe, he launched it again below the falls, and was soon out of sight. At such times, he would step into the canoe, take up his paddle, and, with an air of mystery, start off, looking far down stream, and keeping his own counsel, as if absorbing all the intelligence of forest and stream into himself; but I sometimes detected a little fun in his face, which could yield to my sympathetic smile, for he was thoroughly good-humored. We meanwhile scrambled along the shore with our packs, without any path. This was the last of *our* boating for the day.

The prevailing rock here was a kind of slate, standing on its edges, and my companion, who was recently from California, thought it exactly like that in which the gold is found, and said that if he had had a pan he would have liked to wash a little of the sand here.

The Indian now got along much faster than we, and waited for us from time to time. I found here the only cool spring that I drank at anywhere on this excursion, a little water filling a hollow in the sandy bank. It was a quite memorable event, and due to the elevation of the country, for wherever else we had been the water in the rivers and the streams emptying in was dead and warm, compared with that of a mountainous region. It was very bad walking along the shore over fallen and drifted trees and bushes, and rocks, from time to time swinging ourselves round over the water, or else taking to a gravel bar or going inland. At one place, the Indian being ahead, I was obliged to take off all my clothes in order to ford a small but deep stream emptying in, while my companion, who was inland, found a rude bridge, high up in the woods, and I saw no more of him for some time. I saw there very fresh moose tracks, found a new goldenrod to me (perhaps *Solidago thyrsoidea*), and I passed one white-pine log, which had lodged, in the forest near the edge of the stream, which was quite five feet in diameter at the butt. Probably its size detained it.

Shortly after this I overtook the Indian at the edge of some burnt land, which extended three or four miles at least, beginning about three miles above Second Lake, which we were expecting to reach that night, and which is about ten miles from Telos Lake. This burnt region was still more rocky than before, but, though comparatively open, we could not yet see the lake. Not having seen my companion for some time, I climbed, with the Indian, a singular high rock on the edge of the river, forming a narrow ridge only a foot or two wide at top, in order to look for him; and, after calling many times, I at length heard him answer from a considerable distance inland, he having taken a trail which led off from the river, perhaps directly to the lake, and was now in search of the river again. Seeing a much higher rock, of the same character, about one third of a mile farther east, or down stream, I proceeded toward it, through the burnt land, in order to look for the lake from its summit, supposing that the Indian would keep down the stream in his canoe, and hallooing all the while that my companion might join me on the way.

Before we came together I noticed where a moose, which possibly I had scared by my shouting, had apparently just run along a large rotten trunk of a pine, which made a bridge, thirty or forty feet long, over a hollow, as convenient for him as for me. The tracks were as large as those of an ox, but an ox could not have crossed there.

This burnt land was an exceedingly wild and desolate region. Judging by the weeds and sprouts, it appeared to have been burnt about two years before. It was covered with charred trunks, either prostrate or standing, which crocked our clothes and hands, and we could not easily have distinguished a bear there by his color. Great shells of trees, sometimes unburnt without, or burnt on one side only, but black within, stood twenty or forty feet high. The fire had run up inside, as in a chimney, leaving the sap-wood. Sometimes we crossed a rocky ravine fifty feet wide, on a fallen trunk; and there were great fields of fire-weed (*Epilobium angustifolium*) on all sides, the most extensive that I ever saw, which presented great masses of pink. Intermixed with these were blueberry and raspberry bushes.

Having crossed a second rocky ridge like the first, when I was beginning to ascend the third, the Indian, whom I had left on the shore some fifty rods behind, beckoned to me to come to him, but I made sign that I would first ascend the highest rock before me, whence I expected to see the lake. My companion accompanied me to the top. This was formed just like the others. Being struck with the perfect parallelism of these singular rock hills, however much one might be in advance of another, I took out my compass and found that they lay northwest and southeast, the rock being on its edge, and sharp edges they were. This one, to speak from memory, was perhaps a third of a mile in length, but quite narrow, rising gradually from the northwest to the height of about eighty feet, but steep on the southeast end. The southwest side was as steep as an ordinary roof, or as we could safely climb; the northeast was an abrupt precipice from which you could jump clean to the bottom, near which the river flowed; while the level top of the ridge, on which you walked along, was only from one to three or four feet in width. For a rude illustration, take the half of a pear cut in two lengthwise, lay it on its flat side, the stem to the northwest, and then halve it vertically in the direction of its length, keeping the southwest half. Such was the general form.

There was a remarkable series of these great rock-waves revealed by the burning; breakers, as it were. No wonder that the river that found its way through them was rapid and obstructed by falls. No doubt the absence of soil on these rocks, or its dryness where there was any, caused this to be a very thorough burning. We could see the lake over the woods, two or three miles ahead, and that the river made an abrupt turn southward around the northwest end of the cliff on which we stood, or a little above us, so that we had cut off a bend, and that there was an important fall in it a short distance below us.

I could see the canoe a hundred rods behind, but now on the opposite shore, and supposed that the Indian had concluded to take out and carry round some bad rapids on that side, and that that might be what he had beckoned to me for; but after waiting a while I could still see nothing of him, and I observed to my companion that I wondered where he was, though I began to suspect that he had gone inland to look for the lake from some hill-top on that side, as we had done. This proved to be the case; for after I had started to return to the canoe, I heard a faint halloo, and descried him on the top of a distant rocky hill on that side.

But as, after a long time had elapsed, I still saw his canoe in the same place, and he had not returned to it, and appeared

in no hurry to do so, and, moreover, as I remembered that he
had previously beckoned to me, I thought that there might be
something more to delay him than I knew, and began to return northwest, along the ridge, toward the angle in the river.
My companion, who had just been separated from us, and
had even contemplated the necessity of camping alone, wishing to husband his steps, and yet to keep with us, inquired
where I was going; to which I answered that I was going far
enough back to communicate with the Indian, and that then
I thought we had better go along the shore together, and
keep him in sight.

When we reached the shore, the Indian appeared from out
the woods on the opposite side, but on account of the roar of
the water it was difficult to communicate with him. He kept
along the shore westward to his canoe, while we stopped at
the angle where the stream turned southward around the
precipice. I again said to my companion, that we would keep
along the shore and keep the Indian in sight. We started to
do so, being close together, the Indian behind us having
launched his canoe again, but just then I saw the latter, who
had crossed to our side, forty or fifty rods behind, beckoning
to me, and I called to my companion, who had just disappeared behind large rocks at the point of the precipice, three
or four rods before me, on his way down the stream, that I
was going to help the Indian a moment.

I did so,—helped get the canoe over a fall, lying with my
breast over a rock, and holding one end while he received it
below,—and within ten or fifteen minutes at most I was back
again at the point where the river turned southward, in order
to catch up with my companion, while Polis glided down the
river alone, parallel with me. But to my surprise, when I
rounded the precipice, though the shore was bare of trees,
without rocks, for a quarter of a mile at least, my companion
was not to be seen.

It was as if he had sunk into the earth. This was the more unaccountable to me, because I knew that his feet were, since our swamp walk, very sore, and that he wished to keep with the party; and besides this was very bad walking, climbing over or about the rocks. I hastened along, hallooing and searching for him, thinking he might be concealed behind a rock, yet doubting if he had not taken the other side of the precipice, but the Indian had got along still faster in his canoe, till he was arrested by the falls, about a quarter of a mile below. He then landed, and said that we could go no farther that night. The sun was setting, and on account of falls and rapids we should be obliged to leave this river and carry a good way into another farther east.

The first thing then was to find my companion, for I was now very much alarmed about him, and I sent the Indian along the shore down stream, which began to be covered with unburnt wood again just below the falls, while I searched backward about the precipice which we had passed. The Indian showed some unwillingness to exert himself, complaining that he was very tired, in consequence of his day's work, that it had strained him very much getting down so many rapids alone; but he went off calling somewhat like an owl. I remembered that my companion was near-sighted, and I feared that he had either fallen from the precipice, or fainted and sunk down amid the rocks beneath it.

I shouted and searched above and below this precipice in the twilight till I could not see, expecting nothing less than to find his body beneath it. For half an hour I anticipated and believed only the worst. I thought what I should do the next day, if I did not find him, what I *could* do in such a wilderness, and how his relatives would feel, if I should return without him. I felt that if he were really lost away from the river there, it would be a desperate undertaking to find him; and where were they who could help you? What would it be to raise the country, where there were only two or three camps, twenty or thirty miles apart, and no road, and perhaps nobody at home? Yet we must try the harder, the less the prospect of success.

I rushed down from this precipice to the canoe in order to fire the Indian's gun, but found that my companion had the caps. I was still thinking of getting it off when the Indian returned. He had not found him, but he said that he had seen his tracks once or twice along the shore. This encouraged me very much. He objected to firing the gun, saying that if my companion heard it, which was not likely, on account of the roar of the stream, it would tempt him to come toward us, and he might break his neck in the dark. For the same reason we refrained from lighting a fire on the highest rock. I proposed that we should both keep down the stream to the lake, or that I should go at any rate, but the Indian said, "No use, can't do anything in the dark; come morning, then we find 'em. No harm,—he make 'em camp. No bad animals here, no gristly bears, such as in California, where he's been,—warm night,— he well off as you and I."

I considered that if he was well he could do without us. He had just lived eight years in California, and had plenty of experience with wild beasts and wilder men, was peculiarly accustomed to make journeys of great length, but if he were sick or dead, he was near where we were. The darkness in the woods was by this so thick that it alone decided the question. We must camp where we were. I knew that he had his knapsack, with blankets and matches, and, if well, would fare no worse than we, except that he would have no supper nor society.

This side of the river being so encumbered with rocks, we crossed to the eastern or smoother shore, and proceeded to camp there, within two or three rods of the falls.[1] We pitched no tent, but lay on the sand, putting a few handfuls of grass and twigs under us, there being no evergreen at hand. For fuel we had some of the charred stumps. Our various bags of provisions had got quite wet in the rapids, and I arranged them about the fire to dry. The fall close by was the principal one on this stream, and it shook the earth under us. It was a cool, because dewy, night; the more so, probably, owing to the nearness of the falls. The Indian complained a good deal, and thought afterward that he got a cold there which occasioned a more serious illness. We were not much troubled by mosquitoes at any rate.

I lay awake a good deal from anxiety, but, unaccountably to myself, was at length comparatively at ease respecting him. At first I had apprehended the worst, but now I had little doubt but that I should find him in the morning. From time to time I fancied that I heard his voice calling through the roar of the falls from the opposite side of the river; but it is doubtful if we could have heard him across the stream there. Sometimes I doubted whether the Indian had really seen his tracks, since he manifested an unwillingness to make much of a search, and then my anxiety returned.

It was the most wild and desolate region we had camped in, where, if anywhere, one might expect to meet with befitting inhabitants, but I heard only the squeak of a night-hawk flitting over. The moon in her first quarter, in the fore part of

[1] Grand Falls on the Hubbard Maps.

the night, setting over the bare rocky hills garnished with tall, charred, and hollow stumps or shells of trees, served to reveal the desolation.

THURSDAY, *July* 30.

I aroused the Indian early this morning to go in search of our companion, expecting to find him within a mile or two, farther down the stream. The Indian wanted his breakfast first, but I reminded him that my companion had had neither breakfast nor supper. We were obliged first to carry our canoe and baggage over into another stream, the main East Branch, about three fourths of a mile distant, for Webster Stream was no farther navigable. We went twice over this carry, and the dewy bushes wet us through like water up to the middle; I hallooed in a high key from time to time, though I had little expectation that I could be heard over the roar of the rapids, and, moreover, we were necessarily on the opposite side of the stream to him.

In going over this portage the last time, the Indian, who was before me with the canoe on his head, stumbled and fell heavily once, and lay for a moment silent as if in pain. I hastily stepped forward to help him, asking if he was much hurt, but after a moment's pause, without replying, he sprang up and went forward. He was all the way subject to taciturn fits, but they were harmless ones.

11. Down the East Branch

WE HAD launched our canoe and gone but little way down the East Branch, when I heard an answering shout from my companion, and soon after saw him standing on a point where there was a clearing a quarter of a mile below, and the smoke of his fire was rising near by. Before I saw him I naturally shouted again and again, but the Indian curtly remarked, "He hears you," as if once was enough. It was just below the mouth of Webster Stream. When we arrived, he was smoking his pipe, and said that he had passed a pretty comfortable night, though it was rather cold, on account of the dew.

It appeared that when we stood together the previous evening, and I was shouting to the Indian across the river, he, being near-sighted, had not seen the Indian nor his canoe, and when I went back to the Indian's assistance, did not see which way I went, and supposed that we were below and not above him, and so, making haste to catch up, he ran away from us. Having reached this clearing, a mile or more below

our camp, the night overtook him, and he made a fire in a
little hollow, and lay down by it in his blanket, still thinking
that we were ahead of him. He thought it likely that he had
heard the Indian call once the evening before, but mistook it
for an owl. He had seen one botanical rarity before it was
dark,—pure white *Epilobium angustifolium* [great willow-
herb] amidst the fields of pink ones, in the burnt lands.

He had already stuck up the remnant of a lumberer's shirt,
found on the point, on a pole by the water-side, for a signal,
and attached a note to it, to inform us that he had gone on to
the lake, and that if he did not find us there, he would be back
in a couple of hours. If he had not found us soon, he had some
thoughts of going back in search of the solitary hunter whom
we had met at Telos Lake, ten miles behind, and, if successful,
hire him to take him to Bangor. But if this hunter had moved
as fast as we, he would have been twenty miles off by this
time, and who could guess in what direction? It would have
been like looking for a needle in a haymow, to search for him
in these woods. He had been considering how long he could
live on berries alone.[1]

We substituted for his note a card containing our names
and destination, and the date of our visit, which Polis neatly
inclosed in a piece of birch-bark to keep it dry. This has probably been read by some hunter or explorer ere this. We all had
good appetites for the breakfast which we made haste to
cook here, and then, having partially dried our clothes, we
glided swiftly down the winding stream toward Second Lake.

As the shores became flatter with frequent gravel and sand-
bars, and the stream more winding in the lower land near the
lake, elms and ash-trees made their appearance; also the wild

---

[1] The woodsman who is never lost in the woods but who on occasion may
not know just where he is, follows two simple rules. First, always go downhill,
for this will lead you to water. Then follow the water downstream, for this
will always take you, as he phrases it, "out into the clear."

yellow lily (*Lilium Canadense*), some of whose bulbs I collected for a soup. On some ridges the burnt land extended as far as the lake. This was a very beautiful lake, two or three miles long, with high mountains on the southwest side, the (as our Indian said) *Nerlumskeechticook, i. e.,* Dead-Water Mountain. It appears to be the same called Carbuncle Mountain on the map. According to Polis, it extends in separate elevations all along this and the next lake, which is much larger. The lake, too, I think, is called by the same name, or perhaps with the addition of *gamoc* or *mooc*.

The morning was a bright one, and perfectly still and serene, the lake as smooth as glass, we making the only ripple as we paddled into it.[1] The dark mountains about it were seen

---

[1] Matangamooksis or Second Lake. The East Branch ascends from here up through Third Lake to Fourth Lake above which and the adjacent Stink Pond, it takes its rise.

through a glaucous mist, and the brilliant white stems of canoe-birches mingled with the other woods around it. The wood-thrush sang on the distant shore, and the laugh of some loons, sporting in a concealed western bay, as if inspired by the morning, came distinct over the lake to us, and, what was remarkable, the echo which ran round the lake was much louder than the original note; probably because, the loon being in a regularly curving bay under the mountain, we were exactly in the focus of many echoes, the sound being reflected like light from a concave mirror. The beauty of the scene may have been enhanced to our eyes by the fact that we had just come together again after a night of some anxiety. This reminded me of the Ambejijis Lake on the West Branch, which I crossed in my first coming to Maine.

Having paddled down three quarters of the lake, we came to a standstill, while my companion let down for fish. A white (or whitish) gull sat on a rock which rose above the surface in mid-lake not far off, quite in harmony with the scene; and as we rested there in the warm sun, we heard one loud crushing or crackling sound from the forest, forty or fifty rods distant, as of a stick broken by the foot of some large animal. Even this was an interesting incident there. In the midst of our dreams of giant lake-trout, even then supposed to be nibbling, our fishermen drew up a diminutive red perch, and we took up our paddles again in haste.

It was not apparent where the outlet of this lake was, and while the Indian thought it was in one direction, I thought it was in another. He said, "I bet you fourpence it is there," but he still held on in my direction, which proved to be the right one. As we were approaching the outlet, it being still early in the forenoon, he suddenly exclaimed, "Moose! moose!" and told us to be still. He put a cap on his gun, and, standing up in the stern, rapidly pushed the canoe straight toward the shore and the moose.

It was a cow-moose, about thirty rods off, standing in the water by the side of the outlet, partly behind some fallen timber and bushes, and at that distance she did not look very large. She was flapping her large ears, and from time to time poking off the flies with her nose from some part of her body. She did not appear much alarmed by our neighborhood, only occasionally turned her head and looked straight at us, and then gave her attention to the flies again. As we approached nearer, she got out of the water, stood higher and regarded us more suspiciously. Polis pushed the canoe steadily forward in the shallow water, and I for a moment forgot the moose in attending to some pretty rose-colored Polygonums [water persicaria] just rising above the surface, but the canoe soon grounded in the mud eight or ten rods distant from the moose, and the Indian seized his gun and prepared to fire.

After standing still a moment, she turned slowly, as usual, so as to expose her side, and he improved this moment to fire, over our heads. She thereupon moved off eight or ten rods at a moderate pace, across a shallow bay, to an old standing-place of hers, behind some fallen red maples, on the opposite shore, and there she stood still again a dozen or four-teen rods from us, while the Indian hastily loaded and fired twice at her, without her moving. My companion, who passed him his caps and bullets, said that Polis was as ex-cited as a boy of fifteen, that his hand trembled, and he once put his ramrod back upside down. This was remarkable for so experienced a hunter. Perhaps he was anxious to make a good shot before us. The white hunter had told me that the Indians were not good shots, because they were ex-cited, though he said that we had got a good hunter with us.

The Indian now pushed quickly and quietly back, and a long distance round, in order to get into the outlet,—for he had fired over the neck of a peninsula between it and the lake,—till we approached where the moose had stood, when he exclaimed, "She is a goner!" and was surprised that we did not see her as soon as he did. There, to be sure, she lay perfectly dead, with her tongue hanging out, just where she had stood to receive the last shots, looking unexpectedly large and horse-like, and we saw where the bullets had scarred the trees.

Using a tape, I found that the moose measured just six feet from the shoulder to the tip of the hoof, and was eight feet long as she lay. Some portions of the body, for a foot in diameter, were almost covered with flies, apparently the common fly of our woods, with a dark spot on the wings, and not the very large ones which occasionally pursued us in mid-stream, though both are called moose-flies.

Polis, preparing to skin the moose, asked me to help him find a stone on which to sharpen his large knife. It being all a flat alluvial ground where the moose had fallen, covered with red maples, etc., this was no easy matter; we searched far and wide, a long time, till at length I found a flat kind of slate-stone, and soon after he returned with a similar one, on which he soon made his knife very sharp.

While he was skinning the moose, I proceeded to ascertain what kind of fishes were to be found in the sluggish and muddy outlet. The greatest difficulty was to find a pole. It was almost impossible to find a slender, straight pole ten or twelve feet long in these woods. You might search half an hour in vain. They are commonly spruce, arbor-vitæ, fir, etc., short, stout, and branchy, and do not make good fish-poles, even after you have patiently cut off all their tough and scraggy branches. The fishes were red perch and chivin.

The Indian having cut off a large piece of sirloin, the upper lip, and the tongue, wrapped them in the hide, and placed them in the bottom of the canoe, observing that there was "one man," meaning the weight of one. Our load had previously been reduced some thirty pounds, but a hundred pounds were now added, a serious addition, which made our quarters still more narrow, and considerably increased the danger on the lakes and rapids, as well as the labor of the carries. The skin was ours according to custom, since the Indian was in our employ, but we did not think of claiming it. He being a skillful dresser of moose-hides, would make it worth seven or eight dollars to him, as I was told. He said that he sometimes earned fifty or sixty dollars in a day at them; he had killed ten moose in one day, though the skinning and all took two days. This was the way he had got his property. There were the tracks of a calf thereabouts, which he said would come "by, by," and he could get it if we cared to wait, but I cast cold water on the project.

We continued along the outlet toward Grand Lake, through a swampy region, by a long, winding, and narrow dead water, very much choked up by wood, where we were obliged to land sometimes in order to get the canoe over a log. It was hard to find any channel, and we did not know but we should be lost in the swamp. It abounded in ducks, as usual. At length we reached Grand Lake, which the Indian called *Matungamook*. At the head of this we saw, coming in from the southwest, with a sweep apparently from a gorge in the mountains, Trout Stream, or *Uncardnerheese,* which name, the Indian said, had something to do with mountains.

We stopped to dine on an interesting high rocky island, soon after entering Matungamook Lake, securing our canoe to the cliffy shore. It is always pleasant to step from a boat on to a large rock or cliff. Here was a good opportunity to dry our dewy blankets on the open sunny rock. Indians had recently camped here, and accidentally burned over the western end of the island, and Polis picked up a gun-case of blue broadcloth, and said that he knew the Indian it belonged to, and would carry it to him. His tribe is not so large but he may know all its effects. We proceeded to make a fire and cook our dinner amid some pines, where our predecessors had done the same, while the Indian busied himself about his moose-hide on the shore, for he said that he thought it a good plan for one to do all the cooking, *i. e.,* I suppose, if that one were not himself.

A peculiar evergreen overhung our fire, which at first glance looked like a pitch pine (*P. rigida*), with leaves little more than an inch long, spruce-like, but we found it to be the *Pinus Banksiana,*—"Banks's, or the Labrador Pine," also called Scrub Pine, Gray Pine, etc., a new tree to us. These must have been good specimens, for several were thirty or thirty-five feet high. Richardson found it forty feet high and upward, and states that the porcupine feeds on its bark. Here also grew the Red Pine (*Pinus resinosa*).

I saw where the Indians had made canoes in a little secluded hollow in the woods, on the top of the rock, where they were out of the wind, and large piles of whittlings remained. This must have been a favorite resort for their ancestors, and, indeed, we found here the point of an arrow-head, such as they have not used for two centuries and now know not how to make. The Indian, picking up a stone, remarked to me, "That very strange lock (rock)." It was a piece of hornstone, which I told him his tribe had probably brought here centuries before to make arrow-heads of. He also picked up a yellowish curved bone by the side of our fireplace and asked me to guess what it was. It was one of the upper incisors of a beaver, on which some party had feasted within a year or two. I found also most of the teeth, and the skull, etc. We here dined on fried moose-meat.

One who was my companion in my two previous excursions to these woods, tells me that when hunting up the

Caucomgomoc, about two years ago, he found himself dining one day on moose-meat, mud-turtle, trout, and beaver, and he thought that there were few places in the world where these dishes could easily be brought together on one table.

After the almost incessant rapids and falls of the Madunkchunk (Height-of-Land, or Webster Stream), we had just passed through the dead-water of Second Lake, and were now in the much larger dead-water of Grand Lake, and I thought the Indian was entitled to take an extra nap here. Ktaadn, near which we were to pass the next day, is said to mean "Highest Land." So much geography is there in their names.

The Indian navigator naturally distinguishes by a name those parts of a stream where he has encountered quick water and forks, and again, the lakes and smooth water where he can rest his weary arms, since those are the most interesting and more arable parts to him. The very sight of the *Nerlumskeechticook*, or Dead-Water Mountains, a day's journey off over the forest, as we first saw them, must awaken in him pleasing memories. And not less interesting is it to the white traveler, when he is crossing a placid lake in these out-of-the-way woods, perhaps thinking that he is in some sense one of the earlier discoverers of it, to be reminded that it was thus well known and suitably named by Indian hunters perhaps a thousand years ago.

Ascending the precipitous rock which formed this long narrow island, I was surprised to find that its summit was a narrow ridge, with a precipice on one side, and that its axis of elevation extended from northwest to southeast exactly like that of the great rocky ridge at the commencement of the Burnt Ground, ten miles northwesterly. The same arrangement prevailed here, and we could plainly see that

the mountain ridges on the west of the lake trended the
same way. Splendid large harebells nodded over the edge
and in the clefts of the cliff, and the blueberries (*Vaccinium
Canadense*) were for the first time really abundant in the
thin soil on its top. There was no lack of them hencefor-
ward on the East Branch.

There was a fine view hence over the sparkling lake, which
looked pure and deep, and had two or three, in all, rocky
islands in it. Our blankets being dry, we set out again, the
Indian as usual having left his gazette on a tree.[1] This time
it was we three in a canoe, my companion smoking. We
paddled southward down this handsome lake, which appeared to extend nearly as far east as south, keeping near
the western shore, just outside a small island, under the dark
Nerlumskeechticook mountain. For I had observed on my
map that this was the course. It was three or four miles
across it. It struck me that the outline of this mountain on
the southwest of the lake, and of another beyond it, was not
only like that of the huge rock waves of Webster Stream, but
in the main like Kineo, on Moosehead Lake, having a similar
but less abrupt precipice at the southeast end; in short, that
all the prominent hills and ridges hereabouts were larger or
smaller Kineos, and that possibly there was such a relation
between Kineo and the rocks of Webster Stream.

The Indian did not know exactly where the outlet was,
whether at the extreme southwest angle or more easterly,
and had asked to see my plan at the last stopping-place,
but I had forgotten to show it to him. As usual, he went feeling his way by a middle course between two probable points,
from which he could diverge either way at last without losing much distance. In approaching the south shore, as the
clouds looked gusty and the waves ran pretty high, we so
steered as to get partly under the lee of an island, though at a

---

[1] The reference is to the Indian's record of his having camped there.

great distance from it. I could not distinguish the outlet till we were almost in it, and heard the water falling over the dam there.

Here was a considerable fall, and a very substantial dam, but no sign of a cabin or camp. The hunter whom we met at Telos Lake had told us that there were plenty of trout here, but at this hour they did not rise to the bait, only cousin trout, from the very midst of the rushing waters. There are not so many fishes in these rivers as in the Concord. While we loitered here, Polis took occasion to cut with his big knife some of the hair from his moose-hide, and so lightened and prepared it for drying. I noticed at several old Indian camps in the woods the pile of hair which they had cut from their hides.

Having carried over the dam, he darted down the rapids, leaving us to walk a mile or more, where for the most part there was no path, but very thick and difficult traveling near the stream. At length he would call to let us know where he was waiting for us with his canoe, when, on account of the windings of the stream, we did not know where the shore was, but he did not call often enough, forgetting that we were not Indians. He seemed to be very saving of his breath,—yet he would be surprised if we went by, or did not strike the right spot. This was not because he was un-accommodating, but a proof of superior manners. Indians like to get along with the least possible communication and ado. He was really paying us a great compliment all the while, thinking that we preferred a hint to a kick.

At length, climbing over the willows and fallen trees, when this was easier than to go round or under them, we overtook the canoe, and glided down the stream in smooth but swift water for several miles. I here observed again, as at Webster Stream, and on a still larger scale the next day, that the river was a smooth and regularly inclined plane down which we coasted. As we thus glided along we started the first black ducks which we had distinguished.

We decided to camp early to-night, that we might have ample time before dark; so we stopped at the first favorable shore, where there was a narrow gravelly beach on the western side, some five miles below the outlet of the lake. It was an interesting spot, where the river began to make a great bend to the east, and the last of the peculiar moose-faced

Nerlumskeechticook mountains not far southwest of Grand Lake rose dark in the northwest a short distance behind, displaying its gray precipitous southeast side, but we could not see this without coming out upon the shore.

Two steps from the water on either side, and you come to the abrupt bushy and rooty if not turfy edge of the bank, four or five feet high, where the interminable forest begins, as if the stream had but just cut its way through it. It is surprising on stepping ashore anywhere into this unbroken wilderness to see so often, at least within a few rods of the river, the marks of the axe, made by lumberers who have either camped here or driven logs past in previous springs. You will see perchance where, going on the same errand that you do, they have cut large chips from a tall white-pine stump for their fire.

While we were pitching the camp and getting supper, the Indian cut the rest of the hair from his moose-hide, and proceeded to extend it vertically on a temporary frame between two small trees, half a dozen feet from the opposite side of the fire, lashing and stretching it with arbor-vitæ bark which was always at hand, and in this case was stripped from one of the trees it was tied to. Asking for a new kind of tea, he made us some, pretty good, of the checkerberry (*Gaultheria procumbens*), which covered the ground, dropping a little bunch of it tied up with cedar bark into the kettle; but it was not quite equal to the *Chiogenes*. We called this therefore Checkerberry-tea Camp.

I was struck with the abundance of the *Linnæa borealis* [Linnæa], checkerberry, and *Chiogenes hispidula* [creeping snowberry] almost everywhere in the Maine woods. The wintergreen (*Chimaphila umbellata*) was still in bloom here, and *Clintonia* berries were abundant and ripe. This handsome plant is one of the most common in that forest. We here first noticed the moose-wood in fruit on the banks. The prevailing trees were spruce (commonly black), arbor-vitæ, canoe-birch (black ash and elms beginning to appear), yellow birch, red maple, and a little hemlock skulking in the forest. The Indian said that the white-maple punk was the best for tinder, that yellow-birch punk was pretty good, but hard. After supper he put the moose tongue and lips to boil, cutting out the *septum*. He showed me how to write on the under side of birch bark, with a black spruce twig, which is hard and tough and can be brought to a point.

The Indian wandered off into the woods a short distance just before night, and, coming back, said, "Me found great treasure,—fifty, sixty dollars worth." "What's that?" we asked. "Steel traps, under a log, thirty or forty, I didn't count 'em. I guess Indian work,—worth three dollars apiece." It was a singular coincidence that he should have chanced to walk to and look under that particular log, in that trackless forest.

I saw chivin and chub in the stream when washing my

hands, but my companion tried in vain to catch them. I also heard the sound of bull-frogs from a swamp on the opposite side, thinking at first that they were moose; a duck paddled swiftly by; and sitting in that dusky wilderness, under that dark mountain, by the bright river which was full of reflected light, still I heard the wood-thrush sing, as if no higher civilization could be attained. By this time the night was upon us.

You commonly make your camp just at sundown, and are collecting wood, getting your supper, or pitching your tent while the shades of night are gathering around and adding to the already dense gloom of the forest. You have no time to explore or look around you before it is dark. You may penetrate half a dozen rods farther into that twilight wilderness, after some dry bark to kindle your fire with, and wonder what mysteries lie hidden still deeper in it, say at the end of a long day's walk; or you may run down the shore for a dipper of water, and get a clearer view for a short distance up or down the stream, and while you stand there, see a fish leap, or duck alight in the river, or hear a wood-thrush or robin sing in the woods. That is as if you had been to town or civilized parts.

But there is no sauntering off to see the country, and ten or fifteen rods seems a great way from your companions, and you come back with the air of a much traveled man, as from a long journey, with adventures to relate, though you may have heard the crackling of the fire all the while, —and at a hundred rods you might be lost past recovery, and have to camp out. It is all mossy and *moosey*. In some of those dense fir and spruce woods there is hardly room for the smoke to go up. The trees are a *standing* night, and every fir and spruce which you fell is a plume plucked from night's raven wing. Then at night the general stillness is more impressive than any sound, but occasionally you hear the note of an owl farther or nearer in the woods, and if near a lake, the semi-human cry of the loons at their unearthly revels.

To-night the Indian lay between the fire and his stretched moose-hide, to avoid the mosquitoes. Indeed, he also made a small smoky fire of damp leaves at his head and his feet, and then as usual rolled up his head in his blanket. We with our veils and our wash were tolerably comfortable, but it would be difficult to pursue any sedentary occupation in the woods at this season; you cannot see to read much by the light of a fire through a veil in the evening, nor handle pencil and paper well with gloves or anointed fingers.

FRIDAY, *July* 31.

The Indian said, "You and I kill moose last night, therefore use 'em best wood. Always use hard wood to cook moose-meat." His "best wood" was rock-maple. He cast the moose's lip into the fire, to burn the hair off, and then rolled it up with the meat to carry along. Observing that we were sitting down to breakfast without any pork, he said, with a very grave look, "Me want some fat," so he was told that he might have as much as he would fry.

We had smooth but swift water for a considerable distance, where we glided rapidly along, scaring up ducks and kingfishers. But as usual, our smooth progress erelong came to an end, and we were obliged to carry canoe and all about half a mile down the right bank, around some rapids or falls. It required sharp eyes sometimes to tell which side was the carry, before you went over the falls, but Polis never failed to land us rightly. The raspberries were particularly abundant and large here, and all hands went to eating them, the Indian remarking on their size.

Often on bare rocky carries the trail was so indistinct that I repeatedly lost it, but when I walked behind him I observed that he could keep it almost like a hound, and rarely hesitated, or, if he paused a moment on a bare rock, his eye immediately detected some sign which would have escaped me. Frequently *we* found no path at all at these places, and were to him unaccountably delayed. He would only say it was "ver strange."

We had heard of a Grand Fall on this stream, and thought that each fall we came to must be it, but after christening several in succession with this name, we gave up the search. There were more Grand or Petty Falls than I can remember.[1]

I cannot tell how many times we had to walk on account of falls or rapids. We were expecting all the while that the river would take a final leap and get to smooth water, but there was no improvement this forenoon. However, the carries were an agreeable variety. So surely as we stepped out of the canoe and stretched our legs we found ourselves in a blueberry and raspberry garden, each side of our rocky trail around the falls being lined with one or both. There was not a carry on the main East Branch where we did not find an abundance of both these berries, for these were the rockiest places, and partially cleared, such as these plants prefer, and there had been none to gather the finest before us.

In our three journeys over the carries, for we were obliged to go over the ground three times whenever the canoe was taken out, we did full justice to the berries, and they were just what we wanted to correct the effect of our hard bread and pork diet. Another name for making a portage would have been going a-berrying.[2]

---

[1] The falls and rips coming down the East Branch after leaving Grand Lake, taken from the Hubbard Maps, comprise Stair Falls, Haskell Rock Pitch, Pond Pitch, Grand Pitch, Hulling Machine Falls, Bowlin Falls, Whetstone Falls, Burnt Land Rips, Crowfoot Falls, Grindstone Falls, Rocky Rips, and Ledge Falls.

[2] Thoreau had more to say about raspberries. See Appendix, page 327, for a quotation from his Journal.

We also found a few *Amelanchier* [shadbush], or *service* berries, though most were abortive, but they held on rather more generally than they do in Concord. The Indian called them *Pemoymenuk*, and said that they bore much fruit in some places. He sometimes also ate the northern wild red cherries, saying that they were good medicine, but they were scarcely edible. We bathed and dined at the foot of one of these carries. It was the Indian who commonly reminded us that it was dinner-time, sometimes even by turning the prow to the shore. He once made an indirect, but lengthy apology, by saying that we might think it strange, but that one who worked hard all day was very particular to have his dinner in good season.

At the most considerable fall on this stream, when I was walking over the carry, close behind the Indian, he observed a track on the rock, which was but slightly covered with soil, and, stooping, muttered "caribou." When we returned, he observed a much larger track near the same place, where some animal's foot had sunk into a small hollow in the rock, partly filled with grass and earth, and he exclaimed with surprise, "What that?" "Well, what is it?" I asked. Stooping and laying his hand in it, he answered with a mysterious air, and in a half whisper, "Devil (that is, Indian Devil, or cougar) lodges about here—very bad animal—pull 'em *locks* all to pieces." "How long since it was made?" I asked. "To-day or yesterday," said he. But when I asked him afterward if he was sure it was the devil's track, he said he did not know. I had been told that the scream of a cougar was heard about Ktaadn recently, and we were not far from that mountain.

We spent at least half the time in walking to-day, and the walking was as bad as usual, for the Indian being alone, commonly ran down far below the foot of the carries before he waited for us. The carry-paths themselves were more than usually indistinct, often the route being revealed only by the countless small holes in the fallen timber made by the tacks in the drivers' boots, or where there *was* a slight trail we did not find it. It was a tangled and perplexing thicket, through which we stumbled and threaded our way, and when we had finished a mile of it, our starting-point seemed far away. We were glad that we had not got to walk to Bangor along the banks of this river, which would be a journey of more than a hundred miles. Think of the denseness of the forest, the fallen trees and rocks, the windings of the river, the streams emptying in, and the frequent swamps to be crossed. It made you shudder.

Yet the Indian from time to time pointed out to us where he had thus crept along day after day when he was a boy of ten, and in a starving condition. He had been hunting far north of this with two grown Indians. The winter came on unexpectedly early, and the ice compelled them to leave their canoe at Grand Lake, and walk down the bank. They shouldered their furs and started for Oldtown. The snow was not deep enough for snowshoes, or to cover the inequalities of the ground. Polis was soon too weak to carry any burden; but he managed to catch one otter.

This was the most they all had to eat on this journey, and he remembered how good the yellow-lily roots were, made into a soup with the otter oil. He shared this food equally with the other two, but being so small he suffered much more than they. He waded through the Mattawamkeag at its mouth, when it was freezing cold and came up to his chin, and he, being very weak and emaciated, expected to be swept away. The first house which they reached was at Lincoln, and thereabouts they met a white teamster with supplies, who, seeing their condition, gave them as much of his load as they could eat. For six months after getting home, he was very low, and did not expect to live, and was perhaps always the worse for it.

We could not find much more than half of this day's journey on our maps (the "Map of the Public Lands of Maine and Massachusetts," and "Colton's Railroad and Township Map of Maine," which copies the former). By the maps there was not more than fifteen miles between camps at the outside, and yet we had been busily progressing all day, and much of the time very rapidly.

For seven or eight miles below that succession of "Grand" falls, the aspect of the banks as well as the character of the stream was changed. After passing a tributary from the northeast, perhaps Bowlin Stream, we had good swift smooth water, with a regular slope, such as I have described. Low, grassy banks and muddy shores began. Many elms, as well as maples, and more ash-trees, overhung the stream, and supplanted the spruce.

My lily-roots having been lost when the canoe was taken out at a carry, I landed late in the afternoon, at a low and grassy place amid maples, to gather more. It was slow work, grubbing them up amid the sand, and the mosquitoes were all the while feasting on me. Mosquitoes, black flies, etc., pursued us in mid-channel, and we were glad sometimes to get into violent rapids, for then we escaped them.

A red-headed woodpecker flew across the river, and the Indian remarked that it was good to eat. As we glided swiftly down the inclined plane of the river, a great cat-owl launched itself away from a stump on the bank, and flew heavily across the stream, and the Indian, as usual, imitated its note. Soon the same bird flew back in front of us, and we afterwards passed it perched on a tree. Soon afterward a white-headed eagle sailed down the stream before us. We drove him several miles, while we were looking for a good place to camp, for we expected to be overtaken by a shower,—and still we could distinguish him by his white tail, sailing away from time to time from some tree by the shore still farther down the stream. Some shecorways, being surprised by us, a part of them dived, and we passed directly over them, and could trace their course here and there by a bubble on the surface, but we did not see them come up.[1]

Polis detected once or twice what he called a "tow" road, an indistinct path leading into the forest. In the meanwhile we passed the mouth of the Seboois on our left. This did not look so large as our stream, which was indeed the main one. It was some time before we found a camping-place, for the shore was either too grassy and muddy, where mosquitoes abounded, or too steep a hillside. The Indian said that there were but few mosquitoes on a steep hillside. We examined a good place, where somebody had camped a long time; but it seemed pitiful to occupy an old site, where there was so much room to choose, so we continued on. We at length found a place to our minds, on the west bank, about a mile below the mouth of the Seboois, where, in a very dense spruce wood above a gravelly shore, there seemed to be but few insects. The trees were so thick that we were obliged to clear a space to build our fire and lie down in, and the young spruce trees that were left were like the wall of an apartment rising around us. We were obliged to pull ourselves up a steep bank to get there. But the place which you have selected for your camp, though never so rough and grim, begins at once to have its attractions, and becomes a very centre of civilization to you: "Home is home, be it never so homely."

It turned out that the mosquitoes were more numerous here than we had found them before, and the Indian com-

---

[1] Thoreau made a list of birds which he saw on this trip. See Appendix, page 334.

HENRY
BUGBEL
KANT

plained a good deal, though he lay, as the night before, between three fires and his stretched hide. As I sat on a stump by the fire, with a veil and gloves on, trying to read, he observed, "I make you candle" and in a minute he took a piece of birch bark about two inches wide and rolled it hard, like an allumette fifteen inches long, lit it, and fixed it by the other end horizontally in a split stick three feet high, stuck it in the ground, turning the blazing end to the wind, and telling me to snuff it from time to time. It answered the purpose of a candle pretty well.

I noticed, as I had done before, that there was a lull among the mosquitoes about midnight, and that they began again in the morning. Nature is thus merciful. But apparently they need rest as well as we. Few if any creatures are equally active all night. As soon as it was light I saw, through my veil, that the inside of the tent about our heads was quite blackened with myriads, each one of their wings when flying, as has been calculated, vibrating some three thousand times in a minute, and their combined hum was almost as bad to endure as their stings. I had an uncomfortable night on this account, though I am not sure that one succeeded in his attempt to sting me.

We did not suffer so much from insects on this excursion as the statements of some who have explored these woods in midsummer led us to anticipate. Yet I have no doubt that at some seasons and in some places they are a much more serious pest. The Jesuit Hierome Lalemant, of Quebec, reporting the death of Father Reni Menard, who was abandoned, lost his way, and died in the woods, among the Ontarios near Lake Superior, in 1661, dwells chiefly on his probable sufferings from the attacks of mosquitoes when too weak to defend himself, adding that there was a frightful number of them in those parts, "and so insupportable," says he, "that the three Frenchmen who have made that voyage affirm that there was no other means of defending one's self but to run always without stopping, and it was even necessary for two of them to be employed in driving off these creatures while the third wanted to drink, otherwise he could not have done it." I have no doubt that this was said in good faith.

August 1.

I caught two or three large red chivin (*Leuciscus pulchellus*) early this morning, within twenty feet of the camp, which, added to the moose-tongue, that had been left in the kettle boiling over-night, and to our other stores, made a sumptuous breakfast. The Indian made us some hemlock tea instead of coffee, and we were not obliged to go as far as China for it; indeed, not quite so far as for the fish. This was tolerable, though he said it was not strong enough. It was interesting to see so simple a dish as a kettle of water with a handful of green hemlock sprigs in it, boiling over the huge fire in the open air, the leaves fast losing their lively green color, and know that it was for our breakfast.

We were glad to embark once more, and leave some of the mosquitoes behind. We had passed the *Wassataquoik* without perceiving it. This, according to the Indian, is the name of the main East Branch itself, and not properly applied to this small tributary alone, as on the maps.[1] We found that we had camped about a mile above Hunt's, which is on the east bank, and is the last house for those who ascend Ktaadn on this side.

We also had expected to ascend it from this point, but omitted it on account of the chafed feet of one of my companions. The Indian, however, suggested that perhaps he might get a pair of moccasins at this place, and that he could walk very easily in them without hurting his feet, wearing

---

[1] Hubbard gives Wassadegwewick as the Indian name of the East Branch.

several pairs of stockings, and he said beside that they were
so porous that when you had taken in water it all drained out
again in a little while. We stopped to get some sugar, but
found that the family had moved away, and the house was
unoccupied, except temporarily by some men who were
getting the hay. They told me that the road to Ktaadn left
the river eight miles above; also that perhaps we could get
some sugar at Fisk's, fourteen miles below. I do not remember that we saw the mountain at all from the river.

I noticed a seine here stretched on the bank, which probably had been used to catch salmon. Just below this, on the
west bank, we saw a moose-hide stretched, and with it a
bear-skin, which was comparatively very small. I was the
more interested in this sight, because it was near here that
a townsman of ours, then quite a lad, and alone, killed a large
bear some years ago. The Indian said that they belonged
to Joe Aitteon, my last guide, but how he told I do not
know. He was probably hunting near, and had left them for
the day. Finding that we were going directly to Oldtown,
he regretted that he had not taken more of the moose-meat
to his family, saying that in a short time, by drying it, he
could have made it so light as to have brought away the
greater part, leaving the bones. We once or twice inquired
after the lip, which is a famous tid-bit, but he said, "That go
Oldtown for my old woman; don't get it every day."

Maples grew more and more numerous. It was lowering,
and rained a little during the forenoon, and, as we expected
a wetting, we stopped early and dined on the east side of
a small expansion of the river, just above what are probably
called Whetstone Falls, about a dozen miles below Hunt's.
There were pretty fresh moose-tracks by the water-side.
There were singular long ridges hereabouts, called "horse-
backs," covered with ferns. My companion having lost his
pipe asked the Indian if he could not make him one. "Oh.

yer," said he, and in a minute rolled up one of birch bark, telling him to wet the bowl from time to time. Here also he left his gazette on a tree.

We carried round the falls just below, on the west side. The rocks were on their edges, and very sharp. The distance was about three fourths of a mile. When we had carried over one load, the Indian returned by the shore, and I by the path, and though I made no particular haste, I was nevertheless surprised to find him at the other end as soon as I. It was remarkable how easily he got along over the worst ground. He said to me, "I take canoe and you take the rest, suppose you can keep along with me?" I thought that he meant, that while he ran down the rapids I should keep along the shore, and be ready to assist him from time to time, as I had done before; but as the walking would be very bad, I answered, "I suppose you will go too fast for me, but I will try." But I was to go by the path, he said. This I thought would not help the matter, I should have so far to go to get to the riverside when he wanted me. But neither was this what he meant.

He was proposing a race over the carry, and asked me if I thought I could keep along with him by the same path, adding that I must be pretty smart to do it. As his load, the canoe, would be much the heaviest and bulkiest, though the simplest, I thought that I ought to be able to do it, and said that I would try. So I proceeded to gather up the gun, axe, paddle, kettle, frying-pan, plates, dippers, carpets, etc., etc., and while I was thus engaged he threw me his cow-hide boots. "What, are these in the bargain?" I asked. "Oh, yer," said he; but before I could make a bundle of my load I saw him disappearing over a hill with the canoe on his head; so, hastily scraping the various articles together, I started on the run, and immediately went by him in the bushes, but I had no sooner left him out of sight in a rocky hollow, than the greasy plates, dippers, etc., took to themselves wings,

and while I was employed in gathering them up again, he
went by me; but hastily pressing the sooty kettle to my side,
I started once more, and soon passing him again, I saw him
no more on the carry.

I do not mention this as anything of a feat, for it was but
poor running on my part, and he was obliged to move with
great caution for fear of breaking his canoe as well as his
neck. When he made his appearance, puffing and panting
like myself, in answer to my inquiries where he had been, he
said, "Locks (rocks) cut 'em feet," and laughing added, "Oh,
me love to play sometimes." He said that he and his companions when they came to carries several miles long used to
try who would get over first; each perhaps with a canoe on
his head. I bore the sign of the kettle on my brown linen
sack for the rest of the voyage.

We made a second carry on the west side, around some
falls about a mile below this. On the mainland were Norway
pines, indicating a new geological formation, and it was such
a dry and sandy soil as we had not noticed before. As we
approached the mouth of the East Branch, we passed two
or three huts, the first sign of civilization after Hunt's, though
we saw no road as yet; we heard a cow-bell, and even saw
an infant held up to a small square window to see us pass, but
apparently the infant and the mother that held it were the
only inhabitants then at home for several miles.

This took the wind out of our sails, reminding us that we
were travelers surely, while it was a native of the soil, and
had the advantage of us. Conversation flagged. I would only

hear the Indian, perhaps, ask my companion, "You load my pipe?" He said that he smoked alder bark, for medicine. On entering the West Branch at Nicketow it appeared much larger than the East. Polis remarked that the former was all gone and lost now, that it was all smooth water hence to Oldtown, and he threw away his pole which was cut on the Umbazookskus. Thinking of the rapids, he said once or twice, that you wouldn't catch him to go East Branch again; but he did not by any means mean all that he said.

Things are quite changed since I was here eleven years ago. Where there were but one or two houses, I now found quite a village with saw mills and a store (the latter was locked, but its contents were so much the more safely stored), and there was a stage-road to Mattawamkeag, and the rumor of a stage.[1]

---

[1] Disappointed in their plan to ascend Ktaadn from the east because of the condition of Edward Hoar's feet, which had been in bad shape since his arduous efforts on the passage from Umbazookskus to Chamberlain Lake, they headed down the Penobscot for Oldtown. This portion of their excursion traversing the habitat of the Penobscot Indian will be found on p. 305 ff.

12. Up the West Branch

What was "quite a village" in 1857 and is today the town of Medway at the junction of the East and the West Branch, had been but a clearing when Thoreau went through in 1846 on his way to ascend Ktaadn. This was his first trip. Accompanied by his relative (Thatcher), he left Bangor in a buggy on September 1. Passing through Stillwater and Oldtown and there ferrying across the river, they followed the Houlton Road up the east bank of the Penobscot, crossing "the Sunkhaze, a summery Indian name, the Olemmon, Passadumkeag, and other streams." Then, "leaving the river awhile for shortness," they spent the night in Enfield.

The next morning driving on past Cold Stream Pond, they rejoined the Houlton Road—"here called the military road"

—at Lincoln. Here occurred a detour. Crossing the Penobscot in a canoe, they went over to one of the Indian islands to procure a guide to the mountain. Arrangements were soon made whereby two Indians—one of them bore the fantastic name of Louis Neptune—who were shortly starting up river to hunt moose at Chesuncook, should join them at Five Islands just below Mattawamkeag. By noon they had reached Matta-wamkeag. This was distinguished by being the end of the stage line and by a "substantial covered bridge across the Mattawamkeag"; here they put up "at a frequented house." Intrigued by tales of an ancient Indian battle near by, Thoreau records:

"After dinner we strolled down to the 'Point' formed by the junction of the two rivers, which is said to be the scene of an ancient battle between the Eastern Indians and the Mohawks, and searched there carefully for relics, though the men at the bar-room had never heard of such things; but we found only some flakes of arrow-head stone, some points of arrow-heads, one small leaden bullet, and some colored beads, the last to be referred, perhaps, to early fur-trader days."

Here, while awaiting the arrival of two companions who were coming up from Bangor to join them, Thoreau records on September 2, 1846: [1]

"The last edition of Greenleaf's Map of Maine hung on the

---

[1] The identity of the "two more Bangoreans" has eluded investigation. Thoreau's relative—George Augustus Thatcher—was the husband of his cousin, Rebecca Jane Billings. Her sister, Mary Ann Thoreau Billings married Caleb Lowell, also of Bangor. They were the daughters of his aunt, Nancy (Thoreau) Billings. In characteristic vein, Thoreau referred to his Bangor relations as "the Penobscot tribe." In a letter written a year later (October 24, 1847) to his sister Sophia, who was to spend the winter at Bangor, he said:

"Give my respects to the whole Penobscot tribe and tell them that I trust we are good brothers still, and endeavor to keep the chain of friendship bright, though I dig up a hatchet now and then. . . ."

"From your   Brother Henry"

*wall here, and, as we had no pocket-map, we resolved to trace
a map of the lake country. So, dipping a wad of tow into the
lamp, we oiled a sheet of paper on the oiled table-cloth, and,
in good faith, traced what we afterwards ascertained to be a
labyrinth of errors, carefully following the outlines of the im-
aginary lakes which the map contains. The Map of the Public
Lands of Maine and Massachusetts is the only one I have seen
that at all deserves the name. It was while we were engaged
in this operation that our companions arrived. They had seen
the Indians' fire on the Five Islands, and so we concluded that
all was right."*

Early the next morning we had mounted our packs, and
prepared for a tramp up the West Branch, my companion
having turned his horse out to pasture for a week or ten
days, thinking that a bite of fresh grass, and a taste of running water would do him as much good as backwoods fare
and new country influences his master. Leaping over a fence,
we began to follow an obscure trail up the northern bank of
the Penobscot. There was now no road further, the river being the only highway, and but half a dozen log-huts confined to its banks, to be met with for thirty miles. On either
hand, and beyond, was a wholly uninhabited wilderness,
stretching to Canada. Neither horse nor cow, nor vehicle of
any kind, had ever passed over this ground; the cattle, and
the few bulky articles which the loggers use, being got up in
the winter on the ice, and down again before it breaks up.

The evergreen woods had a decidedly sweet and bracing
fragrance; the air was a sort of diet-drink, and we walked on
buoyantly in Indian file, stretching our legs. Occasionally
there was a small opening on the bank, made for the purpose of log-rolling, where we got a sight of the river,—always
a rocky and rippling stream. The roar of the rapids, the note
of a whistler-duck on the river, of the jay and chickadee
around us, and of the pigeon-woodpecker in the openings,

were the sounds that we heard. This was what you might call a bran-new country; the only roads were of Nature's making, and the few houses were camps. Here, then, one could no longer accuse institutions and society, but must front the true source of evil.

There are three classes of inhabitants who either frequent or inhabit the country which we had now entered;—first, the loggers, who, for a part of the year, the winter and spring, are far the most numerous, but in the summer, except a few explorers for timber, completely desert it; second, the few settlers, the only permanent inhabitants, who live on the verge of it, and help raise supplies for the former; third, the hunters, mostly Indians, who range over it in their season.

At the end of three miles we came to the Mattaseunk stream and mill, where there was even a rude wooden railroad running down to the Penobscot, the last railroad we were to see. We crossed one tract, on the bank of the river, of more than a hundred acres of heavy timber, which had just been felled and burnt over, and was still smoking. Our trail lay through the midst of it, and was wellnigh blotted out. The trees lay at full length, four or five feet deep, and crossing each other in all directions, all black as charcoal, but perfectly sound within, still good for fuel or for timber; soon they would be cut into lengths and burnt again. Here were thousands of cords, enough to keep the poor of Boston and New York amply warm for a winter, which only cumbered the ground and were in the settler's way. And the whole of that solid and interminable forest is doomed to be gradually devoured thus by fire, like shavings, and no man be warmed by it.

At Crocker's log-hut, at the mouth of Salmon River, seven miles from the Point, one of the party commenced distributing a store of small, cent picture-books among the children, to teach them to read, and also newspapers, more or less recent, among the parents, than which notbing can be more acceptable to a backwoods people. It was really an important item in our outfit, and, at times, the only currency that would circulate. I walked through Salmon River with my shoes on, it being low water, but not without wetting my feet. A few miles farther we came to "Marm Howard's," at the end of an extensive clearing, where there were two or three log-huts in sight at once, one on the opposite side of the river, and a few graves, even surrounded by a wooden paling, where already the rude forefathers of *a* hamlet lie, and a thousand years hence, perchance, some poet will write his "Elegy in a Country Churchyard." The "Village Hampdens," the "mute, inglorious Miltons," and Cromwells, "guiltless of" their "country's blood," were yet unborn.

> "Perchance in this *wild* spot *there will be* laid
>   Some heart once pregnant with celestial fire;
>   Hands that the rod of empire might have swayed,
>   Or waked to ecstasy the living lyre."

The next house was Fisk's, ten miles from the Point at the mouth of the East Branch, opposite to the island Nicketow, or the Forks, the last of the Indian islands. I am particular to give the names of the settlers and the distances, since every log-hut in these woods is a public house, and such information is of no little consequence to those who may have occasion to travel this way. Our course here crossed the Penobscot, and followed the southern bank. One of the party, who entered the house in search of some one to set us over, reported a very neat dwelling, with plenty of books, and a new wife, just imported from Boston, wholly new to the woods.

We found the East Branch a large and rapid stream at its mouth, and much deeper than it appeared. Having with some difficulty discovered the trail again, we kept up the south side of the West Branch, or main river, passing by some rapids called Rock-Ebeeme, the roar of which we heard through the woods, and, shortly after, in the thickest of the wood, some empty loggers' camps, still new, which were occupied the previous winter. Though we saw a few more afterwards, I will make one account serve for all. These were such houses as the lumberers of Maine spend the winter in, in the wilderness.

There were the camps and the hovels for the cattle, hardly distinguishable, except that the latter had no chimney. These camps were about twenty feet long by fifteen wide, built of logs,—hemlock, cedar, spruce or yellow birch,—one kind alone, or all together, with the bark on; two or three large ones first, one directly above another, and notched together at the ends, to the height of three or four feet, then of smaller logs resting upon transverse ones at the ends, each of the last successively shorter than the other, to form the roof. The chimney was an oblong square hole in the middle, three or four feet in diameter, with a fence of logs as high as the ridge. The interstices were filled with moss, and the roof was shingled with long and handsome splints of cedar, or spruce, or pine, rifted with a sledge and cleaver.

The fire-place, the most important place of all, was in shape and size like the chimney, and directly under it, defined by a log fence or fender on the ground, and a heap of ashes, a foot or two deep within, with solid benches of split logs running round it. Here the fire usually melts the snow, and dries the rain before it can descend to quench it. The faded beds of arbor-vitæ leaves extended under the eaves on either hand. There was the place for the water-pail, pork-barrel, and wash-basin, and generally a dingy pack of cards left on a log.

Usually a good deal of whittling was expended on the latch, which was made of wood, in the form of an iron one. These houses are made comfortable by the huge fires, which can be afforded night and day. Usually the scenery about them is drear and savage enough; and the loggers' camp is as completely in the woods as a fungus at the foot of a pine

in a swamp; no outlook but to the sky overhead; no more
clearing than is made by cutting down the trees of which
it is built, and those which are necessary for fuel. If only
it be well sheltered and convenient to his work, and near a
spring, he wastes no thought on the prospect. They are very
proper forest houses, the stems of the trees collected together
and piled up around a man to keep out wind and rain,—made
of living green logs, hanging with moss and lichen, and with
the curls and fringes of the yellow-birch bark, and dripping
with resin, fresh and moist, and redolent of swampy odors,
with that sort of vigor and perennialness even about them
that toadstools suggest.[1]

The logger's fare consists of tea, molasses, flour, pork
(sometimes beef), and beans. A great proportion of the beans
raised in Massachusetts find their market here. On expeditions it is only hard bread and pork, often raw, slice upon
slice, with tea or water, as the case may be.

The primitive wood is always and everywhere damp and
mossy, so that I traveled constantly with the impression that
I was in a swamp; and only when it was remarked that this
or that tract, judging from the quality of the timber on it,
would make a profitable clearing, was I reminded, that if
the sun were let in it would make a dry field, like the few I
had seen, at once. The best shod for the most part travel with
wet feet. If the ground was so wet and spongy at this, the
dryest part of a dry season, what must it be in the spring?
The woods hereabouts abounded in beech and yellow birch,

---

[1] Springer in his *Forest Life* (1851), says that they first remove the leaves
and turf from the spot where they intend to build a camp, for fear of fire; also,
that "the spruce-tree is generally selected for camp-building, it being light,
straight, and quite free from sap"; that "the roof is finally covered with the
boughs of the fir, spruce, and hemlock, so that when the snow falls upon the
whole, the warmth of the camp is preserved in the coldest weather"; and that
they make a long seat before the fire, called the "Deacon's Seat," of a spruce or
fir split in halves, with three or four stout limbs left on one side for legs, which
are not likely to get loose. [Thoreau]

of which last there were some very large specimens; also spruce, cedar, fir, and hemlock; but we saw only the stumps of the white-pine here, some of them of great size, these having been already culled out, being the only tree much sought after, even as low down as this. Only a little spruce and hemlock beside had been logged here. The Eastern wood which is sold for fuel in Massachusetts all comes from below Bangor. It was the pine alone, chiefly the white-pine, that had tempted any but the hunter to precede us on this route.

Waite's farm, thirteen miles from the Point, is an extensive and elevated clearing, from which we got a fine view of the river, rippling and gleaming far beneath us. My companions had formerly had a good view of Ktaadn and the other mountains here, but to-day it was so smoky that we could see nothing of them. We could overlook an immense country of uninterrupted forest, stretching away up the East Branch toward Canada on the north and northwest, and toward the Aroostook valley on the northeast; and imagine what wild life was stirring in its midst. Here was quite a field of corn for this region, whose peculiar dry scent we perceived a third of a mile off, before we saw it.

Eighteen miles from the Point brought us in sight of Mc-Causlin's, or "Uncle George's," as he was familiarly called by my companions, to whom he was well known, where we intended to break our long fast. His house was in the midst of an extensive clearing of intervale, at the mouth of the Little Schoodic River, on the opposite or north bank of the Penobscot. So we collected on a point of the shore, that we might be seen, and fired our gun as a signal, which brought out his dogs forthwith, and thereafter their master, who in due time took us across in his batteau. This clearing was bounded abruptly, on all sides but the river, by the naked stems of the forest, as if you were to cut only a few feet square in the midst of a thousand acres of mowing, and set down a thimble therein. He had a whole heaven and horizon to himself, and the sun seemed to be journeying over his clearing only the livelong day. Here we concluded to spend the night, and wait for the Indians, as there was no stopping-place so convenient above. He had seen no Indians pass, and this did not often happen without his knowledge. He thought that his dogs sometimes gave notice of the approach of Indians half an hour before they arrived.

McCauslin was a Kennebec man, of Scotch descent, who had been a waterman twenty-two years, and had driven on the lakes and headwaters of the Penobscot five or six springs in succession, but was now settled here to raise supplies for the lumberers and for himself. He entertained us a day or two with true Scotch hospitality, and would accept no recompense for it. A man of a dry wit and shrewdness, and a general intelligence which I had not looked for in the backwoods. In fact, the deeper you penetrate into the woods, the more intelligent, and, in one sense, less countrified do you find the inhabitants; for always the pioneer has been a traveler, and, to some extent, a man of the world; and, as the distances with which he is familiar are greater, so is his information more general and far reaching than the villagers. If I were to look for a narrow, uninformed, and countrified mind, as opposed to the intelligence and refinement which are thought to emanate from cities, it would be among the rusty inhabitants of an old-settled country, on farms all run out and gone to seed with life-everlasting, in the towns about Boston, even on the high-road in Concord, and not in the backwoods of Maine.

Supper was got before our eyes in the ample kitchen, by a fire which would have roasted an ox; many whole logs, four feet long, were consumed to boil our tea-kettle,—birch, or beech, or maple, the same summer and winter; and the dishes were soon smoking on the table, late the arm-chair, against the wall, from which one of the party was expelled. The arms of the chair formed the frame on which the table rested; and, when the round top was turned up against the wall, it formed the back of the chair, and was no more in the way than the wall itself. This, we noticed, was the prevailing fashion in these log-houses, in order to economize in room.

There were piping-hot wheaten cakes, the flour having been brought up the river in batteaux,— no Indian bread, for the upper part of Maine, it will be remembered, is a wheat country,—and ham, eggs, and potatoes, and milk and cheese, the produce of the farm; and also shad and salmon, tea sweetened with molasses, and sweet cakes, in contradistinction to the hot cakes not sweetened, the one white, the other yellow, to wind up with. Such we found was the prevailing fare, ordinary and extraordinary, along this river. Mountain cranberries (*Vaccinium Vitis-Idæa*), stewed and sweetened, were the common dessert. Everything here was in profusion, and the best of its kind. Butter was in such plenty that it was commonly used, before it was salted, to grease boots with.

In the night we were entertained by the sound of rain-drops on the cedar-splints which covered the roof, and awaked the next morning with a drop or two in our eyes. It had set in for a storm, and we made up our minds not to forsake such comfortable quarters with this prospect, but wait for Indians and fair weather. It rained and drizzled and gleamed by turns, the livelong day. What we did there, how we killed the time would perhaps be idle to tell; how many times we buttered our boots, and how often a drowsy one was seen to sidle off to the bedroom. When it held up, I strolled up and down the bank, and gathered the harebell and cedar-berries, which grew there; or else we tried by turns the long-handled axe on the logs before the door. The axehelves here were made to chop standing on the log,—a primitive log of course,—and were, therefore, nearly a foot longer than with us.

One while we walked over the farm and visited his well-filled barns with McCauslin. There were one other man and two women only here. He kept horses, cows, oxen, and sheep. I think he said that he was the first to bring a plough and a cow so far; and he might have added the last, with only two exceptions. The potato-rot had found him out here, too, the previous year, and got half or two thirds of his crop, though the seed was of his own raising. Oats, grass, and potatoes were his staples; but he raised, also, a few carrots and turnips, and "a little corn for the hens," for this was all that he dared risk, for fear that it would not ripen. Melons, squashes, sweet-corn, beans, tomatoes, and many other vegetables, could not be ripened there.

The very few settlers along this stream were obviously tempted by the cheapness of the land mainly. When I asked McCauslin why more settlers did not come in, he answered, that one reason was, they could not buy the land, it belonged to individuals or companies who were afraid that their wild lands would be settled, and so incorporated into towns, and they be taxed for them; but to settling on the States' land there was no such hindrance. For his own part, he wanted no neighbors,—he didn't wish to see any road by his house. Neighbors, even the best, were a trouble and expense, especially on the score of cattle and fences. They might live across the river, perhaps, but not on the same side.

The chickens here were protected by the dogs. As McCauslin said, "The old one took it up first, and she taught the pup, and now they had got it into their heads that it wouldn't do to have anything of the bird kind on the premises." A hawk hovering over was not allowed to alight, but barked off by the dogs circling underneath; and a pigeon, or a "yellow-

hammer," as they called the pigeon-woodpecker, on a dead limb or stump, was instantly expelled. It was the main business of their day, and kept them constantly coming and going. One would rush out of the house on the least alarm given by the other.

When it rained hardest, we returned to the house, and took down a tract from the shelf. There was the "Wandering Jew," cheap edition, and fine print, the "Criminal Calendar," and "Parish's Geography," and flash novels two or three. Under the pressure of circumstances, we read a little in these. With such aid, the press is not so feeble an engine, after all. This house, which was a fair specimen of those on this river, was built of huge logs, which peeped out everywhere, and were chinked with clay and moss. It contained four or five rooms. There were no sawed boards, or shingles, or clapboards, about it; and scarcely any tool but the axe had been used in its construction. The partitions were made of long clapboard-like splints, of spruce or cedar, turned to a delicate salmon color by the smoke.

The roof and sides were covered with the same, instead of shingles and clapboards, and some of a much thicker and larger size were used for the floor. These were all so straight and smooth, that they answered the purpose admirably, and a careless observer would not have suspected that they were not sawed and planed. The chimney and hearth were of vast size, and made of stone. The broom was a few twigs of arbor-vitæ tied to a stick; and a pole was suspended over the hearth, close to the ceilings, to dry stockings and clothes on. I noticed that the floor was full of small, dingy holes, as if made with a gimlet, but which were, in fact, made by the spikes, nearly an inch long, which the lumberers wear in their boots to prevent their slipping on wet logs. Just above McCauslin's, there is a rocky rapid, where logs jam in the spring; and many "drivers" are there collected, who frequent his house for supplies; these were their tracks which I saw.

At sundown McCauslin pointed away over the forest, across the river, to signs of fair weather amid the clouds,—some evening redness there. For even there the points of compass held; and there was a quarter of the heavens appropriated to sunrise and another to sunset.

The next morning, the weather proving fair enough for our purpose, we prepared to start, and, the Indians having failed us, persuaded McCauslin, who was not unwilling to revisit the scenes of his driving, to accompany us in their stead, intending to engage one other boatman on the way. A strip of cotton cloth for a tent, a couple of blankets, which would suffice for the whole party, fifteen pounds of hard bread, ten pounds of "clear" pork, and a little tea, made up "Uncle George's" pack. The last three articles were calculated to be provision enough for six men for a week, with what we might pick up. A tea-kettle, a frying-pan, and an axe, to be obtained at the last house, would complete our outfit.

We were soon out of McCauslin's clearing, and in the evergreen woods again. The obscure trail made by the two settlers above, which even the woodman is sometimes puzzled to discern, erelong crossed a narrow, open strip in the woods overrun with weeds, called the Burnt Land, where a fire had raged formerly, stretching northward nine or ten miles, to Millinocket Lake. At the end of three miles, we reached Shad Pond, or Noliseemack, an expansion of the river. Hodge, the Assistant State Geologist, who passed through this on the 25th of June, 1837, says, "We pushed our boat through an acre or more of buck-beans, which had taken root at the bottom, and bloomed above the surface in the greatest profusion and beauty." Thomas Fowler's house is four miles from McCauslin's, on the shore of the pond, at the mouth of the Millinocket River, and eight miles from the lake of the same name, on the latter stream. This lake affords a more direct course to Ktaadn, but we preferred to follow the Penobscot and the Pamadumcook lakes.

Fowler was just completing a new log-hut, and was sawing out a window through the logs, nearly two feet thick, when we arrived. He had begun to paper his house with spruce-bark, turned inside out, which had a good effect, and was in keeping with the circumstances. Instead of water we got here a draught of beer, which, it was allowed, would be better; clear and thin, but strong and stringent as the cedar-sap. It was as if we sucked at the very teats of Nature's pine-clad bosom in these parts,—the sap of all Millinocket botany commingled,—the topmost, most fantastic, and spiciest sprays of the primitive wood, and whatever invigorating and stringent gum or essence it afforded steeped and dissolved in it,—a lumberer's drink, which would acclimate and naturalize a man at once,—which would make him see green, and, if he slept, dream that he heard the wind sough among the pines. Here was a fife, praying to be played on, through which we breathed a few tuneful strains,—brought hither to tame wild beasts.

As we stood upon the pile of chips by the door, fish-hawks were sailing overhead; and here, over Shad Pond, might daily be witnessed the tyranny of the bald-eagle over that bird. Tom pointed away over the lake to a bald-eagle's nest, which was plainly visible more than a mile off, on a pine, high above the surrounding forest, and was frequented from year to year by the same pair, and held sacred by him. There were these two houses only there, his low hut and the eagles' airy cart-load of fagots.

Thomas Fowler, too, was persuaded to join us, for two men were necessary to manage the batteau, which was soon to be our carriage, and these men needed to be cool and skillful for the navigation of the Penobscot. Tom's pack was soon made, for he had not far to look for his waterman's boots, and a red flannel shirt. This is the favorite color with lumbermen; and red flannel is reputed to possess some mysterious virtues, to be most healthful and convenient in respect to perspiration. In every gang there will be a large proportion of red birds. We took here a poor and leaky batteau, and began to pole up the Millinocket two miles, to the elder Fowler's, in order to avoid the Grand Falls of the Penobscot, intending to exchange our batteau there for a better.

The Millinocket is a small, shallow, and sandy stream, full of what I took to be lamprey-eels' or suckers' nests, and lined with musquash cabins, but free from rapids, according to Fowler, excepting at its outlet from the lake. He was at this time engaged in cutting the native grass—rush-grass and meadow-clover, as he called it—on the meadows and small, low islands of this stream. We noticed flattened places in the grass on either side, where, he said, a moose had laid down the night before, adding, that there were thousands in these meadows.

Old Fowler's, on the Millinocket, six miles from McCauslin's, and twenty-four from the Point, is the last house. Gibson's, on the Sowadnehunk, is the only clearing above, but that had proved a failure, and was long since deserted. Fowler is the oldest inhabitant of these woods. He formerly lived a few miles from here, on the south side of the West Branch, where he built his house sixteen years ago, the first house built above the Five Islands. Here our new batteau was to be carried over the first portage of two miles, round the Grand Falls of the Penobscot, on a horse-sled made of saplings, to jump the numerous rocks in the way; but we had to wait a couple of hours for them to catch the horses, which were pastured at a distance, amid the stumps, and had wandered still farther off. The last of the salmon for this season had just been caught, and were still fresh in pickle, from which enough was extracted to fill our empty kettle, and so graduate our introduction to simpler forest fare.

The week before they had lost nine sheep here out of their first flock, by the wolves. The surviving sheep came round the house, and seemed frightened, which induced them to go and look for the rest, when they found seven dead and lacerated, and two still alive. These last they carried to the house, and, as Mrs. Fowler said, they were merely scratched in the throat, and had no more visible wound than would be produced by the prick of a pin. She sheared off the wool from their throats, and washed them, and put on some salve, and turned them out, but in a few moments they were missing, and had not been found since. In fact, they were all poisoned, and those that were found swelled up at once, so that they saved neither skin nor wool. This realized the old fables of the wolves and the sheep, and convinced me that that ancient hostility still existed. Verily, the shepherd-boy did not need to sound a false alarm this time. There were steel traps by the door, of various sizes, for wolves, otter, and bears, with large claws instead of teeth, to catch in their sinews. Wolves are frequently killed with poisoned bait.

At length, after we had dined here on the usual backwoods fare, the horses arrived, and we hauled our batteau out of the water, and lashed it to its wicker carriage, and, throwing in our packs, walked on before, leaving the boatmen and driver, who was Tom's brother, to manage the concern. The route, which led through the wild pasture where the sheep were killed, was in some places the roughest ever traveled by horses, over rocky hills, where the sled bounced and slid along, like a vessel pitching in a storm; and one man was as necessary to stand at the stern, to prevent the boat from being wrecked, as a helmsman in the roughest sea. The philosophy of our progress was something like this: when the runners struck a rock three or four feet high, the sled bounced back and upwards at the same time; but, as the horses never ceased pulling, it came down on the top of the rock, and so we got over. This portage probably followed the trail of an ancient Indian carry round these falls. By two o'clock we, who had walked on before, reached the river above the falls, not far from the outlet of Quakish Lake, and waited for the batteau to come up.

We had been here but a short time, when a thunder-shower was seen coming up from the west, over the still invisible lakes, and that pleasant wilderness which we were so eager to become acquainted with; and soon the heavy drops began to patter on the leaves around us. I had just selected the prostrate trunk of a huge pine, five or six feet in diameter, and was crawling under it, when, luckily, the boat arrived. It would have amused a sheltered man to witness the manner in which it was unlashed, and whirled over, while the first water-spout burst upon us. It was no sooner in the hands of the eager company than it was abandoned to the first revolutionary impulse, and to gravity, to adjust it; and they might have been seen all stooping to its shelter, and wriggling under like so many eels, before it was fairly deposited on the ground.

When all were under, we propped up the lee side, and busied ourselves there whittling thole-pins for rowing, when we should reach the lakes; and made the woods ring, between the claps of thunder, with such boat-songs as we could remember. The horses stood sleek and shining with the rain, all

drooping and crestfallen, while deluge after deluge washed over us; but the bottom of a boat may be relied on for a tight roof. At length, after two hours' delay at this place, a streak of fair weather appeared in the northwest, whither our course now lay, promising a serene evening for our voyage; and the driver returned with his horses, while we made haste to launch our boat, and commence our voyage in good earnest.[1]

There were six of us, including the two boatmen. With our packs heaped up near the bows, and ourselves disposed as baggage to trim the boat, with instructions not to move in case we should strike a rock, more than so many barrels of pork, we pushed out into the first rapid, a slight specimen of the stream we had to navigate. With Uncle George in the stern, and Tom in the bows, each using a spruce pole about twelve feet long, pointed with iron,[2] and poling on the same side, we shot up the rapids like a salmon, the water rushing and roaring around, so that only a practiced eye could distinguish a safe course, or tell what was deep water and what

[1] An interesting description of the manufacture of batteaux will be found in the Appendix on page 328.

[2] The Canadians call it *picquer de fond*. [Thoreau]

rocks, frequently grazing the latter on one or both sides, with a hundred as narrow escapes as ever the Argo had in passing through the Symplegades.

I, who had had some experience in boating, had never experienced any half so exhilarating before. We were lucky to have exchanged our Indians, whom we did not know, for these men, who, together with Tom's brother, were reputed the best boatmen on the river, and were at once indispensable pilots and pleasant companions. The canoe is smaller, more easily upset, and sooner worn out; and the Indian is said not to be so skillful in the management of the batteau. He is, for the most part, less to be relied on, and more disposed to sulks and whims. The utmost familiarity with dead streams, or with the ocean, would not prepare a man for this peculiar navigation; and the most skillful boatman anywhere else would here be obliged to take out his boat and carry round a hundred times, still with great risk, as well as delay, where the practiced batteau-man poles up with comparative ease and safety. The hardy "voyageur" pushes with incredible perseverance and success quite up to the foot of the falls, and then only carries round some perpendicular ledge, and launches again in

"The torrent's smoothness, ere it dash below,"

to struggle with the boiling rapids above. The Indians say that the river once ran both ways, one half up and the other half down, but that, since the white man came, it all runs down, and now they must laboriously pole their canoes against the stream, and carry them over numerous portages.

In the summer, all stores—the grindstone and the plough of the pioneer, flour, pork, and utensils for the explorer,— must be conveyed up the river in batteaux; and many a cargo and many a boatman is lost in these waters. In the winter, however, which is very equable and long, the ice is the great highway, and the loggers' team penetrates to Chesuncook

Lake, and still higher up, even two hundred miles above Bangor. Imagine the solitary sled-track running far up into the snowy and evergreen wilderness, hemmed in closely for a hundred miles by the forest, and again stretching straight across the broad surfaces of concealed lakes!

We were soon in the smooth water of the Quakish Lake, and took our turns at rowing and paddling across it. It is a small, irregular, but handsome lake, shut in on all sides by the forest, and showing no traces of man but some low boom in a distant cove, reserved for spring use. The spruce and cedar on its shores, hung with gray lichens, looked at a distance like the ghosts of trees. Ducks were sailing here and there on its surface, and a solitary loon, like a more living wave,—a vital spot on the lake's surface,—laughed and frolicked, and showed its straight leg, for our amusement. Joe Merry Mountain appeared in the northwest, as if it were looking down on this lake especially; and we had our first, but a partial view of Ktaadn, its summit veiled in clouds, like a dark isthmus in that quarter, connecting the heavens with the earth. After two miles of smooth rowing across this lake, we found ourselves in the river again, which was a continuous rapid for one mile, to the dam, requiring all the strength and skill of our boatmen to pole up it.

This dam is a quite important and expensive work for this country, whither cattle and horses cannot penetrate in the summer, raising the whole river ten feet, and flooding, as they said, some sixty square miles by means of the innumerable lakes with which the river connects. It is a lofty and solid structure, with sloping piers, some distance above, made of frames of logs filled with stones, to break the ice.[1] Here every log pays toll as it passes through the sluices.

---

[1] Even the Jesuit missionaries, accustomed to the St. Lawrence and other rivers of Canada, in their first expeditions to the Abenaquinois, speak of rivers *ferrées de rochers,* shod with rocks. See also No. 10 *Relations,* for 1647, p. 185. [Thoreau]

We filed into the rude loggers' camp at this place, such as I have described, without ceremony, and the cook, at that moment the sole occupant, at once set about preparing tea for his visitors. His fireplace, which the rain had converted into a mud-puddle, was soon blazing again, and we sat down on the log benches around it to dry us. On the well-flattened and somewhat faded beds of arbor-vitæ leaves, which stretched on either hand under the eaves behind us, lay an odd leaf of the Bible, some genealogical chapter out of the Old Testament; and, half buried by the leaves, we found Emerson's Address on West India Emancipation, which had been left here formerly by one of our company, and *had made two converts to the Liberty party here,* as I was told; also, an odd number of the Westminster Review, for 1834, and a pamphlet entitled History of the Erection of the Monument on the grave of Myron Holly. This was the readable or reading matter in a lumberer's camp in the Maine woods, thirty miles from a road, which would be given up to the bears in a fortnight. These things were well thumbed and soiled.

This gang was headed by one John Morrison, a good specimen of a Yankee; and was necessarily composed of men not bred to the business of dam-building, but who were Jacks-at-all-trades, handy with the axe, and other simple implements, and well skilled in wood and water craft.[1] We had hot cakes for our supper even here, white as snowballs, but without butter, and the never-failing sweet cakes, with which we filled our pockets, foreseeing that we should not soon meet with the like again. Such delicate puff-balls seemed a singular diet for backwoodsmen. There was also tea without milk, sweetened with molasses. And so, exchanging a word with John Morrison and his gang when we had returned to the shore, and also exchanging our batteau for a better still, we made haste to improve the little daylight that remained.

---

[1] For further characterization of Yankees see the Appendix, page 329.

This camp, exactly twenty-nine miles from Mattawamkeag Point by the way we had come, and about one hundred from Bangor by the river, was the last human habitation of any kind in this direction. Beyond, there was no trail, and the river and lakes, by batteaux and canoes, was considered the only practicable route. We were about thirty miles by the river from the summit of Ktaadn, which was in sight, though not more than twenty, perhaps, in a straight line.

13. Warping Up

It being about the full of the moon, and a warm and pleasant evening, we decided to row five miles by moonlight to the head of the North Twin Lake, lest the wind should rise on the morrow. After one mile of river, or what the boatmen call "thoroughfare,"—for the river becomes at length only the connecting link between the lakes,—and some slight rapid which had been mostly made smooth water by the dam, we entered the North Twin Lake just after sundown, and steered across for the river "thoroughfare," four miles distant.

This is a noble sheet of water, where one may get the impression which a new country and a "lake of the woods" are fitted to create. There was the smoke of no log-hut nor camp of any kind to greet us, still less was any lover of nature or musing traveler watching our batteau from the distant hills; not even the Indian hunter was there, for he rarely climbs them, but hugs the river like ourselves. No face welcomed us but the fine fantastic sprays of free and happy evergreen trees, waving one above another in their ancient home. At first the red clouds hung over the western shore as gorgeously as if over a city, and the lake lay open to the light with even a civilized aspect, as if expecting trade and commerce, and towns and villas.

We could distinguish the inlet to the South Twin, which is said to be the larger, where the shore was misty and blue, and it was worth the while to look thus through a narrow opening across the entire expanse of a concealed lake to its own yet more dim and distant shore. The shores rose gently to ranges of low hills covered with forests; and though, in fact, the most valuable white-pine timber, even about this lake, had been culled out, this would never have been suspected by the voyager. The impression, which indeed corresponded with the fact, was, as if we were upon a high table-land between the States and Canada, the northern side of which is drained by the St. John and Chaudière, the southern by the Penobscot and Kennebec. There was no bold mountainous shore, as we might have expected, but only isolated hills and mountains rising here and there from the plateau.

The country is an archipelago of lakes,—the lake-country of New England. Their levels vary but a few feet, and the boatmen, by short portages, or by none at all, pass easily from one to another. They say that at very high water the Penobscot and the Kennebec flow into each other, or at any rate, that you may lie with your face in the one and your toes in the other. Even the Penobscot and St. John have been connected by a canal, so that the lumber of the Allegash, instead of going down the St. John, comes down the Penobscot; and the Indian's tradition, that the Penobscot once ran both ways for his convenience, is, in one sense, partially realized to-day.

None of our party but McCauslin had been above this lake, so we trusted to him to pilot us, and we could not but confess the importance of a pilot on these waters. While it is river, you will not easily forget which way is up stream; but when you enter a lake, the river is completely lost, and you scan the distant shores in vain to find where it comes in. A stranger is, for the time at least, lost, and must set about a voyage of discovery first of all to find the river. To follow the windings of the shore when the lake is ten miles, or even more, in length, and of an irregularity which will not soon be mapped, is a wearisome voyage, and will spend his time and his provisions.

They tell a story of a gang of experienced woodmen sent to a location on this stream, who were thus lost in the wilderness of lakes. They cut their way through thickets, and carried their baggage and their boats over from lake to lake, sometimes several miles. They carried into Millinocket Lake, which is on another stream, and is ten miles square, and contains a hundred islands. They explored its shores thoroughly, and then carried into another, and another, and it was a week of toil and anxiety before they found the Penobscot River again, and then their provisions were exhausted, and they were obliged to return.

While Uncle George steered for a small island near the head of the lake, now just visible, like a speck on the water,

we rowed by turns swiftly over its surface, singing such boatsongs as we could remember. The shores seemed at an indefinite distance in the moonlight. Occasionally we paused in our singing and rested on our oars, while we listened to hear if the wolves howled, for this is a common serenade, and my companions affirmed that it was the most dismal and unearthly of sounds; but we heard none this time. If we did not *hear*, however, we did *listen*, not without a reasonable expectation; that at least I have to tell,—only some utterly uncivilized, big-throated owl hooted loud and dismally in the drear and boughy wilderness, plainly not nervous about his solitary life, nor afraid to hear the echoes of his voice there. We remembered also that possibly moose were silently watching us from the distant coves, or some surly bear or timid caribou had been startled by our singing. It was with new emphasis that we sang there the Canadian boat-song,—

> "Row, brothers, row, the stream runs fast,
>   The Rapids are near and the daylight's past!"—

which describes precisely our own adventure, and was inspired by the experience of a similar kind of life,—for the rapids were ever near, and the daylight long past; the woods on shore looked dim, and many an Utawas' tide here emptied into the lake.

> "Why should we yet our sail unfurl?
>   There is not a breath the blue wave to curl!
>   But, when the wind blows off the shore,
>   Oh, sweetly we'll rest our weary oar."

> "Utawas' tide! this trembling moon
>   Shall see us float o'er thy surges soon."

At last we glided past the "green isle," which had been our landmark, all joining in the chorus; as if by the watery links of rivers and of lakes we were about to float over unmeasured zones of earth, bound on unimaginable adventures,—

> "Saint of this green isle! hear our prayers,
>   Oh, grant us cool heavens and favoring airs!"

About nine o'clock we reached the river, and ran our boat into a natural haven between some rocks, and drew her out on the sand. This camping-ground McCauslin had been familiar with in his lumbering days, and he now struck it unerringly in the moonlight, and we heard the sound of the rill which would supply us with cool water emptying into the lake. The first business was to make a fire, an operation which was a little delayed by the wetness of the fuel and the ground, owing to the heavy showers of the afternoon. The fire is the main comfort of the camp, whether in summer or winter, and is about as ample at one season as at another. It is as well for cheerfulness as for warmth and dryness. It forms one side of the camp; one bright side at any rate. Some were dispersed to fetch in dead trees and boughs, while Uncle George felled the birches and beeches which stood convenient, and soon we had a fire some ten feet long by three or four high, which rapidly dried the sand before it. This was calculated to burn all night.

We next proceeded to pitch our tent; which operation was performed by sticking our two spike-poles into the ground in a slanting direction, about ten feet apart, for rafters, and then drawing our cotton cloth over them, and tying it down at the ends, leaving it open in front, shed-fashion. But this evening the wind carried the sparks on to the tent and burned it. So we hastily drew up the batteau just within the edge of the woods before the fire, and propping up one side three or four feet high, spread the tent on the ground to lie on; and with the corner of a blanket, or what more or less we could get to put over us, lay down with our heads and bodies under the boat, and our feet and legs on the sand toward the fire.

At first we lay awake, talking of our course, and finding ourselves in so convenient a posture for studying the heavens, with the moon and stars shining in our faces, our conversation naturally turned upon astronomy, and we recounted by turns the most interesting discoveries in that science. But at length we composed ourselves seriously to sleep. It was interesting, when awakened at midnight, to watch the grotesque and fiend-like forms and motions of some one of the party, who, not being able to sleep, had got up silently to arouse the fire, and add fresh fuel, for a change; now stealthily lugging a dead tree from out the dark, and heaving it on, now stirring up the embers with his fork, or tiptoeing about to observe the stars, watched, perchance, by half the prostrate party in breathless silence; so much the more intense because they were awake, while each supposed his neighbor sound asleep.

Thus aroused, I, too, brought fresh fuel to the fire, and then rambled along the sandy shore in the moonlight, hoping to meet a moose come down to drink, or else a wolf. The little rill tinkled the louder, and peopled all the wilderness for me; and the glassy smoothness of the sleeping lake, laving the shores of a new world, with the dark, fantastic rocks rising here and there from its surface, made a scene not easily described. It has left such an impression of stern, yet gentle, wildness on my memory as will not soon be effaced. Not far from midnight we were one after another awakened by rain falling on our extremities; and as each was made aware of the fact by cold or wet, he drew a long sigh and then drew up his legs, until gradually we had all sidled round from lying at right angles with the boat, till our bodies formed an acute angle with it, and were wholly protected. When next we awoke, the moon and stars were shining again, and there were signs of dawn in the east. I have been thus particular in order to convey some idea of a night in the woods.

We had soon launched and loaded our boat, and, leaving our fire blazing, were off again before breakfast. The lumberers rarely trouble themselves to put out their fires, such is the dampness of the primitive forest; and this is one cause, no doubt, of the frequent fires in Maine, of which we hear so much on smoky days in Massachusetts. The forests are held cheap after the white-pine has been culled out; and the explorers and hunters pray for rain only to clear the atmosphere of smoke. The woods were so wet today, however, that there was no danger of our fire spreading.[1]

After poling up half a mile of river, or thoroughfare, we rowed a mile across the foot of Pamadumcook Lake, which is the name given on the map to this whole chain of lakes, as if there was but one, though they are, in each instance, distinctly separated by a reach of the river, with its narrow and rocky channel and its rapids. This lake, which is one of the largest, stretched northwest ten miles, to hills and mountains in the distance. McCauslin pointed to some distant, and as yet inaccessible, forests of white-pine, on the sides of a mountain in that direction. The Joe Merry Lakes, which lay between us and Moosehead, on the west, were recently, if they are not still, "surrounded by some of the best timbered land in the State." By another thoroughfare we passed into Deep Cove, a part of the same lake, which makes up two miles, toward the northeast, and rowing two miles across this, by another short thoroughfare, entered Ambejijis Lake.

At the entrance to a lake we sometimes observed what is technically called "fencing stuff," or the unhewn timbers of which booms are formed, either secured together in the water, or laid up on the rocks and lashed to trees, for spring use. But it was always startling to discover so plain a trail of civilized man there. I remember that I was strangely affected, when we were returning, by the sight of a ring-bolt well drilled into a rock, and fastened with lead, at the head of this solitary Ambejijis Lake.

---

[1] "The surface of the ground in the Maine woods is everywhere spongy and saturated with moisture"—so recorded Thoreau of his trip in 1853. His description is of virgin growth where the moss was sometimes knee-deep. It was not without reason that the loggers spoke of "letting daylight into the swamp." There was no underbrush as there is nowadays in second growth. To leave a campfire ablaze in the Maine woods today is a misdemeanor punishable by heavy fine.

It was easy to see that driving logs must be an exciting as well as arduous and dangerous business. All winter long the logger goes on piling up the trees which he has trimmed and hauled in some dry ravine at the head of a stream, and then in the spring he stands on the bank and whistles for Rain and Thaw, ready to wring the perspiration out of his shirt to swell the tide, till suddenly, with a whoop and halloo from him, shutting his eyes, as if to bid farewell to the existing state of things, a fair proportion of his winter's work goes scrambling down the country, followed by his faithful dogs, Thaw and Rain and Freshet and Wind, the whole pack in full cry, toward the Orono Mills.

Every log is marked with the owner's name, cut in the sapwood with an axe or bored with an auger, so deep as not to be worn off in the driving, and yet not so as to injure the timber; and it requires considerable ingenuity to invent new and simple marks where there are so many owners. They have quite an alphabet of their own, which only the practiced can read. One of my companions read off from his memorandum book some marks of his own logs, among which there were crosses, belts, crow's feet, girdles, etc., as, "Y—girdle—crowfoot," and various other devices.

When the logs have run the gauntlet of innumerable rapids and falls, each on its own account, with more or less jamming and bruising, those bearing various owners' marks being mixed up together,—since all must take advantage of the same freshet,—they are collected together at the heads of the lakes, and surrounded by a boom fence of floating logs, to prevent their being dispersed by the wind, and are thus towed all together, like a flock of sheep, across the lake, where there is no current, by a windlass, or boom-head, such as we sometimes saw standing on an island or headland, and, if circumstances permit, with the aid of sails and oars. Sometimes, notwithstanding, the logs are dispersed over many miles of lake surface in a few hours by winds and freshets and thrown up on distant shores, where the driver can pick up only one or two at a time, and return with them to the thoroughfare; and before he gets his flock well through Ambejijis or Pamadumcook, he makes many a wet and uncomfortable camp on the shore.

He must be able to navigate a log as if it were a canoe, and be as indifferent to cold and wet as a muskrat. He uses a few efficient tools,—a lever commonly of rock-maple, six or seven feet long, with a stout spike in it, strongly ferruled on, and a long spike-pole, with a screw at the end of the spike to make it hold.[1] The boys along shore learn to walk on floating logs as city boys on sidewalks. Sometimes the logs are thrown up on rocks in such positions as to be irrecoverable but by another freshet as high, or they jam together at rapids and falls,

---

[1] A dozen years later a Yankee blacksmith by the name of Peavey devised a vast improvement on the "lever" described by Thoreau. A curving iron hook was made to swing up and down with the lever but *not* sidewise by attaching the upper end of the hook to a bolt inserted *through the lips* of an iron collar tightly clasping the handle. Thus, whenever and from whatever angle the handle was lifted above or hauled against a log, the "dog" or hook *always* bit into it securely. With the older tool, called a swing dog, the user always had to adjust the hook by hand. Also, a steel pick was inserted in the end of the handle. With this tool log-rolling became a fine art embellished with such refinements as the Bangor flip. Directly the term "peavey" became synonymous with "cant dog" in the Penobscot region. Today a drive of long timber is rare; the bulk of it is pulp.

and accumulate in vast piles, which the driver must start at
the risk of his life. Such is the lumber business, which depends
on many accidents, as the early freezing of the rivers, that the
teams may get up in season, a sufficient freshet in the spring,
to fetch the logs down, and many others.[1]

I quote Michaux on Lumbering on the Kennebec, then the
source of the best white-pine lumber carried to England.
"The persons engaged in this branch of industry are generally
emigrants from New Hampshire. . . . In the summer they
unite in small companies, and traverse these vast solitudes in
every direction, to ascertain the places in which the pines
abound. After cutting the grass and converting it into hay for
the nourishment of the cattle to be employed in their labor,
they return home. In the beginning of the winter they enter
the forests again, establish themselves in huts covered with
the bark of the canoe-birch, or the arbor-vitæ; and, though
the cold is so intense that the mercury sometimes remains for
several weeks from 40° to 50° [Fahr.] below the point of con-
gelation, they persevere, with unabated courage, in their
work."

According to Springer, the company consists of choppers,
swampers,—who make roads,—barker and loader, teamster,
and cook. "When the trees are felled, they cut them into logs
from fourteen to eighteen feet long, and, by means of their
cattle, which they employ with great dexterity, drag them to
the river, and, after stamping on them a mark of property, roll
them on its frozen bosom. At the breaking of the ice, in the
spring, they float down with the current. . . . The logs that
are not drawn the first year," adds Michaux, "are attacked by
large worms, which form holes about two lines in diameter, in

---

[1] "A steady current or pitch of water is preferable to one either rising or
diminishing; as, when rising rapidly, the water at the middle of the river is considerably higher than at the shores,—so much so as to be distinctly perceived
by the eye of a spectator on the banks, presenting an appearance like a turn-
pike road. The lumber, therefore, is always sure to incline from the centre of
the channel toward either shore."—Springer. [Thoreau]

every direction; but, if stripped of their bark, they will remain uninjured for thirty years." [1]

Ambejijis, this quiet Sunday morning, struck me as the most beautiful lake we had seen. It is said to be one of the deepest. We had the fairest view of Joe Merry, Double Top, and Ktaadn, from its surface. The summit of the latter had a singularly flat, table-land appearance, like a short highway, where a demigod might be let down to take a turn or two in an afternoon, to settle his dinner. We rowed a mile and a half to near the head of the lake, and, pushing through a field of lily-pads, landed, to cook our breakfast, by the side of a large rock, known to McCauslin. Our breakfast consisted of tea, with hard bread and pork, and fried salmon, which we ate with forks neatly whittled from alder-twigs, which grew there, off strips of birch-bark for plates. The tea was black tea, without milk to color or sugar to sweeten it, and two tin dippers were our teacups. This beverage is as indispensable to the loggers as to any gossiping old woman in the land, and they, no doubt, derive great comfort from it.

Here was the site of an old logger's camp, remembered by McCauslin, now overgrown with weeds and bushes. In the midst of a dense underwood we noticed a whole brick, on a rock, in a small run, clean and red and square as in a brick-yard, which had been brought thus far formerly for tamping. Some of us afterward regretted that we had not carried this on with us to the top of the mountain, to be left there for our mark. It would certainly have been a simple evidence of civilized man. McCauslin said that large wooden crosses, made of oak, still sound, were sometimes found standing in this wilderness, which were set up by the first Catholic missionaries who came through to the Kennebec.

---

[1] Thoreau's description of lumbering operations on the lower Penobscot will be found in the Appendix on page 329.

In the next nine miles, which were the extent of our voyage, and which it took us the rest of the day to get over, we rowed across several small lakes, poled up numerous rapids and thoroughfares, and carried over four portages. I will give the names and distances, for the benefit of future tourists. First, after leaving Ambejijis Lake, we had a quarter of a mile of rapids to the portage, or carry of ninety rods around Ambejijis Falls; then a mile and a half through Passamagamet Lake, which is narrow and river-like, to the falls of the same name, —Ambejijis stream coming in on the right; then two miles through Katepskonegan Lake to the portage of ninety rods around Katepskonegan Falls, which name signifies "carrying-place,"—Passamagamet stream coming in on the left; then three miles through Pockwockomus Lake, a slight expansion of the river, to the portage of forty rods around the falls of the same name,—Katepskonegan stream coming in on the left; then three quarters of a mile through Aboljacarmegus Lake, similar to the last, to the portage of forty rods around the falls of the same name; then half a mile of rapid water to the Sowadnehunk dead-water, and the Aboljacknagesic stream.

This is generally the order of names as you ascend the river: First, the lake, or, if there is no expansion, the dead-water; then the falls; then the stream emptying into the lake, or river above, all of the same name. First we came to Passamagamet Lake, then to Passamagamet Falls, then to Passamagamet stream, emptying in. This order and identity of names, it will be perceived, is quite philosophical, since the dead-water or lake is always at least partially produced by the stream emptying in above; and the first fall below, which is the outlet of that lake, and where that tributary water makes its first plunge, also naturally bears the same name.

At the portage around Ambejijis Falls I observed a pork-barrel on the shore, with a hole eight or nine inches square cut in one side, which was set against an upright rock; but the bears, without turning or upsetting the barrel, had gnawed a hole in the opposite side, which looked exactly like an enormous rat-hole, big enough to put their heads in; and at the bottom of the barrel were still left a few mangled and slabbered slices of pork. It is usual for the lumberers to leave such supplies as they cannot conveniently carry along with them at carries or camps, to which the next comers do not scruple to help themselves, they being the property, commonly, not of an individual, but a company, who can afford to deal liberally.

I will describe particularly how we got over some of these portages and rapids, in order that the reader may get an idea of the boatman's life. At Ambejijis Falls, for instance, there was the roughest path imaginable cut through the woods; at first up hill, at an angle of nearly forty-five degrees, over rocks and logs without end. This was the manner of the portage. We first carried over our baggage, and deposited it on the shore at the other end; then, returning to the batteau, we dragged it up the hill by the painter, and onward, with frequent pauses, over half the portage. But this was a bungling way, and would soon have worn out the boat.

Commonly, three men walk over with a batteau weighing from three to five or six hundred pounds on their heads and shoulders, the tallest standing under the middle of the boat, which is turned over, and one at each end, or else there are two at the bows. More cannot well take hold at once. But this requires some practice, as well as strength, and is in any case extremely laborious, and wearing to the constitution, to follow. We were, on the whole, rather an invalid party, and could render our boatmen but little assistance.

Our two men at length took the batteau upon their shoulders, and, while two of us steadied it, to prevent it from rocking and wearing into their shoulders, on which they placed their hats folded, walked bravely over the remaining distance, with two or three pauses. In the same manner they accomplished the other portages. With this crushing weight they must climb and stumble along over fallen trees and slippery rocks of all sizes, where those who walked by the sides were continually brushed off, such was the narrowness of the path. But we were fortunate not to have to cut our path in the first place. Before we launched our boat, we scraped the bottom smooth again, with our knives, where it had rubbed on the rocks, to save friction.

To avoid the difficulties of the portage, our men determined to "warp up" the Passamagamet Falls; so while the rest walked over the portage with the baggage, I remained in the batteau, to assist in warping up. We were soon in the midst of the rapids, which were more swift and tumultuous than any we had poled up, and had turned to the side of the stream for the purpose of warping, when the boatmen, who felt some pride in their skill, and were ambitious to do something more than usual, for my benefit, as I surmised, took one more view of the rapids, or rather the falls; and, in answer to our question, whether we couldn't get up there, the other answered that he guessed he'd try it. So we pushed again into the midst of the stream, and began to struggle with the current.

I sat in the middle of the boat to trim it, moving slightly to the right or left as it grazed a rock. With an uncertain and wavering motion we wound and bolted our way up, until the bow was actually raised two feet above the stern at the steepest pitch; and then, when everything depended upon his exertions, the bowman's pole snapped in two; but before he had time to take the spare one, which I reached him, he had saved himself with the fragment upon a rock; and so we got up by a hair's breadth; and Uncle George exclaimed that that was never done before, and he had not tried it if he had not known whom he had got in the bow, nor he in the bow, if he had not known him in the stern.

At this place there was a regular portage cut through the woods, and our boatmen had never known a batteau to ascend the falls. As near as I can remember, there was a perpendicular fall here, at the worst place of the whole Penobscot River, two or three feet at least. I could not sufficiently admire the skill and coolness with which they performed this feat, never speaking to each other. The bowman, not looking behind, but knowing exactly what the other is about, works as if he worked alone. Now sounding in vain for a bottom in fifteen feet of water, while the boat falls back several rods, held straight only with the greatest skill and exertion; or, while the sternman obstinately holds his ground, like a turtle, the bowman springs from side to side with wonderful suppleness and dexterity, scanning the rapids and the rocks with a thousand eyes; and now, having got a bite at last, with a lusty shove, which makes his pole bend and quiver, and the whole boat tremble, he gains a few feet upon the river.

To add to the danger, the poles are liable at any time to be caught between the rocks, and wrenched out of their hands, leaving them at the mercy of the rapids,—the rocks, as it were, lying in wait, like so many alligators, to catch them in their teeth, and jerk them from your hands, before you have stolen an effectual shove against their palates. The pole is set close to the boat, and the prow is made to overshoot, and just turn the corners of the rocks, in the very teeth of the rapids. Nothing but the length and lightness, and the slight draught of the batteau, enables them to make any headway. The bowman must quickly choose his course; there is no time to deliberate. Frequently the boat is shoved between rocks where both sides touch, and the waters on either hand are a perfect maelstrom.

Half a mile above this two of us tried our hands at poling

up a slight rapid; and we were just surmounting the last
difficulty, when an unlucky rock confounded our calculations;
and while the batteau was sweeping round irrecoverably
amid the whirlpool, we were obliged to resign the poles to
more skillful hands.

Katepskonegan is one of the shallowest and weediest of the
lakes, and looked as if it might abound in pickerel. The falls of
the same name, where we stopped to dine, are considerable
and quite picturesque. Here Uncle George had seen trout
caught by the barrelful; but they would not rise to our bait at
this hour. Halfway over this carry, thus far in the Maine wilderness on its way to the Provinces, we noticed a large, flam-
ing, Oak Hall hand-bill, about two feet long, wrapped round
the trunk of a pine, from which the bark had been stripped,
and to which it was fast glued by the pitch. This should be
recorded among the advantages of this mode of advertising,
that so, possibly, even the bears and wolves, moose, deer,
otter, and beaver, not to mention the Indian, may learn where
they can fit themselves according to the latest fashion, or, at
least, recover some of their own lost garments. We christened
this the Oak Hall carry.

The forenoon was as serene and placid on this wild stream
in the woods, as we are apt to imagine that Sunday in summer
usually is in Massachusetts. We were occasionally startled by
the scream of a bald-eagle, sailing over the stream in front of
our batteau; or of the fish-hawks, on whom he levies his con-
tributions. There were, at intervals, small meadows of a few
acres on the sides of the stream, waving with uncut grass,
which attracted the attention of our boatmen, who regretted
that they were not nearer to their clearings, and calculated
how many stacks they might cut. Two or three men sometimes spend the summer by themselves, cutting the grass in
these meadows, to sell to the loggers in the winter, since it

will fetch a higher price on the spot than in any market in the State.

On a small isle, covered with this kind of rush, or cut grass, on which we landed to consult about our further course, we noticed the recent track of a moose, a large, roundish hole in the soft, wet ground, evincing the great size and weight of the animal that made it. They are fond of the water, and visit all these island-meadows, swimming as easily from island to island as they make their way through the thickets on land. Now and then we passed what McCauslin called a pokelogan, an Indian term for what the drivers might have reason to call a poke-logs-in, an inlet that leads nowhere. If you get in, you have got to get out again the same way. These, and the frequent "run-rounds" which come into the river again, would embarrass an inexperienced voyager not a little.

The carry around Pockwockomus Falls was exceedingly rough and rocky, the batteau having to be lifted directly from the water up four or five feet on to a rock, and launched again down a similar bank. The rocks on this portage were covered with the *dents* made by the spikes in the lumberers' boots while staggering over under the weight of their batteaux; and you could see where the surface of some large rocks on which they had rested their batteaux was worn quite smooth with use. As it was, we had carried over but half the usual portage at this place for this stage of the water, and launched our boat in the smooth wave just curving to the fall, prepared to struggle with the most violent rapid we had to encounter. The rest of the party walked over the remainder of the portage, while I remained with the boatmen to assist in warping up.

One had to hold the boat while the others got in to prevent it from going over the falls. When we had pushed up the rapids as far as possible, keeping close to the shore, Tom seized the painter and leaped out upon a rock just visible in

the water, but he lost his footing, notwithstanding his spiked
boots, and was instantly amid the rapids; but recovering himself by good luck, and reaching another rock, he passed the
painter to me, who had followed him, and took his place again
in the bows. Leaping from rock to rock in the shoal water,
close to the shore, and now and then getting a bite with the
rope round an upright one, I held the boat while one reset his
pole, and then all three forced it upward against any rapid.
This was "warping up." When a part of us walked round at
such a place, we generally took the precaution to take out the
most valuable part of the baggage for fear of being swamped.

As we poled up a swift rapid for half a mile above Aboljacarmegus Falls, some of the party read their own marks on
the huge logs which lay piled up high and dry on the rocks on
either hand, the relics probably of a jam which had taken
place here in the Great Freshet in the spring.[1] Many of these
would have to wait for another great freshet, perchance, if
they lasted so long, before they could be got off. It was singular enough to meet with property of theirs which they had
never seen, and where they had never been before, thus
detained by freshets and rocks when on its way to them. Methinks that must be where all my property lies, cast up on the
rocks on some distant and unexplored stream, and waiting for
an unheard-of freshet to fetch it down. O make haste, ye gods,
with your winds and rains, and start the jam before it rots!

The last half mile carried us to the Sowadnehunk dead-
water, so called from the stream of the same name, signifying
"running between mountains," an important tributary which
comes in a mile above. Here we decided to camp, about
twenty miles from the Dam, at the mouth of Murch Brook
and the Aboljacknagesic, mountain streams, broad off from

---

[1] Thoreau's comments on this freshet in the spring of 1846 are to be found
in the Appendix on page 330.

Ktaadn, and about a dozen miles from its summit, having made fifteen miles this day.

We had been told by McCauslin that we should here find trout enough; so, while some prepared the camp, the rest fell to fishing. Seizing the birch poles which some party of Indians, or white hunters, had left on the shore, and baiting our hooks with pork, and with trout, as soon as they were caught, we cast our lines into the mouth of the Aboljacknagesic, a clear, swift, shallow stream, which came in from Ktaadn. Instantly a shoal of white chivin (*Leucisci pulchelli*), silvery roaches, cousin-trout, or what not, large and small, prowling thereabouts, fell upon our bait, and one after another were landed amidst the bushes. Anon their cousins, the true trout, took their turn, and alternately the speckled trout, and the silvery roaches, swallowed the bait as fast as we could throw in; and the finest specimens of both that I have ever seen, the largest one weighing three pounds, were heaved upon the shore, though at first in vain, to wriggle down into the water again, for we stood in the boat; but soon we learned to remedy this evil; for one, who had lost his hook, stood on shore to catch them as they fell in a perfect shower around him,— sometimes, wet and slippery, full in his face and bosom, as his arms were outstretched to receive them.

While yet alive, before their tints had faded, they glistened like the fairest flowers, the product of primitive rivers; and he could hardly trust his senses, as he stood over them, that these jewels should have swam away in that Aboljacknagesic water for so long, so many dark ages;—these bright fluviatile flowers, seen of Indians only, made beautiful, the Lord only knows why, to swim there! I could understand better for this, the truth of mythology, the fables of Proteus, and all those

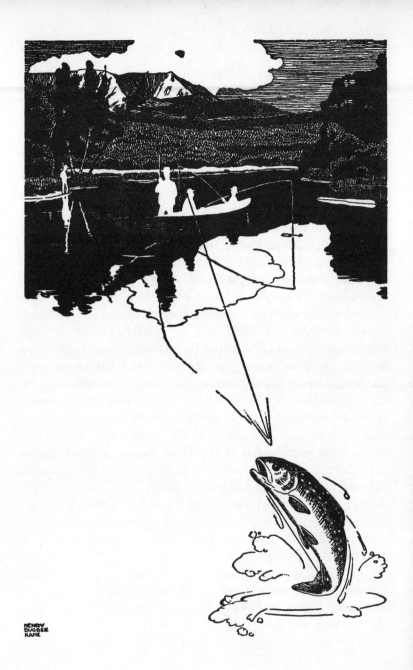

beautiful sea-monsters,—how all history, indeed, put to a terrestrial use, is mere history; but put to a celestial, is my- thology always.

But there is the rough voice of Uncle George, who com- mands at the frying-pan, to send over what you've got, and then you may stay till morning. The pork sizzles and cries for fish. Luckily for the foolish race, and this particularly foolish generation of trout, the night shut down at last, not a little deepened by the dark side of Ktaadn, which, like a perma- nent shadow, reared itself from the eastern bank. Lescarbot, writing in 1609, tells us that the Sieur Champdoré, who, with one of the people of the Sieur de Monts, ascended some fifty leagues up the St. John in 1608, found the fish so plenty, "qu'en mettant la chaudière sur le feu ils en avoient pris suffisamment pour eux dîsner avant que l'eau fust chaude." Their descendants here are no less numerous.

So we accompanied Tom into the woods to cut cedar-twigs for our bed. While he went ahead with the axe and lopped off the smallest twigs of the flat-leaved cedar, the arbor-vitæ of the gardens, we gathered them up, and returned with them to the boat, until it was loaded. Our bed was made with as much care and skill as a roof is shingled; beginning at the foot, and laying the twig end of the cedar upward, we advanced to the head, a course at a time, thus successively covering the stub-ends, and producing a soft and level bed. For us six it was about ten feet long by six in breadth. This time we lay under our tent, having pitched it more prudently with refer- ence to the wind and the flame, and the usual huge fire blazed in front. Supper was eaten off a large log, which some freshet had thrown up. This night we had a dish of arbor-vitæ, or cedar-tea, which the lumberer sometimes uses when other herbs fail,—

> "A quart of arbor-vitæ,
> To make him strong and mighty,"

but I had no wish to repeat the experiment. It had too medicinal a taste for my palate. There was the skeleton of a moose here, whose bones some Indian hunters had picked on this very spot.

In the night I dreamed of trout-fishing; and, when at length I awoke, it seemed a fable that this painted fish swam there so near my couch, and rose to our hooks the last evening, and I doubted if I had not dreamed it all. So I arose before dawn to test its truth, while my companions were still sleeping. There stood Ktaadn with distinct and cloudless outline in the moonlight; and the rippling of the rapids was the only sound to break the stillness. Standing on the shore, I once more cast my line into the stream, and found the dream to be real and the fable true. The speckled trout and silvery roach, like flying-fish, sped swiftly through the moonlight air, describing bright arcs on the dark side of Ktaadn, until moonlight, now fading into daylight, brought satiety to my mind, and the minds of my companions who had joined me.

Note—They were fishing in the mouth of the Aboljack-nagesic. This is today called Abol Stream for shortness. The other stream entering the West Branch and described by Thoreau as Murch Brook appears on the Hubbard Maps as the Aboljackarmegas and is today known as Ktaadn Stream.

14. Ktaadn

By six o'clock, having mounted our packs and a good blanketful of trout, ready dressed, and swung up such baggage and provision as we wished to leave behind upon the tops of saplings, to be out of the reach of bears, we started for the summit of the mountain, distant, as Uncle George said the boatmen called it, about four miles, but as I judged, and as it proved, nearer fourteen.[1] He had never been any nearer the mountain than this, and there was not the slightest trace of man to guide us farther in this direction.

At first, pushing a few rods up the Aboljacknagesic, or "open-land stream," we fastened our batteau to a tree, and

---

[1] Ktaadn, whose name is an Indian word signifying highest land, was first ascended by white men in 1804. It was visited by Professor J. W. Bailey of West Point in 1836; by Dr. Charles T. Jackson, the State Geologist, in 1837; and by two young men from Boston in 1845. All these have given accounts of their expeditions. Since I was there, two or three other parties have made the excursion, and told their stories. Besides these, very few, even among backwoodsmen and hunters, have ever climbed it, and it will be a long time before the tide of fashionable travel sets that way.

traveled up the north side, through burnt lands, now partially overgrown with young aspens and other shrubbery; but soon, recrossing this stream, where it was about fifty or sixty feet wide, upon a jam of logs and rocks,—and you could cross it by this means almost anywhere,—we struck at once for the highest peak, over a mile or more of comparatively open land, still very gradually ascending the while. Here it fell to my lot, as the oldest mountain-climber, to take the lead. So, scanning the woody side of the mountain, which lay still at an indefinite distance, stretched out some seven or eight miles in length before us, we determined to steer directly for the base of the highest peak, leaving a large slide, by which, as I have since learned, some of our predecessors ascended, on our left.

This course would lead us parallel to a dark seam in the forest, which marked the bed of a torrent, and over a slight spur, which extended southward from the main mountain, from whose bare summit we could get an outlook over the country, and climb directly up the peak, which would then be close at hand. Seen from this point, a bare ridge at the extremity of the open land, Ktaadn presented a different aspect from any mountain I have seen, there being a greater proportion of naked rock rising abruptly from the forest; and we looked up at this blue barrier as if it were some fragment of a wall which anciently bounded the earth in that direction. Setting the compass for a northeast course, which was the bearing of the southern base of the highest peak, we were soon buried in the woods.[1]

We soon began to meet with traces of bears and moose, and those of rabbits were everywhere visible. The tracks of moose, more or less recent, to speak literally, covered every

---

[1] The ascent was made roughly parallel with and somewhat to the eastward of the route later known as the Abol Trail. An interesting discussion of Thoreau's ascent, comparing it with other early attempts, will be found in *Appalachia*, June, 1946.

square rod on the sides of the mountains; and these animals are probably more numerous there now than ever before, being driven into this wilderness, from all sides, by the settlements. The track of a full-grown moose is like that of a cow, or larger, and of the young, like that of a calf. Sometimes we found ourselves traveling in faint paths, which they had made, like cow-paths in the woods, only far more indistinct, being rather openings, affording imperfect vistas through the dense underwood, than trodden paths; and everywhere the twigs had been browsed by them, clipped as smoothly as if by a knife. The bark of trees was stripped up by them to the height of eight or nine feet, in long, narrow strips, an inch wide, still showing the distinct marks of their teeth.

We expected nothing less than to meet a herd of them every moment, and our Nimrod held his shooting-iron in readiness; but we did not go out of our way to look for them, and, though numerous, they are so wary that the unskillful hunter might range the forest a long time before he could get sight of one. They are sometimes dangerous to encounter, and will not turn out for the hunter, but furiously rush upon him and trample him to death, unless he is lucky enough to avoid them by dodging round a tree. The largest are nearly as large as a horse, and weigh sometimes one thousand pounds; and it is said that they can step over a five-foot gate in their ordinary walk.

They are described as exceedingly awkward-looking animals, with their long legs and short bodies, making a ludicrous figure when in full run, but making great headway, nevertheless. It seemed a mystery to us how they could thread this woods, which it required all our suppleness to accomplish,—climbing, stooping, and winding, alternately. They are said to drop their long and branching horns, which usually spread five or six feet, on their backs, and make their way easily by the weight of their bodies. Our boatmen said, but I know not with how much truth, that their horns are apt to be gnawed away by vermin while they sleep. Their flesh, which is more like beef than venison, is common in Bangor market.

We had proceeded on thus seven or eight miles, till about noon, with frequent pauses to refresh the weary ones, crossing a considerable mountain stream, which we conjectured to be Murch Brook, at whose mouth we had camped, all the time in woods, without having once seen the summit, and rising very gradually, when the boatmen beginning to despair a little, and fearing that we were leaving the mountain on one side of us, for they had not entire faith in the compass, McCauslin climbed a tree, from the top of which he could see the peak, when it appeared that we had not swerved from a right line, the compass down below still ranging with his arm, which pointed to the summit.

By the side of a cool mountain rill, amid the woods, where the water began to partake of the purity and transparency of the air, we stopped to cook some of our fishes, which we had brought thus far in order to save our hard bread and pork, in the use of which we had put ourselves on short allowance. We soon had a fire blazing, and stood around it, under the damp and sombre forest of firs and birches, each with a sharpened stick, three or four feet in length, upon which he had spitted his trout, or roach, previously well gashed and salted, our sticks radiating like the spokes of a wheel from one centre, and each crowding his particular fish into the most desirable exposure, not with the truest regard always to his neighbor's rights. Thus we regaled ourselves, drinking meanwhile at the spring, till one man's pack, at least, was considerably lightened, when we again took up our line of march.

At length we reached an elevation sufficiently bare to

afford a view of the summit, still distant and blue, almost as if retreating from us. A torrent, which proved to be the same we had crossed, was seen tumbling down in front, literally from out of the clouds. But this glimpse at our whereabouts was soon lost, and we were buried in the woods again. The wood was chiefly yellow birch, spruce, fir, mountain-ash, or round-wood, as the Maine people call it, and moose-wood. It was the worst kind of traveling; sometimes like the densest scrub-oak patches with us. The cornel, or bunch-berries, were very abundant, as well as Solomon's seal and mooseberries. Blueberries were distributed along our whole route; and in one place the bushes were drooping with the weight of the fruit, still as fresh as ever. It was the 7th of September.

Such patches afforded a grateful repast, and served to bait the tired party forward. When any lagged behind, the cry

of "blueberries" was most effectual to bring them up. Even at this elevation we passed through a moose-yard, formed by a large flat rock, four or five rods square, where they tread down the snow in winter. At length, fearing that if we held a direct course to the summit, we should not find any water near our camping-ground, we gradually swerved to the west, till, at four o'clock, we struck again the torrent which I have mentioned, and here, in view of the summit, the weary party decided to camp that night.

While my companions were seeking a suitable spot for this purpose, I improved the little daylight that was left in climbing the mountain alone. We were in a deep and narrow ravine, sloping up to the clouds, at an angle of nearly forty-five degrees, and hemmed in by walls of rock, which were at first covered with low trees, then with impenetrable thickets of scraggy birches and spruce-trees, and with moss, but at last bare of all vegetation but lichens, and almost continually draped in clouds. Following up the course of the torrent which occupied this,—and I mean to lay some emphasis on this word *up,*—pulling myself up by the side of perpendicular falls of twenty or thirty feet, by the roots of firs and birches, and then, perhaps, walking a level rod or two in the thin stream, for it took up the whole road, ascending by huge steps, as it were, a giant's stairway, down which a river flowed, I had soon cleared the trees, and paused on the successive shelves, to look back over the country.

The torrent was from fifteen to thirty feet wide, without a tributary, and seemingly not diminishing in breadth as I advanced; but still it came rushing and roaring down, with a copious tide, over and amidst masses of bare rock, from the very clouds, as though a waterspout had just burst over the mountain. Leaving this at last, I began to work my way, scarcely less arduous than Satan's anciently through Chaos, up the nearest, though not the highest peak. At first scrambling on all fours over the tops of ancient black spruce-trees (*Abies nigra*), old as the flood, from two to ten or twelve feet in height, their tops flat and spreading, and their foliage blue, and nipped with cold, as if for centuries they had ceased growing upward against the bleak sky, the solid cold.

I walked some good rods erect upon the tops of these trees, which were overgrown with moss and mountain-cranberries. It seemed that in the course of time they had filled up the intervals between the huge rocks, and the cold wind had uniformly leveled all over. Here the principle of vegetation was hard put to it. There was apparently a belt of this kind running quite round the mountain, though, perhaps, nowhere so remarkable as here. Once slumping through, I looked down ten feet, into a dark and cavernous region, and saw the stem of a spruce, on whose top I stood, as on a mass of coarse basket-work, fully nine inches in diameter at the ground. These holes were bears' dens, and the bears were even then at home. This was the sort of garden I made my way *over*, for an eighth of a mile, at the risk, it is true, of treading on some of the plants, not seeing any path *through* it,—certainly the most treacherous and porous country I ever traveled.

> "Nigh foundered on he fares,
> Treading the crude consistence, half on foot,
> Half flying."

But nothing could exceed the toughness of the twigs,— not one snapped under my weight, for they had slowly grown. Having slumped, scrambled, rolled, bounced, and walked, by turns, over this scraggy country, I arrived upon a side-hill, or rather side-mountain, where rocks, gray, silent rocks, were the flocks and herds that pastured, chewing a rocky cud at sunset. They looked at me with hard gray eyes, without a bleat or a low. This brought me to the skirt of a cloud, and bounded my walk that night. But I had already seen that Maine country when I turned about, waving, flowing, rippling, down below.

When I returned to my companions, they had selected a

camping-ground on the torrent's edge, and were resting on the ground; one was on the sick list, rolled in a blanket, on a damp shelf of rock. It was a savage and dreary scenery enough; so wildly rough, that they looked long to find a level and open space for the tent. We could not well camp higher, for want of fuel; and the trees here seemed so evergreen and sappy, that we almost doubted if they would acknowledge the influence of fire; but fire prevailed at last, and blazed here, too, like a good citizen of the world. Even at this height we met with frequent traces of moose, as well as bears. As here was no cedar, we made our bed of coarser feathered spruce; but at any rate the feathers were plucked from the live tree.

It was, perhaps, even a more grand and desolate place for a night's lodging than the summit would have been, being in the neighborhood of those wild trees, and of the torrent. Some more aerial and finer-spirited winds rushed and roared through the ravine all night, from time to time arousing our fire, and dispersing the embers about. It was as if we lay in the very nest of a young whirlwind. At midnight, one of my bed-fellows, being startled in his dreams by the sudden blazing up to its top of a fir-tree, whose green boughs were dried by the heat, sprang up, with a cry, from his bed, thinking the world on fire, and drew the whole camp after him.

In the morning, after whetting our appetite on some raw pork, a wafer of hard bread, and a dipper of condensed cloud or waterspout, we all together began to make our way up the falls, which I have described; this time choosing the right hand, or highest peak, which was not the one I had approached before. But soon my companions were lost to my sight behind the mountain ridge in my rear, which still seemed ever retreating before me, and I climbed alone over

huge rocks, loosely poised, a mile or more, still edging toward the clouds; for though the day was clear elsewhere, the summit was concealed by mist.

The mountain seemed a vast aggregation of loose rocks, as if some time it had rained rocks, and they lay as they fell on the mountain sides, nowhere fairly at rest, but leaning on each other, all rocking-stones, with cavities between, but scarcely any soil or smoother shelf. They were the raw materials of a planet dropped from an unseen quarry, which the vast chemistry of nature would anon work up, or work down, into the smiling and verdant plains and valleys of earth. This was an undone extremity of the globe; as in lignite, we see coal in the process of formation.

At length I entered within the skirts of the cloud which seemed forever drifting over the summit, and yet would never be gone, but was generated out of that pure air as fast as it flowed away; and when, a quarter of a mile farther, I reached the summit of the ridge, which those who have seen in clearer weather say is about five miles long, and contains a thousand acres of table-land, I was deep within the hostile ranks of clouds, and all objects were obscured by them. Now the wind would blow me out a yard of clear sunlight, wherein I stood; then a gray, dawning light was all it could accomplish, the cloud-line ever rising and falling with the wind's intensity. Sometimes it seemed as if the summit would be cleared in a few moments, and smile in sunshine; but what was gained on one side was lost on another. It was like sitting in a chimney and waiting for the smoke to blow away.

It was, in fact, a cloud factory,—these were the cloud-works, and the wind turned them off done from the cool, bare rocks. Occasionally, when the windy columns broke in to me, I caught sight of a dark, damp crag to the right or left, the mist driving ceaselessly between it and me. It reminded me of the creations of the old epic and dramatic poets, of Atlas, Vulcan, the Cyclops, and Prometheus. Such was Caucasus and the rock where Prometheus was bound. Æschylus had no doubt visited such scenery as this. It was vast, Titanic, and such as man never inhabits. Some part of the beholder, even some vital part, seems to escape through the loose grating of his ribs as he ascends. He is more lone than you can imagine. There is less of substantial thought and fair understanding in him than in the plains where men inhabit. His reason is dispersed and shadowy, more thin and subtile, like the air.

Vast, Titanic, inhuman Nature has got him at disadvantage, caught him alone, and pilfers him of some of his divine faculty. She does not smile on him as in the plains. She seems to say sternly, Why came ye here before your time. This ground is not prepared for you. Is it not enough that I smile in the valleys? I have never made this soil for thy feet, this air for thy breathing, these rocks for thy neighbors. I cannot pity nor fondle thee here, but forever relentlessly drive thee hence to where I *am* kind. Why seek me where I have not called thee, and then complain because you find me but a stepmother? Shouldst thou freeze or starve, or shudder thy life away, here is no shrine, nor altar, nor any access to my ear.

> "Chaos and ancient Night, I come no spy
> With purpose to explore or to disturb
> The secrets of your realm, but . . .
> .   .   .   .   .   as my way
> Lies through your spacious empire up to light."

The tops of mountains are among the unfinished parts of the globe, whither it is a slight insult to the gods to climb and pry into their secrets, and try their effect on our humanity. Only daring and insolent men, perchance, go there. Simple races, as savages, do not climb mountains,—their tops are sacred and mysterious tracts never visited by them. Pomola is always angry with those who climb to the summit of Ktaadn.

According to Jackson, who, in his capacity of geological surveyor of the State, has accurately measured it,—the altitude of Ktaadn is 5300 feet, or a little more than one mile above the level of the sea,—and he adds, "It is then evidently the highest point in the State of Maine, and is the most abrupt granite mountain in New England." [1] The peculiarities of that spacious table-land on which I was standing, as well as the remarkable semi-circular precipice or basin on the eastern side, were all concealed by the mist. I had brought my whole pack to the top, not knowing but I should have to make my descent to the river, and possibly to the settled portion of the State alone, and by some other route, and wishing to have a complete outfit with me.

But at length, fearing that my companions would be anxious to reach the river before night, and knowing that the clouds might rest on the mountain for days, I was compelled to descend. Occasionally, as I came down, the wind would blow me a vista open, through which I could see the country eastward, boundless forests, and lakes, and streams, gleaming in the sun, some of them emptying into the East Branch. There were also new mountains in sight in that direction. Now and then some small bird of the sparrow family would flit away before me, unable to command its course, like a fragment of the gray rock blown off by the wind.

I found my companions where I had left them, on the side of the peak, gathering the mountain-cranberries, which

---

[1] The *United States Geodetic Survey* map gives the altitude as 5267 feet. The publications of the Appalachian Mountain Club give it as 5273 feet. It is also stated that the official spelling adopted by the United States Geographic Board in 1893 is Kahtahdin. The spelling of place names in the Maine woods is a variable feast. Here as well as elsewhere, Thoreau's usage, which accords interestingly enough with that on the Hubbard maps, has been followed.

filled every crevice between the rocks, together with blueberries, which had a spicier flavor the higher up they grew,
but were not the less agreeable to our palates. When the
country is settled, and roads are made, these cranberries will
perhaps become an article of commerce. From this elevation, just on the skirts of the clouds, we could overlook the
country, west and south, for a hundred miles. There it was,
the State of Maine, which we had seen on the map, but not
much like that,—immeasurable forest for the sun to shine
on, that eastern *stuff* we hear of in Massachusetts. No clearing, no house. It did not look as if a solitary traveler had cut
so much as a walking-stick there.

Countless lakes,—Moosehead in the southwest, forty miles
long by ten wide, like a gleaming silver platter at the end of
the table; Chesuncook, eighteen long by three wide, without an island; Millinocket, on the south, with its hundred
islands; and a hundred others without a name; and moun-

tains, also, whose names, for the most part, are known only to the Indians. The forest looked like a firm grass sward, and the effect of these lakes in its midst has been well compared, by one who has since visited this same spot, to that of a "mirror broken into a thousand fragments, and wildly scattered over the grass, reflecting the full blaze of the sun." It was a large farm for somebody, when cleared. According to the Gazetteer, which was printed before the boundary question was settled, this single Penobscot county, in which we were, was larger than the whole State of Vermont, with its fourteen counties; and this was only a part of the wild lands of Maine.[1]

We are concerned now, however, about natural, not political limits. We were about eighty miles, as the bird flies, from Bangor, or one hundred and fifteen, as we had ridden, and walked, and paddled. We had to console ourselves with the reflection that this view was probably as good as that from the peak, as far as it went; and what were a mountain without its attendant clouds and mists? Like ourselves, neither Bailey nor Jackson had obtained a clear view from the summit.

Setting out on our return to the river, still at an early hour in the day, we decided to follow the course of the torrent, which we supposed to be Murch Brook, as long as it would not lead us too far out of our way. We thus traveled about four miles in the very torrent itself, continually crossing and recrossing it, leaping from rock to rock, and jumping with the stream down falls of seven or eight feet, or sometimes

---

[1] The Gazetteer was not abreast of affairs in the State of Maine. In 1846 the north of Maine lay, as it does today, in four counties ranging from west to east: Somerset (1809), Piscataquis (1838), Penobscot (1816), with Aroostook (1839) overtopping them all. Ktaadn is in Piscataquis County.

sliding down on our backs in a thin sheet of water. This ravine had been the scene of an extraordinary freshet in the spring, apparently accompanied by a slide from the mountain. It must have been filled with a stream of stones and water, at least twenty feet above the present level of the torrent. For a rod or two, on either side of its channel, the trees were barked and splintered up to their tops, the birches bent over, twisted, and sometimes finely split, like a stablebroom; some, a foot in diameter, snapped off, and whole clumps of trees bent over with the weight of rocks piled on them. In one place we noticed a rock, two or three feet in diameter, lodged nearly twenty feet high in the crotch of a tree. For the whole four miles, we saw but one rill emptying in, and the volume of water did not seem to be increased from the first.

We traveled thus very rapidly with a downward impetus, and grew remarkably expert at leaping from rock to rock, for leap we must, and leap we did, whether there was any rock at the right distance or not. It was a pleasant picture when the foremost turned about and looked up the winding ravine, walled in with rocks and the green forest, to see, at intervals of a rod or two, a red-shirted or green-jacketed mountaineer against the white torrent, leaping down the channel with his pack on his back, or pausing upon a convenient rock in the midst of the torrent to mend a rent in his clothes, or unstrap the dipper at his belt to take a draught of the water. At one place we were startled by seeing, on a little sandy shelf by the side of the stream, the fresh print of a man's foot, and for a moment realized how Robinson Crusoe felt in a similar case; but at last we remembered that we had struck this stream on our way up, though we could not have told where, and one had descended into the ravine for a drink. The cool air above and the continual bathing of our bodies in mountain water, alternate foot, sitz, douche.

and plunge baths, made this walk exceedingly refreshing, and we had traveled only a mile or two, after leaving the torrent before every thread of our clothes was as dry as usual, owing perhaps to a peculiar quality in the atmosphere.

After leaving the torrent, being in doubt about our course, Tom threw down his pack at the foot of the loftiest spruce-tree at hand, and shinned up the bare trunk some twenty feet, and then climbed through the green tower, lost to our sight, until he held the topmost spray in his hand.[1] Mc-Causlin, in his younger days, had marched through the wilderness with a body of troops, under General Somebody, and with one other man did all the scouting and spying service. The General's word was, "Throw down the top of that tree," and there was no tree in the Maine woods so high that it did not lose its top in such a case. I have heard a story of two men being lost once in these woods, nearer to the settlements than this, who climbed the loftiest pine they could find, some six feet in diameter at the ground, from whose top they discovered a solitary clearing and its smoke. When at this height, some two hundred feet from the ground, one of them became dizzy, and fainted in his companion's arms, and the latter had to accomplish the descent with him, alternately fainting and reviving, as best he could.

To Tom we cried, Where away does the summit bear? where the burnt lands? The last he could only conjecture; he descried, however, a little meadow and pond, lying probably in our course, which we concluded to steer for. On reach-

---

[1] "The spruce-tree," says Springer in '51, "is generally selected, principally for the superior facilities which its numerous limbs afford the climber. To gain the first limbs of this tree, which are from twenty to forty feet from the ground, a smaller tree is undercut and lodged against it, clambering up which the top of the spruce is reached. In some cases, when a very elevated position is desired, the spruce-tree is lodged against the trunk of some lofty pine, up which we ascend to a height twice that of the surrounding forest."

To indicate the direction of pines, one throws down a branch, and a man on the ground takes the bearing. [Thoreau]

ing this secluded meadow, we found fresh tracks of moose on the shore of the pond, and the water was still unsettled as if they had fled before us. A little farther, in a dense thicket, we seemed to be still on their trail. It was a small meadow, of a few acres, on the mountain side, concealed by the forest, and perhaps never seen by a white man before, where one would think that the moose might browse and bathe, and rest in peace. Pursuing this course, we soon reached the open land, which went sloping down some miles toward the Penobscot.

Perhaps I most fully realized that this was primeval, untamed, and forever untamable *Nature,* or whatever else men call it, while coming down this part of the mountain. We were passing over "Burnt Lands," burnt by lightning, perchance, though they showed no recent marks of fire, hardly so much as a charred stump, but looked rather like a natural pasture for the moose and deer, exceedingly wild and desolate, with occasional strips of timber crossing them, and low poplars springing up, and patches of blueberries here and there. I found myself traversing them familiarly, like some pasture run to waste, or partially reclaimed by man; but when I reflected what man, what brother or sister or kinsman of our race made it and claimed it, I expected the proprietor to rise up and dispute my passage.

It is difficult to conceive of a region uninhabited by man. We habitually presume his presence and influence everywhere. And yet we have not seen pure Nature, unless we have seen her thus vast and drear and inhuman, though in the midst of cities. Nature was here something savage and awful, though beautiful. I looked with awe at the ground I trod on, to see what the Powers had made there, the form and fashion and material of their work. This was that Earth of which we have heard, made out of Chaos and Old Night. Here was no man's garden, but the unhandseled globe. It was not lawn, nor pasture, nor mead, nor woodland, nor lea, nor arable, nor waste land.

It was the fresh and natural surface of the planet Earth, as it was made forever and ever,—to be the dwelling of man, we say,—so Nature made it, and man may use it if he can. Man was not to be associated with it. It was Matter, vast, terrific,—not his Mother Earth that we have heard of, not for him to tread on, or be buried in,—no, it were being too familiar even to let his bones lie there,—the home, this, of Necessity and Fate. There was clearly felt the presence of a force not bound to be kind to man. It was a place for heathenism and superstitious rites,—to be inhabited by men nearer of kin to the rocks and to wild animals than we.

We walked over it with a certain awe, stopping, from time to time, to pick the blueberries which grew there, and had a smart and spicy taste. Perchance where *our* wild pines stand, and leaves lie on their forest floor, in Concord, there were once reapers, and husbandmen planted grain; but here not even the surface had been scarred by man, but it was a specimen of what God saw fit to make this world. What is it to be admitted to a museum, to see a myriad of particular things, compared with being shown some star's surface, some hard matter in its home! I stand in awe of my body, this matter to which I am bound has become so strange to me. I fear not spirits, ghosts, of which I am one,—*that* my body might, —but I fear bodies, I tremble to meet them. What is this Titan that has possession of me? Talk of mysteries! Think of our life in nature,—daily to be shown matter, to come in contact with it,—rocks, trees, wind on our cheeks! the *solid* earth! the *actual* world! the *common sense! Contact! Contact!* Who are we? *where* are we?

Erelong we recognized some rocks and other features in the landscape which we had purposely impressed on our memories, and, quickening our pace, by two o'clock we reached the batteau.[1] Here we had expected to dine on trout, but in this glaring sunlight they were slow to take the bait, so we were compelled to make the most of the crumbs of our hard bread and our pork, which were both nearly exhausted. Meanwhile we deliberated whether we should go up the river a mile farther, to Gibson's clearing, on the Sowadnehunk, where there was a deserted log-hut in order to get a half-inch auger, to mend one of our spike-poles with. There were young spruce-trees enough around us, and we had a spare spike, but nothing to make a hole with. But as it was uncertain whether we should find any tools left there, we patched up the broken pole, as well as we could, for the downward voyage, in which there would be but little use for it.

Moreover, we were unwilling to lose any time in this expedition, lest the wind should rise before we reached the larger lakes, and detain us; for a moderate wind produces quite a sea on these waters, in which a batteau will not live for a moment; and on one occasion McCauslin had been delayed a week at the head of the North Twin, which is only four miles across. We were nearly out of provisions, and ill prepared in this respect for what might possibly prove a week's journey round by the shore, fording innumerable streams, and threading a trackless forest, should any accident happen to our boat.

---

[1] The bears had not touched things on our possessions. They sometimes tear a batteau to pieces for the sake of the tar with which it is besmeared.

15. Shooting the Rapids in a Batteau

IT WAS with regret that we turned our backs on Chesuncook, which McCauslin had formerly logged on, and the Allegash lakes. There were still longer rapids and portages above; among the last the Ripogenus Portage, which he described as the most difficult on the river, and three miles long. The whole length of the Penobscot is two hundred and seventy-five miles, and we are still nearly one hundred miles from its source. Hodge, the assistant State Geologist, passed up this river in 1837, and by a portage of only one mile and three quarters crossed over into the Allegash, and so went down that into the St. John, and up the Madawaska to the Grand Portage across to the St. Lawrence. His is the only account that I know of an expedition through to Canada in this direction.

He thus describes his first sight of the latter river, which, to compare small things with great, is like Balboa's first sight of the Pacific from the mountains of the Isthmus of Darien. "When we first came in sight of the St. Lawrence," he says, "from the top of a high hill, the view was most striking, and much more interesting to me from having been shut up in the woods for the two previous months. Directly before us lay the broad river, extending across nine or ten miles, its surface broken by a few islands and reefs, and two ships riding at anchor near the shore. Beyond, extended ranges of uncultivated hills, parallel with the river. The sun was just going down behind them, and gilding the whole scene with its parting rays."

About four o'clock, the same afternoon, we commenced our return voyage, which would require but little if any poling. In shooting rapids the boatmen use large and broad paddles, instead of poles, to guide the boat with. Though we glided so swiftly, and often smoothly, down, where it had cost us no slight effort to get up, our present voyage was attended with far more danger; for if we once fairly struck one of the thousand rocks by which we were surrounded the boat would be swamped in an instant. When a boat is swamped under these circumstances, the boatmen commonly find no difficulty in keeping afloat at first, for the current keeps both them and their cargo up for a long way down the stream; and if they can swim, they have only to work their way gradually to the shore.

The greatest danger is of being caught in an eddy behind some larger rock, where the water rushes up stream faster than elsewhere it does down, and being carried round and round under the surface till they are drowned. McCauslin pointed out some rocks which had been the scene of a fatal

accident of this kind. Sometimes the body is not thrown out
for several hours. He himself had performed such a circuit
once, only his legs being visible to his companions; but he
was fortunately thrown out in season to recover his breath.[1]

In shooting the rapids, the boatman has this problem to
solve: to choose a circuitous and safe course amid a thousand sunken rocks, scattered over a quarter or half a mile,
at the same time that he is moving steadily on at the rate of
fifteen miles an hour. Stop he cannot; the only question is,
where will he go? The bowman chooses the course with all
his eyes about him, striking broad off with his paddle, and
drawing the boat by main force into her course. The sternman faithfully follows the bow.

We were soon at the Aboljacarmegus Falls. Anxious to
avoid the delay, as well as the labor, of the portage here,
our boatmen went forward first to reconnoitre, and concluded to let the batteau down the falls, carrying the baggage only over the portage. Jumping from rock to rock until
nearly in the middle of the stream, we were ready to receive the boat and let her down over the first fall, some six
or seven feet perpendicular. The boatmen stand upon the
edge of a shelf of rock, where the fall is perhaps nine or ten
feet perpendicular, in from one to two feet of rapid water,
one on each side of the boat, and let it slide gently over, till
the bow is run out ten or twelve feet in the air; then, letting
it drop squarely, while one holds the painter, the other leaps
in, and his companion following, they are whirled down the
rapids to a new fall, or to smooth water.

---

[1] I cut this from a newspaper. "On the 11th (instant?) [May, '49], on Rap-
pogenes Falls, Mr. John Delantee, of Orono, Me., was drowned while running
logs. He was a citizen of Orono, and was twenty-six years of age. His companions found his body, enclosed it in bark, and buried it in the solemn
woods." [Thoreau]

Thoreau's guide in 1853, Joe Aitteon, was later drowned on a West Branch
drive. In keeping with the tradition on the Penobscot, his mates identified
the place where he was last seen alive on the river. There they hung his
caulked boots from a branch of a tall pine.

In a very few minutes they had accomplished a passage
in safety, which would be as foolhardy for the unskillful to
attempt as the descent of Niagara itself. It seemed as if it
needed only a little familiarity, and a little more skill, to
navigate down such falls as Niagara itself with safety. At any
rate, I should not despair of such men in the rapids above
Table-Rock, until I saw them actually go over the falls, so
cool, so collected, so fertile in resources are they. One might
have thought that these were falls, and that falls were not
to be waded through with impunity, like a mud-puddle.
There was really danger of their losing their sublimity in losing their power to harm us. Familiarity breeds contempt.
The boatman pauses, perchance, on some shelf beneath a
table-rock under the fall, standing in some cove of back-
water two feet deep, and you hear his rough voice come up
through the spray, coolly giving directions how to launch the
boat this time.

Having carried round Pockwockomus Falls, our oars soon
brought us to the Katepskonegan, or Oak Hall carry, where
we decided to camp half-way over, leaving our batteau to
be carried over in the morning on fresh shoulders. One shoulder of each of the boatmen showed a red spot as large as one's
hand, worn by the batteau on this expedition; and this shoulder, as it did all the work, was perceptibly lower than its fellow, from long service. Such toil soon wears out the strongest
constitution. The drivers are accustomed to work in the cold
water in the spring, rarely ever dry; and if one falls in all
over he rarely changes his clothes till night, if then, even.
One who takes this precaution is called by a particular nick-
name, or is turned off. None can lead this life who are not
almost amphibious.

McCauslin said soberly, what is at any rate a good story to
tell, that he had seen where six men were wholly under water
at once, at a jam, with their shoulders to handspikes. If the
log did not start, then they had to put out their heads to

breathe. The driver works as long as he can see, from dark to dark, and at night has not time to eat his supper and dry his clothes fairly, before he is asleep on his cedar bed. We lay that night on the very bed made by such a party, stretching our tent over the poles which were still standing, but re-shingling the damp and faded bed with fresh leaves.

In the morning we carried our boat over and launched it, making haste lest the wind should rise. The boatmen ran down Passamagamet, and soon after Ambejijis Falls, while we walked round with the baggage. We made a hasty breakfast at the head of Ambejijis Lake on the remainder of our pork, and were soon rowing across its smooth surface again, under a pleasant sky, the mountains being now clear of clouds in the northeast. Taking turns at the oars, we shot rapidly across Deep Cove, the foot of Pamadumcook, and the North Twin, at the rate of six miles an hour, the wind not being high enough to disturb us, and reached the Dam at noon. The boatmen went through one of the log sluices in the batteau, where the fall was ten feet at the bottom, and took us in below.

Here was the longest rapid in our voyage, and perhaps the running this was as dangerous and arduous a task as any. Shooting down sometimes at the rate, as we judged, of fifteen miles an hour, if we struck a rock we were split from end to end in an instant. Now like a bait bobbing for some river monster, amid the eddies, now darting to this side of the stream, now to that, gliding swift and smooth near to our destruction, or striking broad off with the paddle and drawing the boat to right or left with all our might, in order to avoid a rock. I suppose that it was like running the rapids of the Sault Sainte Marie, at the outlet of Lake Superior, and our boatmen probably displayed no less dexterity than the

Indians there do. We soon ran through this mile, and floated in Quakish Lake.

After such a voyage, the troubled and angry waters, which once had seemed terrible and not to be trifled with, appeared tamed and subdued; they had been bearded and worried in their channels, pricked and whipped into submission with the spike-pole and paddle, gone through and through with impunity, and all their spirit and their danger taken out of them, and the most swollen and impetuous rivers seemed but playthings henceforth. I began, at length, to understand the boatman's familiarity with, and contempt for, the rapids.

"Those Fowler boys," said Mrs. McCauslin, "are perfect ducks for the water." They had run down to Lincoln, according to her, thirty or forty miles, in a batteau, in the night, for a doctor, when it was so dark that they could not see a rod before them, and the river was swollen so as to be almost a continuous rapid, so that the doctor *cried*, when they brought him up at daylight, "Why, Tom, how did you see to steer?" "We didn't steer much,—only kept her straight." And yet they met with no accident. It is true, the more difficult rapids are higher up than this.

When we reached the Millinocket opposite to Tom's house, and were waiting for his folks to set us over, for we had left our batteau above the Grand Falls, we discovered two canoes, with two men in each, turning up this stream from Shad Pond, one keeping the opposite side of a small island before us, while the other approached the side where we were standing, examining the banks carefully for muskrats as they came along. The last proved to be Louis Neptune and his companion, now, at last, on their way up to Chesuncook after moose; but they were so disguised that we hardly knew them. At a little distance they might have been taken for Quakers, with their broad-brimmed hats and overcoats with broad capes, the spoils of Bangor, seeking a settlement

in this Sylvania,—or, nearer at hand, for fashionable gentlemen the morning after a spree.

Met face to face, these Indians in their native woods
looked like the sinister and slouching fellows whom you meet
picking up strings and paper in the streets of a city. There
is, in fact, a remarkable and unexpected resemblance between the degraded savage and the lowest classes in a great
city. The one is no more a child of nature than the other.
In the progress of degradation the distinction of races is soon
lost. Neptune at first was only anxious to know what we "kill,"
seeing some partridges in the hands of one of the party, but
we had assumed too much anger to permit of a reply. We
thought Indians had some honor before. But—"Me been
sick. Oh, me unwell now. You make bargain, then me go."
They had in fact been delayed so long by a drunken frolic at
the Five Islands, and they had not yet recovered from its
effects. They had some young musquash in their canoes,
which they dug out of the banks with a hoe, for food, not
for their skins, for musquash are their principal food on these
expeditions. So they went on up the Millinocket, and we kept
down the bank of the Penobscot, after recruiting ourselves
with a draught of Tom's beer, leaving Tom at his home.[1]

Thus a man shall lead his life away here on the edge of
the wilderness, on Indian Millinocket stream, in a new world,
far in the dark of a continent, and have a flute to play at

---

[1] As Thoreau predicted, "the tide of fashionable travel" has finally "set
that way" and the settlements have encroached on the Maine woods. Just
above "old Fowler's" carry from Millinocket Stream to Quakish Lake, is the
paper mill town of Millinocket. Above there the Bangor and Aroostook Railroad cuts from the village of Norcross on North Twin Lake across to the
settlement of Grindstone on the East Branch, at the mouth of which is the
small town of Medway. From there a road follows the course of the West
Branch through East Millinocket and Dolby—where "Uncle George" Mc-
Causlin's setter camp at the mouth of the Little Schoodic River has been
flowed out—then through Millinocket, on past the foot of Ktaadn, ultimately
reaching Greenville by way of Ripogenus Dam at the foot of Chesuncook
Lake.

HENRY
BUGBEE
KANE

evening here, while his strains echo to the stars, amid the howling of wolves; shall live, as it were, in the primitive age of the world, a primitive man. Yet he shall spend a sunny day, and in this century be my contemporary; perchance he shall read some scattered leaves of literature, and sometimes talk with me. Why read history, then, if the ages and the generations are now? He lives three thousand years deep into time, an age not yet described by poets. Can you well go further back in history than this? Ay! ay!—for there turns up but now into the mouth of Millinocket stream a still more ancient and primitive man, whose history is not brought down even to the former.

In a bark vessel sewn with the roots of the spruce, with horn-beam paddles, he dips his way along. He is but dim and misty to me, obscured by the æons that lie between the bark canoe and the batteau. He builds no house of logs, but a wigwam of skins. He eats no hot bread and sweet cake, but musquash and moose meat and the fat of bears. He glides up the Millinocket and is lost to my sight, as a more distant and misty cloud is seen flitting by behind a nearer, and is lost in space. So he goes about his destiny, the red face of man.

After having passed the night, and buttered our boots for the last time, at Uncle George's, whose dogs almost devoured him for joy at his return, we kept on down the river the next day, about eight miles on foot, and then took a batteau, with a man to pole it, to Mattawamkeag, ten more. At the middle of that very night, to make a swift conclusion to a long story, we dropped our buggy over the half-finished bridge at Oldtown, where we heard the confused din and clink of a hundred saws, which never rest, and at six o'clock the next morning one of the party was steaming his way to Massachusetts.

What is most striking in the Maine wilderness is the con-
tinuousness of the forest, with fewer open intervals or glades
than you had imagined. Except the few burnt lands, the
narrow intervals on the rivers, the bare tops of the high
mountains, and the lakes and streams, the forest is uninterrupted. It is even more grim and wild than you had anticipated, a damp and intricate wilderness, in the spring everywhere wet and miry. The aspect of the country, indeed, is
universally stern and savage, excepting the distant views of
the forest from hills, and the lake prospects, which are mild
and civilizing in a degree.

The lakes are something which you are unprepared for;
they lie up so high, exposed to the light, and the forest is
diminished to a fine fringe on their edges, with here and
there a blue mountain, like amethyst jewels set around some
jewel of the first water,—so anterior, so superior, to all the
changes that are to take place on their shores, even now civil
and refined, and fair as they can ever be. These are not
the artificial forests of an English king,—a royal preserve
merely. Here prevail no forest laws but those of nature.
The aborigines have never been dispossessed, nor nature
disforested.

It is a country full of evergreen trees, of mossy silver
birches and watery maples, the ground dotted with insipid,
small, red berries, and strewn with damp and moss-grown
rocks,—a country diversified with innumerable lakes and
rapid streams, peopled with trout and various species of
leucisci, with salmon, shad, and pickerel, and other fishes;
the forest resounding at rare intervals with the note of the
chickadee, the blue-jay, and the woodpecker, the scream of
the fish-hawk and the eagle, the laugh of the loon, and the
whistle of ducks along the solitary streams; at night, with the
hooting of owls and howling of wolves; in summer, swarming

with myriads of black flies and mosquitoes, more formidable than wolves to the white man.

Such is the home of the moose, the bear, the caribou, the wolf, the beaver, and the Indian. Who shall describe the inexpressible tenderness and immortal life of the grim forest, where Nature, though it be mid-winter, is ever in her spring, where the moss-grown and decaying trees are not old, but seem to enjoy a perpetual youth; and blissful, innocent Nature, like a serene infant, is too happy to make a noise, except by a few tinkling, lisping birds and trickling rills?

What a place to live, what a place to die and be buried in! There certainly men would live forever, and laugh at death and the grave. There they could have no such thoughts as are associated with the village graveyard,—that make a grave out of one of those moist evergreen hummocks!

> Die and be buried who will,
> I mean to live here still;
> My nature grows ever more young
> The primitive pines among.

I am reminded by my journey how exceedingly new this country still is. You have only to travel for a few days into the interior and back parts even of many of the old States, to come to that very America which the Northmen, and Cabot, and Gosnold, and Smith, and Raleigh visited. If Columbus was the first to discover the islands, Americus Vespucius and Cabot, and the Puritans, and we their descendants, have discovered only the shores of America. While the republic has already acquired a history world-wide, America is still unsettled and unexplored. Like the English in New Holland, we live only on the shores of a continent even yet, and hardly know where the rivers come from which float our navy. The very timber and boards and shingles of which our houses are made grew but yesterday in a wilderness where the Indian still hunts and the moose runs wild. New York has her wilderness within her own borders; and though the sailors of Europe are familiar with the soundings of her Hudson, and Fulton long since invented the steamboat on its waters, an Indian is still necessary to guide her scientific men to its headwaters in the Adirondack country.

Have we even so much as discovered and settled the shores? Let a man travel on foot along the coast, from the Passamaquoddy to the Sabine, or to the Rio Bravo, or to wherever the end is now, if he is swift enough to overtake it, faithfully following the windings of every inlet and of every cape, and stepping to the music of the surf,—with a desolate fishing-town once a week, and a city's port once a month to cheer him, and putting up at the light-houses, when there are any,—and tell me if it looks like a discovered and settled country, and not rather, for the most part, like a desolate island, and No-Man's Land.

We have advanced by leaps to the Pacific, and left many a lesser Oregon and California unexplored behind us. Though the railroad and the telegraph have been established on the shores of Maine, the Indian still looks out from her interior mountains over all these to the sea. There stands the city of Bangor, fifty miles up the Penobscot, at the head of navigation for vessels of the largest class, the principal lumber depot on this continent, with a population of twelve thousand, like a star on the edge of night, still hewing at the forests of which it is built, already overflowing with the luxuries and refinement of Europe, and sending its vessels to Spain, to England, and to the West Indies for its groceries,—and yet only a few axemen have gone "up river," into the howling wilderness which feeds it.

The bear and deer are still found within its limits; and the moose, as he swims the Penobscot, is entangled amid its shipping, and taken by foreign sailors in its harbor. Twelve miles in the rear, twelve miles of railroad, are Orono and the

Indian Island, the home of the Penobscot tribe, and then commence the batteau and the canoe, and the military road; and sixty miles above, the country is virtually unmapped and unexplored, and there still waves the virgin forest of the New World.

16. The Penobscot Indians

On each of his three trips Thoreau visited Oldtown and the other islands in the Penobscot which had been set aside for the Indians. His interest in them is evidenced by the following passages.

1846

The ferry here took us past the Indian Island. As we left the shore, I observed a short, shabby, washerwoman-looking Indian,—they commonly have the woebegone look of the girl that cried for spilt milk,—just from "up river," land on the Oldtown side near a grocery, and, drawing up his canoe, take out a bundle of skins in one hand, and an empty keg or half-barrel in the other, and scramble up the bank with them. This picture will do to put before the Indian's history, that is, the history of his extinction.

In 1837 there were three hundred and sixty-two souls left

of this tribe.[1] The island seemed deserted today, yet I observed some new houses among the weather-stained ones, as if the tribe had still a design upon life; but generally they have a very shabby, forlorn, and cheerless look, being all back side and woodshed, not homesteads, even Indian homesteads, but instead of home or abroad-steads, for their life is *domi aut militiae*, at home or at war, or now rather *venatus*, that is, a hunting, and most of the latter. The church is the only trim-looking building, but that is not Abenaki, that was Rome's doings. Good Canadian it may be, but it is poor Indian. These were once a powerful tribe. Politics are all the rage with them now. I even thought that a row of wigwams, with a dance of powwows, and a prisoner tortured at the stake, would be more respectable than this.

We landed in Milford, and rode along the east side of the Penobscot, having a more or less constant view of the river, and the Indian islands in it, for they retain all the islands as far up as Nicketow, at the mouth of the East Branch. They are generally well-timbered, and are said to be better soil than the neighboring shores. The river seemed shallow and rocky, and interrupted by rapids, rippling and gleaming in the sun. We paused a moment to see a fish-hawk dive for a fish down straight as an arrow, from a great height, but he missed his prey this time.

.   .   .   .

The next morning we drove along through a high and hilly country, in view of Cold-Stream Pond, a beautiful lake four or five miles long, and came into the Houlton road again, here called the military road, at Lincoln, forty-five miles from Bangor, where there is quite a village for this country,—the principal one above Oldtown. Learning that there were

---

[1] Thoreau's prediction has not been borne out. The tribe now numbers six hundred and eleven.

several wigwams here, on one of the Indian islands, we left our horse and wagon, and walked through the forest half a mile to the river, to procure a guide to the mountains. It was not till after considerable search that we discovered their habitations,—small huts, in a retired place, where the scenery was unusually soft and beautiful, and the shore skirted with pleasant meadows and graceful elms.

We paddled ourselves across to the island side in a canoe, which we found on the shore. Near where we landed sat an Indian girl, ten or twelve years old, on a rock in the water, in the sun, washing, and humming or moaning a song meanwhile. It was an aboriginal strain. A salmon-spear, made wholly of wood, lay on the shore, such as they might have used before white men came. It had an elastic piece of wood fastened to one side of its point, which slipped over and closed upon the fish, somewhat like the contrivance for holding a bucket at the end of a well-pole.

As we walked up to the nearest house, we were met by a sally of a dozen wolfish-looking dogs, which may have been lineal descendants from the ancient Indian dogs, which the first voyageurs describe as "their wolves." I suppose they were. The occupant soon appeared, with a long pole in his hand, with which he beat off the dogs, while he parleyed with us. A stalwart, but dull and greasy-looking fellow, who told us, in his sluggish way, in answer to our questions, as if it were the first serious business he had to do that day, that there *were* Indians going "up river"—he and one other—to-day, before noon. And who was the other? Louis Neptune, who lives in the next house. Well, let us go over and see Louis together. The same doggish reception, and Louis Neptune makes his appearance,—a small, wiry man, with puckered and wrinkled face, yet he seemed the chief man of the two; the same, as I remembered, who had accompanied Jackson to the mountain in '37. The same questions were put to Louis, and the same information obtained, while the other Indian stood by.

It appeared that they were going to start by noon, with two canoes, to go up to Chesuncook to hunt moose,—to be gone a month. "Well, Louis, suppose you get to the Point (to the Five Islands, just below Mattawamkeag) to camp, we walk on up the West Branch to-morrow,—four of us,—and wait for you at the dam, or this side. You overtake us to-morrow or next day, and take us into your canoes. We stop for you, you stop for us. We pay you for your trouble." "Ye!" replied Louis, "may be you carry some provision for all,—some pork,—some bread,—and so pay." He said, "Me sure get some moose;" and when I asked if he thought Pomola would let us go up, he answered that we must plant one bottle of rum on the top; he had planted good many; and when he looked again, the rum was all gone. He had been up two or three times; he had planted letter,—English, German, French, etc. These men were slightly clad in shirt and pantaloons, like laborers with us in warm weather. They did not invite us into their houses, but met us outside. So we left the Indians, thinking ourselves lucky to have secured such guides and companions.[1]

1853

On his return from a-moose-hunting on the West Branch in September, Thoreau spent a day at Oldtown.

The next forenoon we went to Oldtown. One slender old Indian on the Oldtown shore, who recognized my companion, was full of mirth and gestures, like a Frenchman. A Catholic priest crossed to the island in the same batteau with us. The Indian houses are framed, mostly of one story, and in rows one behind another, at the south end of the island, with a few

---

[1] They were disappointed. These were the two who had got drunk at Five Islands and later failed them.

scattered ones. I counted about forty, not including the church and what my companion called the council-house. The last, which I suppose is their town-house, was regularly framed and shingled like the rest. There were several of two stories, quite neat, with front-yards inclosed, and one at least had green blinds. Here and there were moose-hides stretched and drying about them. There were no cart-paths, nor tracks of horses, but foot-paths; very little land cultivated, but an abundance of weeds, indigenous and naturalized; more introduced weeds than useful vegetables, as the Indian is said to cultivate the vices rather than the virtues of the white man.

Yet this village was cleaner than I expected, far cleaner than such Irish villages as I have seen. The children were not particularly ragged nor dirty. The little boys met us with bow in hand and arrow on string, and cried, "Put up a cent." Verily, the Indian has but a feeble hold on his bow now; but the curiosity of the white man is insatiable, and from the first he has been eager to witness this forest accomplishment. That elastic piece of wood with its feathered dart, so sure to be unstrung by contact with civilization, will serve for the type, the coat-of-arms of the savage.

Alas for the Hunter Race! the white man has driven off their game, and substituted a cent in its place. I saw an Indian woman washing at the water's edge. She stood on a rock, and, after dipping the clothes in the stream, laid them on the rock, and beat them with a short club. In the graveyard, which was crowded with graves, and overrun with weeds, I noticed an inscription in Indian, painted on a wooden grave-board. There was a large wooden cross on the island.

Since my companion knew him, we called on Governor Neptune, who lived in a little "ten-footer," one of the humblest of them all. Personalities are allowable in speaking of public men, therefore I will give the particulars of our visit. He was abed. When we entered the room, which was one half of the house, he was sitting on the side of the bed. There was a clock hanging in one corner. He had on a black frock-coat, and black pants, much worn, white cotton shirt, socks, a red silk handkerchief about his neck, and a straw hat. His black hair was only slightly grayed. He had very broad cheeks, and his features were decidedly and refreshingly different from those of any of the upstart Native American party whom I have seen. He was no darker than many old white men.

He told me that he was eighty-nine; but he was going a-moose-hunting that fall, as he had been the previous one. Probably his companions did the hunting. We saw various squaws dodging about. One sat on the bed by his side and helped him out with his stories. They were remarkably corpulent, with smooth, round faces, apparently full of good humor. Certainly our much-abused climate had not dried up their adipose substance. While we were there,—for we stayed a good while,—one went over to Oldtown, returned and cut out a dress, which she had bought, on another bed in the room.

The Governor said that "he could remember when the moose were much larger; that they did not use to be in the woods, but came out of the water, as all deer did. Moose was whale once. Away down Merrimack way, a whale came ashore in a shallow bay. Sea went out and left him, and he

came up on land a moose. What made them know he was a whale was, that at first, before he began to run in bushes, he had no bowels inside, but"—and then the squaw who sat on the bed by his side, as the Governor's aid, and had been putting in a word now and then and confirming the story, asked me what we called that soft thing we find along the seashore. "Jelly-fish," I suggested. "Yes," said he, "no bowels, but jelly-fish."

There may be some truth in what he said about the moose growing larger formerly; for the quaint John Josselyn, a physician who spent many years in this very district of Maine in the seventeenth century, says that the tips of their horns "are sometimes found to be two fathoms asunder,"—and he is particular to tell us that a fathom is six feet,—"and (they are) in height, from the toe of the fore-foot to the pitch of the shoulder, twelve foot, both which hath been taken by some of my sceptique readers to be monstrous lies;" and he adds, "There are certain transcendentia in every creature, which are the indelible character of God, and which discover God." This is a greater dilemma to be caught in than is presented by the cranium of the young Bechuana ox, apparently another of the *transcendentia,* in the collection of Thomas Steel, Upper Brook Street, London, whose "entire length of horn, from tip to tip, along the curve, is 13 ft. 5 in.; distance (straight) between the tips of the horns, 8 ft. 8½ in." However, the size both of the moose and the cougar, as I have found, is generally rather underrated than overrated, and I should be inclined to add to the popular estimate a part of what I subtracted from Josselyn's.

But we talked mostly with the Governor's son-in-law, a very sensible Indian; and the Governor, being so old and deaf, permitted himself to be ignored, while we asked questions about him. The former said that there were two political parties among them,—one in favor of schools, and the other opposed to them, or rather they did not wish to resist the priest, who was opposed to them. The first had just prevailed at the election and sent their man to the legislature. Neptune and Aitteon and he himself were in favor of schools. He said, "If Indians got learning, they would keep their money."

When we asked where Joe's father, Aitteon, was, he knew that he must be at Lincoln, though he was about going a-moose-hunting, for a messenger had just gone to him there to get his signature to some papers. I asked Neptune if they had any of the old breed of dogs yet. He answered, "Yes." "But that," said I, pointing to one that had just come in, "is a Yankee dog." He assented. I said that he did not look like a good one. "Oh, yes!" he said, and he told, with much gusto, how, the year before, he had caught and held by the throat a wolf.

A very small black puppy rushed into the room and made at the Governor's feet, as he sat in his stockings with his legs dangling from the bedside. The Governor rubbed his hands and dared him to come on, entering into the sport with spirit. Nothing more that was significant transpired, to my knowledge, during this interview. This was the first time that I ever called on a governor, but, as I did not ask for an office, I can speak of it with the more freedom.

An Indian who was making canoes behind a house, looking up pleasantly from his work,—for he knew my companion,—said that his name was Old John Pennyweight. I had heard of him long before, and I enquired after one of his contemporaries, Joe Fourpence-ha'penny but alas! he no longer circulates. I made a faithful study of canoe-building, and I thought that I should like to serve an apprenticeship at that trade for one season, going into the woods for bark with my "boss," making the canoe there, and returning in it at last.

His "faithful study of canoe-building," Thoreau recorded in his Journal on September 22, 1853, and again when he

stopped at the Indian Camp on the West Branch at the end of
Northeast Carry on July 25, 1857.[1]

Behind one house, an Indian had nearly finished one canoe
and was just beginning another, outdoors. I looked very
narrowly at the process and had already carefully examined and measured our birch. We asked this Indian his name.
He answered readily and pleasantly, "My name is old John
Pennyweight." Said he got his bark at the head of Passadumkeag, fifty miles off. Took him two days to find one tree that
was suitable; had to look very sharp to be sure the bark was
not imperfect. But once he made two birches out of one tree.
Took the bark off with a shovel made of rock maple, three or
four inches wide.

It took him a fortnight or three weeks to complete a canoe
after he had got the materials ready. They sometimes made
them of spruce bark, and also of skins, but they were not so
good as birch. Boats of three hides were quicker made. This
was the best time to get the birch bark. It would not come
off in the winter. (I had heard Joe [Aitteon] say of a certain
canoe that it was made of summer bark.) They scrape all the
inner bark off, and in the canoe the bark is wrong side out-
ward.[2]

He had the ribs of a canoe, all got out of cedar,—the first
step in making a canoe, after materials (have been) brought
together,—and each one shaped for the particular place it

---

[1] The interested reader may compare Thoreau's account with that appear-
ing on page 284 of *The American Neptune,* October, 1948, under the title,
"A Canoe from the Penobscot River," by Wendell S. Hadlock and Ernest S.
Dodge.

[2] Four years later on the West Branch, Thoreau recorded:

I measured the largest canoe-birch which I saw in this journey near the
end of the carry. It was 14½ feet in circumference at two feet from the ground,
but at five feet divided into three parts. The canoe-birches thereabouts were
commonly marked by conspicuous dark spiral ridges, with a groove between,
so that I thought at first that they had been struck by lightning, but, as the
Indian [Polis] said, it was evidently caused by the grain of the tree.

was to hold in the canoe. As both ends are alike, there will be two ribs alike. These two were placed close together, and the next in succession each way were placed next on each side, and thus tied up in bundles of fourteen to sixteen till all were made. In the bundle I examined, they were two and a half inches wide in the middle and narrowing to the ends.

He would untie a bundle, take out the inmost or longest, or several, and place them on their ends in a very large iron kettle of hot water over a fire turning them from time to time. Then taking one of the inmost or longest ones, he bent and shaped it with much labor over his knee, giving it with his eyes the shape it was to have in the canoe. It was then tied  firmly and held in that shape with the reddish cedar bark. Sometimes he was obliged to tie a straight piece of wood on tangent-wise to the rib, and, with a bark tie, draw out a side of the rib to that. Then each succeeding smaller rib in one half the bundle is forced into this. The first bundles of fourteen or sixteen making two bundles of steamed and bent and tied up ribs; and thus all are left to dry in that shape.

I was sorry that I could not be there to witness the next step in making a canoe, for I was much struck by the *method* of his work, and the process deserves to be minutely described,—as much, at least, as most of the white man's arts, accounts of which now fill the journals. I do not know how the bark is made to hug so tightly the ribs, unless they are driven into place somewhat like a loop. One of the next things must be to make the long, thin sheathing of cedar, less than half an inch thick, of pieces half the length of the birch, reaching each way close together beneath the ribs, and quite thin toward the edges of the canoe.

However, I examined the canoe that was nearly done with minuteness. The edge or taffrail is composed first of two long strips of cedar, rather stout, one on each side. Four narrow hardwood (rock maple) cross-bars, artfully shaped so that no strength may be wasted, keep these apart, give firmness to the whole and answer for seats. The ends of the ribs come up behind or outside this taffrail and are nailed to it with a single nail. Pennyweight said they formerly used wooden pegs. The edge of the bark is brought up level with this, and a very slender triangular cleat of cedar is nailed on over it and flush with the surface of the taffrail. Then there are ties of split white spruce bark (looking like split bamboo) through the bark, between the ribs, and around these two strips of cedar, and over the strips one flat and thin strip covering the ties, making smooth work and coming out flush with the under strips. Thus the edge of the ca- noe is completed. Owing to the form of the canoe, there must be some seams near the edge on the sides about eighteen inches apart, and pieces of bark are put under them. The edges of the bark are carefully sewed to- gether at the ends with the same spruce roots, and, in our canoe, a strip of canvas covered with pitch was laid (doubled) over the edge.

They use rosin now, but pitch formerly. Canoe is nearly straight on bottom;— straight in principle— and not so rounded the other way as is supposed. *Vide* this section in the middle. The sides bulge out an inch or so beyond the rail. There is an additional piece of bark, four or five inches wide, along each side in the middle four or five feet for protection, and a similar protecting strip for eighteen inches on each side at the ends. The canoe rises about one foot in the last five or six feet. There is an oval piece of cedar for stiffness in- side, within a foot of each end, and near this the ribs are bent short to breaking. Beyond there are not ribs, but sheaths and a small keel-like piece, and the hollow is filled with shavings. Lightness, above all, is studied in the construction. Nails and rosin were all the modern things I noticed. The maker used one of those curved knives, and worked very hard at bending the knees.

Four years later in 1857 Thoreau had another opportunity for a close-up observation of canoe-building. This was at Northeast Carry on the West Branch.

Here was a canoe on the stocks, in an earlier stage of its manufacture than I had seen before, and I noticed it particularly. The St. Francis Indian was paring down the long cedar strips, or lining, with his crooked knife.

As near as I could *see*, and *understand* him and Polis, they first lay the bark flat on the ground, outside up, and two of the top rails, the inside and thickest ones, already connected with cross-bars, upon it, in order to get the form; and, with logs and rocks to keep the bark in place, they bend up the birch, cutting down slits in the edges from within three feet of the ends and perpendicularly on all sides about the rails, making a square corner at the ground; and a row of stakes three feet high is then driven into the ground all around, to hold the bark up in its place.

They next lift the frame, *i. e.* two rails connected by cross-bars, to the proper height, and sew the bark strongly to the rails with spruce roots [1] every six inches, the thread passing

---

[1] Apparently the choice of spruce roots provoked a dispute between the Indians, for on the Allegash trip Thoreau records:

Our Indian [Polis] said that *he* used *black* spruce roots to sew canoes with, obtaining it from high lands or mountains. The St. Francis Indian thought that *white* spruce roots might be the best. But the former said, "No good, break, can't split 'em"; also that they were hard to get, deep in the ground, but the black were near the surface, on higher land, as well as tougher. He said that the white spruce was *subekoondark*, black, *skusk*. I told him I thought that I could make a canoe, but he expressed great doubt of it; at any rate, he thought that my work would not be "neat" the first time. An Indian at Greenville had told me that the winter bark, that is, bark taken

around the rail and also *through* the ends of the cross-bars, and sew on strips of bark to protect the sides in the middle.

The canoe is as yet carried out square down at the ends (not ⸺) and is perfectly flat on the bot-tom. (The canoe had advanced thus far.) Then as near as I could learn, they shape the ends (?), put in all the lining of long thin strips, so shaped and shaved as just to fit, and fill up the bark, pressing it out and shaping the canoe. Then they put in the ribs and put on the outer or thinnest rail over the edge of the bark.

The canoe implies a long antiquity in which its manufacture has been gradually perfected. It will ere long, perhaps, be ranked among the lost arts.[1]

1857

After leaving the mouth of the East Branch, Thoreau was in the Indians' country until he reached Bangor two days later.

Things are quite changed since I was here eleven years ago. Where there were but one or two houses, I now found quite a village, with saw-mills and a store (the latter was locked, but its contents were so much the more safely stored), and there was a stage-road to Mattawamkeag, and the rumor of a stage. Indeed, a steamer had ascended thus far once, when the water was very high. But we were not able to get any sugar, only a better shingle to lean our backs against.

We camped about two miles below Nicketow, on the south side of the West Branch, covering with fresh twigs the withered bed of a former traveler, and feeling that we were now in a settled country, especially when in the evening we heard an ox sneeze in its wild pasture across the river. Wherever

off before the sap flows in May, was harder and much better than summer bark.

[1] Journal, July 25, 26, 1857.

you land along the frequented part of the river, you have not far to go to find these sites of temporary inns, the withered bed of flattened twigs, the charred sticks, and perhaps tent-poles. And not long since, similar beds were spread along the Connecticut, the Hudson, and the Delaware, and longer still ago by the Thames and the Seine, and they now help to make the soil where private and public gardens, mansions and palaces are. We could not get fir twigs for our bed here, and the spruce was harsh in comparison, having more twig in proportion to its leaf, but we improved it somewhat with hemlock.

The Indian remarked as before, "Must have hard wood to cook moose-meat," as if that were a maxim, and proceeded to get it. My companion cooked some in California fashion, winding a long string of the meat round a stick and slowly turning it in his hand before the fire. It was very good. But the Indian not approving of the mode, or because he was not allowed to cook it his own way, would not taste it. After the regular supper we attempted to make a lily soup of the bulbs which I had brought along, for I wished to learn all I could before I got out of the woods. Following the Indian's direc-tions, for he began to be sick, I washed the bulbs carefully, minced some moose-meat and some pork, salted and boiled all together, but we had not patience to try the experiment fairly, for he said it must be boiled till the roots were completely softened so as to thicken the soup like flour; but though we left it on all night, we found it dried to the kettle in the morn-ing, and not yet boiled to a flour. Perhaps the roots were not ripe enough, for they commonly gather them in the fall. As it was, it was palatable enough, but it reminded me of the Irish-man's limestone broth. The other ingredients were enough alone. The Indian's name for these bulbs was *Sheepnoc*. I stirred the soup by accident with a striped maple or moose-wood stick, which I had peeled, and he remarked that its bark was an emetic.[1]

He prepared to camp as usual between his moose-hide and the fire, but it beginning to rain suddenly, he took refuge under the tent with us, and gave us a song before falling asleep. It rained hard in the night, and spoiled another box of matches for us, which the Indian had left out, for he was very careless; but, as usual, we had so much the better night for the rain, since it kept the mosquitoes down.

Sunday, *August 2.*

Was a cloudy and unpromising morning. One of us observed to the Indian, "You did not stretch your moose-hide last night, did you, Mr. Polis?" Whereat he replied, in a tone of surprise, though perhaps not of ill humor: "What you ask me that question for? Suppose I stretch 'em, you see 'em. May be your way talking, may be all right, no Indian way." I had observed that he did not wish to answer the same question more than once, and was often silent when it was put again for the sake of certainty, as if he were moody. Not that he was incommunicative, for he frequently commenced a long-winded narrative of his own accord,—repeated at length the tradition of some old battle, or some passage in the recent history of his tribe in which he had acted a prominent part, from time to time drawing a long breath, and resuming the thread of his tale, with the true story-teller's leisureliness, perhaps after shooting a rapid,—prefacing with "we-ll-by-by," etc., as he paddled along. Especially after the day's work was over, and he had put himself in posture for the night, he would be unexpectedly sociable, exhibit even the *bonhommie*

---

[1] These bulbs Thoreau had dug the day before. He had been interested in the possibility of cooking them since Polis had suggested the idea on the West Branch. See Appendix, page 331.

of a Frenchman, and we would fall asleep before he got through his periods.

Nicketow is called eleven miles from Mattawamkeag by the river. Our camp was therefore, about nine miles from the latter place. The Indian was quite sick this morning with the colic. I thought that he was the worse for the moose-meat he had eaten. We reached the Mattawamkeag at half past eight in the morning, in the midst of a drizzling rain, and after buying some sugar set out again.

The Indian growing much worse, we stopped in the north part of Lincoln to get some brandy for him, but failing in this, an apothecary recommended Brandreth's pills, which he refused to take, because he was not acquainted with them. He said to me, "Me doctor,—first study my case, find out what ail 'em,—then I know what to take." We dropped down a little farther, and stopped at mid-forenoon on an island and made him a dipper of tea. Here, too, we dined and did some washing and botanizing, while he lay on the bank. In the afternoon we went on a little farther, though the Indian was no better. "Burntibus," as he called it, was a long, smooth, lake-like reach below the Five Islands. He said that he owned a hundred acres somewhere up this way. As a thunder-shower appeared to be coming up, we stopped opposite a barn on the west bank, in Chester, about a mile above Lincoln. Here at last we were obliged to spend the rest of the day and night, on account of our patient, whose sickness did not abate.

He lay groaning under his canoe on the bank, looking very woe-begone, yet it was only a common case of colic. You would not have thought, if you had seen him lying about thus, that he was the proprietor of so many acres in that neighborhood, was worth $6,000, and had been to Washington. It seemed to me that, like the Irish, he made a greater ado about his sickness than a Yankee does, and was more alarmed about himself. We talked somewhat of leaving him with his people in Lincoln,—for that is one of their homes,—and taking the stage the next day, but he objected on account of the expense, saying, "Suppose me well in morning, you and I go Oldtown by noon."

As we were taking our tea at twilight, while he lay groaning still under his canoe, having at length found out "what ail him," he asked me to get him a dipper of water. Taking the dipper in one hand he seized his powder-horn with the other, and pouring into it a charge or two of powder, stirred it up with his finger, and drank it off. This was all he took to-day after breakfast beside his tea.

To save the trouble of pitching our tent, when we had secured our stores from wandering dogs, we camped in the solitary half-open barn near the bank, with the permission of the owner, lying on new-mown hay four feet deep. The fragrance of the hay, in which many ferns, etc., were mingled, was agreeable, though it was quite alive with grasshoppers which you could hear crawling through it. This served to graduate our approach to houses and feather beds. In the night some large bird, probably an owl, flitted through over our heads, and very early in the morning we were awakened by the twittering of swallows which had their nests there.

MONDAY, *August* 3.

We started early before breakfast, the Indian being considerably better, and soon glided by Lincoln, and after another long and handsome lake-like reach, we stopped to breakfast on the west shore, two or three miles below this town. We frequently passed Indian islands with their small houses on them. The Governor, Aitteon, lives in one of them, in Lincoln.

The Penobscot Indians seem to be more social, even, than the whites. Ever and anon in the deepest wilderness of Maine, you come to the log hut of a Yankee or Canada settler, but a Penobscot never takes up his residence in such a solitude. They are not even scattered about on their islands in the Penobscot, which are all within the settlements, but gathered together on two or three,—though not always on the best soil,—evidently for the sake of society, I saw one or two houses not now used by them, because, as our Indian Polis said, they were too solitary.

The small river emptying in at Lincoln is the Matanancook, which also, we noticed, was the name of a steamer moored there. So we paddled and floated along, looking into the mouths of rivers. When passing the Mohawk Rips, or, as the Indian called them, "Mohog lips," four or five miles below Lincoln, he told us at length the story of a fight between his tribe and the Mohawks there, anciently,—how the latter were overcome by stratagem, the Penobscots using concealed knives,—but they could not for a long time kill the Mohawk chief, who was a very large and strong man, though he was attacked by several canoes at once, when swimming alone in the river.

From time to time we met Indians in their canoes, going up river. Our man did not commonly approach them, but exchanged a few words with them at a distance in his tongue.

These were the first Indians we had met since leaving the Umbazookskus.

At Piscataquis Falls, just above the river of that name, we walked over the wooden railroad on the eastern shore, about one and a half miles long, while the Indian glided down the rapids. The steamer from Oldtown stops here, and passengers take a new boat above. Piscataquis, whose mouth we here passed, means "branch." It is obstructed by falls at its mouth, but can be navigated with batteaux or canoes above through a settled country, even to the neighborhood of Moosehead Lake, and we had thought at first of going that way. We were not obliged to get out of the canoe after this on account of falls or rapids, nor, indeed, was it quite necessary here. We took less notice of the scenery to-day, because we were in quite a settled country. The river became broad and sluggish, and we saw a blue heron winging its way slowly down the stream before us.

We passed the Passadumkeag River on our left and saw the blue Olamon mountains at a distance in the southeast. Hereabouts our Indian told us at length the story of their contention with the priest respecting schools. He thought a great deal of education and had recommended it to his tribe. His argument in its favor was, that if you had been to college and learnt to calculate, you could "keep 'em property,—no other way." He said that his boy was the best scholar in the school at Oldtown, to which he went with whites. He himself is a Protestant, and goes to church regularly at Oldtown. According to his account, a good many of his tribe are Protestants, and many of the Catholics also are in favor of schools.

Some years ago they had a schoolmaster, a Protestant, whom they liked very well. The priest came and said that they must send him away, and finally he had such influence, telling them that they would go to the bad place at last if they retained him, that they sent him away. The school party, though numerous, were about giving up. Bishop Fenwick came from Boston and used his influence against them. But our Indian told his side that they must not give up, must hold on, they were the strongest. If they gave up, then they would have no party. But they answered that it was "no use, priest too strong, we'd better give up." At length he persuaded them to make a stand.

The priest was going for a sign to cut down the liberty-pole. So Polis and his party had a secret meeting about it; he got ready fifteen or twenty stout young men, "stript 'em naked, and painted 'em like old times," and told them that when the priest and his party went to cut down the liberty-pole, they were to rush up, take hold of it, and prevent them, and he assured them that there would be no war, only a noise, "no war where priest is." He kept his men concealed in a house near by, and when the priest's party were about to cut down the liberty-pole, the fall of which would have been a death-blow to the school-party, he gave a signal, and his young men rushed out and seized the pole. There was a great uproar, and they were about coming to blows, but the priest interfered, saying, "No war, no war," and so the pole stands, and the school goes on still.

We thought that it showed a good deal of tact in him, to seize this occasion and take his stand on it; proving how well he understood those with whom he had to deal.

The Olamon River comes in from the east in Greenbush a few miles below the Passadumkeag. When we asked the meaning of this name, the Indian said there was an island opposite its mouth which was called *Olarmon;* that in old times, when visitors were coming to Oldtown, they used to stop there to dress and fix up or paint themselves. "What is that which ladies used?" he asked. Rouge? Red Vermilion?

"Yer," he said, "that is *larmon,* a kind of clay or red paint, which they used to get here."

We decided that we, too, would stop at this island, and fix up our inner man, at least, by dining. It was a large island, with an abundance of hemp nettle, but I did not notice any kind of red paint there. The Olamon River, at its mouth at least, is a dead stream. There was another large island in that neighborhood, which the Indian called *Soogle* (*i. e.,* Sugar) Island.

About a dozen miles before reaching Oldtown he inquired, "How you like 'em your pilot?" But we postponed an answer till we had got quite back again.

The Sunkhaze, another short dead stream, comes in from the east two miles above Oldtown. There is said to be some of the best deer ground in Maine on this stream. Asking the meaning of this name, the Indian said, "Suppose you are going down Penobscot, just like we, and you see a canoe come out of bank and go along before you, but you no see 'em stream. That is *Sunkhaze.*"

He had previously complimented me on my paddling, saying that I paddled "just like anybody," giving me an Indian name which meant "great paddler." When off this stream he said to me, who sat in the bows, "Me teach you paddle." So turning toward the shore he got out, came forward and placed my hands as he wished. He placed one of them quite outside the boat, and the other parallel with the first, grasping the paddle near the end, not over the flat extremity, and told me to slide it back and forth on the side of the canoe. This, I found, was a great improvement which I had not thought of, saving me the labor of lifting the paddle each time, and I wondered that he had not suggested it before. It is true, before our baggage was reduced we had been obliged to sit with our legs drawn up, and our knees above the side of the canoe, which would have prevented our paddling thus, or perhaps he was afraid of wearing out his canoe, by constant friction on the side.

I told him that I had been accustomed to sit in the stern, and lifting my paddle at each stroke, getting a pry on the side each time, and I still paddled partly as if in the stern. He then wanted to see me paddle in the stern. So, changing paddles, for he had the longer and better one, and turning end for end, he sitting flat on the bottom and I on the crossbar, he began to paddle very hard, trying to turn the canoe, looking over his shoulder and laughing, but finding it in vain he relaxed his efforts, though we still sped along a mile or two very swiftly. He said that he had no fault to find with my paddling in the stern, but I complained that he did not paddle according to his own directions in the bows.

Opposite the Sunkhaze is the main boom of the Penobscot, where the logs from far up the river are collected and assorted. As we drew near to Oldtown I asked Polis if he was not glad to get home again; but there was no relenting to his wildness, and he said, "It makes no difference to me where I am." Such is the Indian's pretense always.

We approached the Indian Island through the narrow strait called "Cook." He said, "I 'xpect we take in some water there, river so high,—never see it so high at this season. Very rough water there, but short; swamp steamboat once. Don't you paddle till I tell you, then you paddle right along." It was a very short rapid. When we were in the midst of it he shouted "paddle," and we shot through without taking in a drop.

Soon after the Indian houses came in sight, but I could not at first tell my companion which of two or three large white ones was our guide's. He said it was the one with blinds.[1] We

---

[1] In the course of illustrating *The Maine Woods*, the artist visited Oldtown. Living in Joe Polis's old home on the Indian Island was the widow of his adopted son. Joe Polis, who died in 1884, had no children. His niece, who had

landed opposite his door at about four in the afternoon, having come some forty miles this day. From the Piscataquis we
had come remarkably and unaccountably quick, probably as
fast as the stage or the boat, though the last dozen miles was
dead water. Polis wanted to sell us his canoe, said it would last
seven or eight years, or with care, perhaps ten; but we were
not ready to buy it.

We stopped for an hour at his house, where my companion
shaved with his razor, which he pronounced in very good
condition. Mrs. P. wore a hat and had a silver brooch on her
breast, but she was not introduced to us. The house was
roomy and neat. A large new map of Oldtown and the Indian
Island hung on the wall, and a clock opposite to it. Wishing
to know when the cars left Oldtown, Polis's son brought one
of the last Bangor papers, which I saw was directed to
"Joseph Polis," from the office.

This was the last that I saw of Joe Polis. We took the last
train, and reached Bangor that night.

---

married a Frenchman, had several. Joe picked out and adopted the "darkest
one"—Peter Ranco. He is said to have borne a remarkable resemblance to Joe
Polis, and his photograph served as the model for the sketch of Thoreau's last
guide which heads this chapter.

Appendix

As has been noted, on each of his three trips Thoreau passed through in part the same portions of northern Maine two and even three times. In order that none of his striking passages are omitted in combining the three separate accounts into a single integrated whole, there has been adopted the device of referring the reader to this appendix wherein these pertinent passages are collected.

The following paragraphs comprise the conclusion which Thoreau wrote for his account of his second trip in the Maine woods, when he accompanied his relative a-moose-hunting down the West Branch to Chesuncook in September, 1853.

Humboldt has written an interesting chapter on the primitive forest, but no one has yet described for me the difference between that wild forest which once occupied our oldest townships, and the tame one which I find there to-day. It is a difference which would be worth attending to. The civilized man not only clears the land permanently to a great extent, and cultivates open fields, but he tames and cultivates to a certain extent the forest itself. By his mere presence, almost, he

317

changes the nature of the trees as no other creature does. The sun and
air, and perhaps fire, have been introduced, and grain raised where it
stands. It has lost its wild, damp, and shaggy look, the countless fallen
and decaying trees are gone, and consequently that thick coat of moss
which lived on them is gone too. The earth is comparatively bare and
smooth and dry. The most primitive places left with us are the swamps,
where the spruce still grows shaggy with usnea.

The surface of the ground in the Maine woods is everywhere spongy
and saturated with moisture. I noticed that the plants which cover the
forest floor there are such as are commonly confined to swamps with
us,—the *Clintonia borealis,* orchises, creeping snowberry, and others;
and the prevailing aster there is the *Aster acuminatus,* which with us
grows in damp and shady woods. The asters *cordifolius* and *macrophyllus* also are common, asters of little or no color, and sometimes
without petals. I saw no soft, spreading, second-growth white-pines,
with smooth bark, acknowledging the presence of the wood chopper,
but even the young white-pines were all tall and slender rough-barked
trees.

Those Maine woods differ essentially from ours. There you are never
reminded that the wilderness which you are threading is, after all, some
villager's familiar wood-lot, some widow's thirds, from which her ancestors have sledded fuel for generations, minutely described in some
old deed which is recorded, of which the owner has got a plan, too,
and old bound-marks may be found every forty rods, if you will search.
'Tis true, the map may inform you that you stand on land granted by
the State to some academy, or on Bingham's purchase; but these names
do not impose on you, for you see nothing to remind you of the academy
or of Bingham.

What were the "forests" of England to these? One writer relates of
the Isle of Wight, that in Charles the Second's time "there were woods
in the island so complete and extensive, that it is said a squirrel might
have traveled in several parts many leagues together on the top of the
trees." If it were not for the rivers (and he might go round their heads),
a squirrel could here travel thus the whole breadth of the country.

We have as yet had no adequate account of a primitive pine forest.
I have noticed that in a physical atlas lately published in Massachusetts,
and used in our schools, the "wood land" of North America is limited
almost solely to the valleys of the Ohio and some of the Great Lakes,
and the great pine forests of the globe are not represented. In our
vicinity, for instance, New Brunswick and Maine are exhibited as bare

as Greenland. It may be that the children of Greenville, at the foot of Moosehead Lake, who surely are not likely to be scared by an owl, are referred to the valley of the Ohio to get an idea of a forest; but they would not know what to do with their moose, bear, caribou, beaver, etc., there. Shall we leave it to an Englishman to inform us, that "in North America, both in the United States and Canada, are the most extensive pine forests in the world"? The greater part of New Brunswick, the northern half of Maine, and adjacent parts of Canada, not to mention the northeastern part of New York and other tracts farther off, are still covered with an almost unbroken pine forest.

But Maine, perhaps, will soon be where Massachusetts is. A good part of her territory is already as bare and commonplace as much of our neighborhood, and her villages generally are not so well shaded as ours. We seem to think that the earth must go through the ordeal of sheep-pasturage before it is habitable by man. Consider Nahant, the resort of all the fashion of Boston,—which peninsula I saw but indistinctly in the twilight, when I steamed by it, and thought that it was unchanged since the discovery. John Smith described it in 1614 as "the Mattahunts, two pleasant isles of groves, gardens, and cornfields;" and others tell us that it was once well wooded, and even furnished timber to build the wharves of Boston. Now it is difficult to make a tree grow there, and the visitor comes away with a vision of Mr. Tudor's ugly fences, a rod high, designed to protect a few pear-shrubs.

And what are we coming to in our Middlesex towns?—a bald, staring

town-house, or meeting-house, and a bare liberty-pole, as leafless as it is fruitless, for all I can see. We shall be obliged to import the timber for the last, hereafter, or splice such sticks as we have;—and our ideas of liberty are equally mean with these. The very willow-rows lopped every three years for fuel or powder,—and every sizable pine and oak, or other forest tree, cut down within the memory of man! As if individual speculators were to be allowed to export the clouds out of the sky, or the stars out of the firmament, one by one. We shall be reduced to gnaw the very crust of the earth for nutriment.

They have even descended to smaller game. They have lately, as I hear, invented a machine for chopping up huckleberry-bushes fine, and so converting them into fuel!—bushes which, for fruit alone, are worth all the pear-trees in the country many times over. (I can give you a list of the three best kinds, if you want it.) At this rate, we shall all be obliged to let our beards grow at least, if only to hide the nakedness of the land and make a sylvan appearance. The farmer sometimes talks of "brushing up," simply as if bare ground looked better than clothed ground, than that which wears its natural vesture,—as if the wild hedges, which, perhaps, are more to his children than his whole farm beside, were *dirt*.

I know of one who deserves to be called the Tree-hater, and, perhaps, to leave this for a new patronymic to his children. You would think that he had been warned by an oracle that he would be killed by the fall of a tree, and so was resolved to anticipate them. The journalists think that they cannot say too much in favor of such "improvements" in husbandry; it is a safe theme, like piety; but as for the beauty of one of these "model farms," I would as lief see a patent churn and a man turning it. They are, commonly, places merely where somebody is making money, it may be counterfeiting. The virtue of making two blades of grass grow where only one grew before does not begin to be superhuman.

Nevertheless, it was a relief to get back to our smooth, but still varied landscape. For a permanent residence, it seemed to me that there could be no comparison between this and the wilderness, necessary as the latter is for a resource and a background, the raw material of all our civilization. The wilderness is simple, almost to barrenness. The partially cultivated country it is which chiefly has inspired, and will continue to inspire, the strains of poets, such as compose the mass of any literature. Our woods are sylvan, and their inhabitants woodmen and rustics,—that is, *selvaggia*, and the inhabitants are *salvages*. A civilized man, using the word in the ordinary sense, with his ideas and associations, must at length pine there, like a cultivated plant, which clasps its fibres about a crude and undissolved mass of peat.

At the extreme North, the voyagers are obliged to dance and act plays for employment. Perhaps our own woods and fields,—in the best wooded towns, where we need not quarrel about the huckleberries, —with the primitive swamps scattered here and there in their midst, but not prevailing over them, are the perfection of parks and groves, gardens, arbors, paths, vistas, and landscapes. They are the natural consequence of what art and refinement we as a people have,—the common which each village possesses, its true paradise, in comparison with which all elaborately and willfully wealth-constructed parks and gardens are paltry imitations. Or, I would rather say, such were our groves twenty years ago. The poet's, commonly, is not a logger's path, but a woodman's. The logger and pioneer have preceded him, like John the Baptist; eaten the wild honey, it may be, but the locusts also; banished decaying wood and the spongy mosses which feed on it, and built hearths and humanized Nature for him.

But there are spirits of a yet more liberal culture, to whom no simplicity is barren. There are not only stately pines, but fragile flowers, like the orchises, commonly described as too delicate for cultivation, which derive their nutriment from the crudest mass of peat. These remind us, that, not only for strength, but for beauty, the poet must, from time to time, travel the logger's path and the Indian's trail, to drink at some new and more bracing fountain of the Muses, far in the recesses of the wilderness.

The kings of England formerly had their forests "to hold the king's game," for sport or food, sometimes destroying villages to create or extend them; and I think that they were impelled by a true instinct. Why should not we, who have renounced the king's authority, have our national preserves, where no villages need be destroyed, in which the bear and panther, and some even of the hunter race, may still exist, and not be "civilized off the face of the earth,"—our forests, not to hold the king's game merely, but to hold and preserve the king himself also, the lord of creation,—not for idle sport or food, but for inspiration and our own true recreation? or shall we, like the villains, grub them all up, poaching on our own national domains?

Page 27.

Already we had thought that we saw Moosehead Lake from a hill-top, where an extensive fog filled the distant lowlands, but we were mistaken. It was not till we were within a mile or two of its south end that we got our first view of it—a suitably wild-looking sheet of water, sprinkled with small, low islands, which were covered with shaggy spruce and other wild wood,—seen over the infant port of Greenville with mountains on each side and far in the north, and a steamer's smoke-pipe rising above a roof. A pair of moose horns ornamented a corner of the public house where we left our horse, and a few rods distant lay the small steamer Moosehead, Captain King. There was no village, and no summer road any farther in this direction,—but a winter road, that is, one passable only when deep snow covers its inequalities, from Greenville up the east side of the lake to Lily Bay, about twelve miles.

. . . .

Off Lily Bay it is a dozen miles wide, but it is much broken by islands. The scenery is not merely wild, but varied and interesting; mountains were seen, farther or nearer, on all sides but the northwest, their summits now lost in the clouds; but Mount Kineo is the principal feature of the lake, and more exclusively belongs to it. After leaving Greenville, at the foot, which is the nucleus of a town some eight or ten years old, you see but three or four houses for the whole length of the lake, or about forty miles, three of them the public houses at which the steamer is advertised to stop, and the shore is an unbroken wilderness. The prevailing wood seemed to be spruce, fir, birch, and rock maple. You could easily distinguish the hard wood from the soft, or "black growth," as it is called, at a great distance—the former being smooth, round-topped, and light green, with a bowery and cultivated look.

Page 41.

Mount Kineo, at which the boat touched, is a peninsula with a narrow neck, about midway the lake on the east side. The celebrated precipice is on the east or land side of this, and is so high and perpendicular that you can jump from the top, many hundred feet, into the water, which makes up behind the point. A man on board told us that an anchor had been sunk ninety fathoms at its base before reaching bottom! Probably it will be discovered erelong that some Indian maiden jumped off it for love once, for true love never could have found a path more to its mind. We passed quite close to the rock here, since it is a very bold shore, and I observed marks of a rise of four or five feet on it.

Page 48.

I told the Indian that we would go to church to Chesuncook this (Sunday) morning, some fifteen miles. It was settled weather at last.

A few swallows flitted over the water, we heard the white throats along the shore, the phebe notes of the chickadee, and, I believe, redstarts, and moose-flies of large size pursued us in mid-stream.

The Indian thought we should lie by on Sunday. Said he, "We come here lookum things, look all round; but come Sunday, lock up all that, and then Monday look again." He spoke of an Indian of his acquaintance who had been with some ministers to Ktaadn, and had told him how they conducted. This he described in a low and solemn voice. "They make a long prayer every morning and night, and at every meal. Come Sunday," said he, "they stop 'em, no go at all that day,—keep still,— preach all day,—first one, then another, just like church. Oh, ver good men." "One day," said he, "going along a river, they came to the body of a man in the water, drowned good while, all ready fall to pieces. They go right ashore,—stop there, go no farther that day,—they have meeting there, preach and pray just like Sunday. Then they get poles and lift up the body, and they go back and carry the body with them. Oh, they ver good men."

I judged from this account that their every camp was a camp-meeting, and they had mistaken their route,—they should have gone to Eastham; that they wanted an opportunity to preach somewhere more than to see Ktaadn. I read of another similar party that seem to have spent their time there singing the songs of Zion. I was glad that I did not go to that mountain with such slow coaches.

However, the Indian added, plying the paddle all the while, that if we would go along, he must go with us, he our man, and he suppose that if he no takum pay for what he do Sunday, then ther's no harm, but if he takum pay, then wrong. I told him that he was stricter than white men. Nevertheless, I noticed that he did not forget to reckon in the Sundays at last.

He appeared to be a very religious man, and said his prayers in a loud voice, in Indian, kneeling before the camp, morning and evening,—sometimes scrambling up again in haste when he had forgotten this, and saying them with great rapidity. In the course of the day, he remarked, not very originally, "Poor man rememberum God more than rich."

Page 56.

It appears that in a forest like this the great majority of flowers, shrubs, and grasses are confined to the banks of the rivers and lakes, and to the meadows, more open swamps, burnt lands, and mountain tops; comparatively very few indeed penetrate the woods. There is no such dispersion even of wild-flowers as is commonly supposed, or as exists in a cleared and settled country. Most of our wild-flowers, so called, may be considered as naturalized in the localities where they grow. Rivers and lakes are the great protectors of such plants against the aggressions of the forest, by their annual rise and fall keeping open a narrow strip where these more delicate plants have light and space in which to grow. They are the *protégés* of the rivers. These narrow, and straggling bands and isolated groups are, in a sense, the pioneers of civilization. Birds, quadrupeds, insects, and man also, in the main, follow the flowers, and the latter in his turn makes more room for them and for berry-bearing shrubs, birds, and small quadrupeds. One settler told me that not only blackberries and raspberries, but mountain maples came in, in the clearing and burning.

Though plants are often referred to primitive woods as their locality, it cannot be true of very many, unless the woods are supposed to include such localities as I have mentioned. Only those which require but little light, and can bear the drip of the trees, penetrate the woods, and these have commonly more beauty in their leaves than in their pale and almost colorless blossoms.

.   .   .   .

It appears that I saw about a dozen plants which had accompanied man as far into the woods as Chesuncook, and had naturalized themselves there, in 1853. Plants begin thus early to spring by the side of a logging-path,—a mere vista through the woods, which can only be used in the winter, on account of the stumps and fallen trees,—which at length are the roadside plants in old settlements. The pioneers of such are planted in part by the first cattle, which cannot be summered in the woods.

Page 60.

The prevailing trees (I speak only of what I saw) on the east and west branches of the Penobscot and on the upper part of the Allegash were the fir, spruce (both black and white), and arbor-vitæ, or "cedar." The fir has the darkest foliage, and, together with the spruce, makes a very dense "black growth," especially on the upper parts of the rivers. A dealer in lumber with whom I talked called the former a weed, and it is commonly regarded as fit neither for timber nor fuel. But it is more sought after as an ornamental tree than any other evergreen of these woods except the arbor-vitæ. The black spruce is much more common than the white. Both are tall and slender trees. The arbor-vitæ, which is of a more cheerful hue, with its light-green fans, is also tall and slender, though sometimes two feet in diameter. It often fills the swamps.

Mingled with the former, and also here and there forming extensive and more open woods by themselves, indicating, it is said, a better soil, were canoe and yellow birches (the former was always at hand for kindling a fire,—we saw no small white-birches in that wilderness), and sugar and red maples.

The Aspen (*Populus tremuloides*) was very common on burnt grounds. We saw many straggling white pines, commonly unsound trees, which had therefore been skipped by the choppers; these were the largest trees we saw; and we occasionally passed a small wood in which this was the prevailing tree; but I did not notice nearly so many of these trees as I can see in a single walk in Concord. The speckled or hoary alder (*Alnus incana*) abounds everywhere along the muddy banks of rivers and lakes, and in swamps. Hemlock could commonly be found for tea, but was nowhere abundant. Yet F. A. Michaux states that in Maine, Vermont, and the upper part of New Hampshire, &c., the hemlock forms three fourths of the evergreen woods, the rest being black spruce. It belongs to cold hillsides.

The elm and black ash were very common along the lower and stiller parts of the streams, where the shores were flat and grassy or there were low gravelly islands. They made a pleasing variety in the scenery, and we felt as if nearer home while gliding past them.

The above fourteen trees made the bulk of the woods which we saw.

The larch (Juniper), beech, and Norway pine (*Pinus resinosa*, red pine), were only occasionally seen in particular places. The *Pinus Banksiana* (gray or Northern scrub pine), and a single small red oak (*Quercus rubra*) only, are on islands in Grand Lake, on the East Branch.

The above are almost all peculiarly Northern trees, and found chiefly, if not solely, on mountains southward.

Page 68.

Midway the lake we took on board two manly-looking middle-aged men, with their batteau, who had been exploring for six weeks as far as the Canada line, and had let their beards grow. They had the skin of a beaver, which they had recently caught, stretched on an oval hoop, though the fur was not good at that season. I talked with one of them, telling him that I had come all this distance partly to see where the white-pine, the Eastern stuff of which our houses are built, grew, but that on this and a previous excursion into another part of Maine I had found it a scarce tree; and I asked him where I must look for it. With a smile, he answered, that he could hardly tell me. However, he said that he had found enough to employ two teams the next winter in a place where there was thought to be none left. What was considered a "tip-top" tree now was not looked at twenty years ago, when he first went into the business; but they succeeded very well now with what was considered quite inferior timber then. The explorer used to cut into a tree higher and higher up, to see if it was false-hearted, and if there was a rotten heart as big as his arm, he let it alone; but now they cut such a tree, and sawed it all around the rot, and it made the very best of boards, for in such a case they were never shaky.

Page 102.

We reached the Penobscot about four o'clock and found there some St. Francis Indians encamped on the bank, in the same place where I camped with four Indians four years before. They were making a canoe, and, as then, drying moose meat. The meat looked very suitable to make a *black* broth at least. Our Indian said it was not good. Their camp was covered with spruce-bark. They had got a young moose, taken in the river a fortnight before, confined in a sort of cage of logs piled up cob-fashion, seven or eight feet high. It was quite tame, about four feet high, and covered with moose-flies. There was a large quantity of cornel (*C. stolonifera*), red maple, and also willow and aspen boughs, stuck through between the logs on all sides, butt-ends out, and on their leaves it was browsing. It looked at first as if it were in a bower rather than a pen.

Page 148.

The note of the white-throated sparrow, a very inspiriting but almost wiry sound, was the first heard in the morning, and with this all the woods rang. This was the prevailing bird in the northern part of Maine. The forest generally was all alive with them at this season, and they were proportionally numerous and musical about Bangor. They evidently breed in that State. Wilson did not know where they bred, and says, "Their only note is a kind of chip." Though commonly unseen, their simple *ah, te-te-te, te-te-te, te-te-te,* so sharp and piercing, was as distinct to the ear as the passage of a spark of fire shot into the darkest of the forest would be to the eye. I thought that they commonly uttered it as they flew. I hear this note for a few days only in the spring, as they go through Concord, and in the fall see them again going southward, but then they are mute. We were commonly aroused by their lively strain very early. What a glorious time they must have in that wilderness, far from mankind and election day!

Page 179.

One connected with lumbering operations at Bangor told me that the largest pine belonging to his firm, cut the previous winter, "scaled" in the woods four thousand five hundred feet, and was worth ninety dollars in the log at the Bangor boom in Oldtown. They cut a road three and a half miles long for this tree alone. He thought that the principal locality for the white pine that came down the Penobscot now was at the head of the East Branch and the Allegash, about Webster Stream and Eagle and Chamberlain Lakes. Much timber has been stolen from the public lands (Pray what kind of forest-warden is the Public itself?) I heard of one man who, having discovered some particularly fine trees just within the boundaries of the public lands, and not daring to employ an accomplice, cut them down, and by means of block and tackle, without cattle, tumbled them into a stream, and so succeeded in getting off with them without the least assistance. Surely, stealing pine-trees in this way is not so mean as robbing hen-roosts.

Page 204.

In his Journal on Aug. 3, 1857, Thoreau wrote:
This was the midst of the raspberry season. We found them abundant on every carry on the East Branch and below, and children were carrying them from all sides into Bangor. I observed that they were the prominent dish on the tables, once a low scarlet mountain, garnishing the head of the table in a dish two feet across. Earlier the strawberries are equally abundant, and we even found a few still deep in the grass. Neither of these abound about Boston, and we saw that they were due to the peculiar air of this higher latitude. Though for six weeks before leaving home we had been scarcely able to lie under

more than a single sheet, we experienced no hot weather in Maine. The air was uniformly fresh and bracing like that of a mountain to us, and, though the inhabitants like to make it out that it is as warm there as in Massachusetts, we were not to be cheated. It is so much the more desirable at this season to breathe the raspberry air of Maine.

Page 234.

At Oldtown, we walked into a batteau-manufactory. The making of batteaux is quite a business here for the supply of the Penobscot River. We examined some on the stocks. They are light and shapely vessels, calculated for rapid and rocky streams, and to be carried over long portages on men's shoulders, from twenty to thirty feet long, and only four or four and a half wide, sharp at both ends like a canoe, though broadest forward on the bottom, and reaching seven or eight feet over the water, in order that they may slip over rocks as gently as possible. They are made very slight, only two boards to a side, commonly secured to a few light maple or other hard-wood knees, but inward are of the clearest and widest white-pine stuff, of which there is a great waste on account of their form, for the bottom is left perfectly flat, not only from side to side, but from end to end. Sometimes they become "hogging" even, after long use, and the boatmen then turn them over and straighten them by a weight at each end. They told us that one wore out in two years, or often in a single trip, on the rocks, and sold for from fourteen to sixteen dollars. There was something refreshing and wildly musical to my ears in the very name of the white man's canoe, reminding me of Charlevoix and Canadian Voyageurs. The batteau is a sort of mongrel between the canoe and the boat, a fur-trader's boat.

On his second trip Thoreau took off the measurements of a batteau at Ansell Smith's. His entry in his Journal of September 18, 1853, records:

I measured one of the many batteaux lying about with my two foot ash rule made here. It was not peculiar in any respect that I noticed.

Extreme length	31	feet
Extreme width	5½	feet
Width of bottom	2⁶⁄₁₂	feet
Length of bottom	20⁹⁄₁₂	feet
Length of bow	6¹⁰⁄₁₂	feet
Length of stern	3½	feet
Depth within	17	inches

Page 237.

No people can long continue provincial in character who have the propensity for politics and whittling, and rapid traveling, which the Yankees have, and who are leaving the mother country behind in the variety of their notions and inventions. The possession and exercise of practical talent merely are a sure and rapid means of intellectual culture and independence.

Page 249.

Within a dozen miles of Bangor we passed through the villages of Stillwater and Oldtown, built at the falls of the Penobscot, which furnish the principal power by which the Maine woods are converted into lumber. The mills are built directly over and across the river. Here is a close jam, a hard rub, at all seasons; and then the once green tree, long since white, I need not say as the driven snow, but as a driven log, becomes lumber merely. Here your inch, your two and your three inch stuff begin to be, and Mr. Sawyer marks off those spaces which decide the destiny of so many prostrate forests. Through this steel riddle, more or less coarse, is the arrowy Maine forest, from Ktaadn and Chesuncook, and the head-waters of the St. John, relentlessly sifted, till it comes out boards, clapboards, laths, and shingles such as the wind can take, still, perchance, to be slit and slit again, till men get a size that will suit. Think how stood the white-pine tree on the shore of Chesuncook, its branches soughing with the four winds, and every individual needle trembling in the sunlight,—think how it stands with it now,—sold, perchance, to the New England Friction-Match Company! There were in 1837, as I read, two hundred and fifty saw-mills on the Penobscot and its tributaries above Bangor, the greater part of them in this immediate neighborhood, and they sawed two hundred millions of feet of boards annually. To this is to be added the lumber of the Kennebec, Androscoggin, Saco, Passamaquoddy, and other streams. No wonder that we hear so often of vessels which are becalmed off our coast, being surrounded a week at a time by floating lumber from the Maine woods. The mission of men there seems to be, like so many busy demons, to drive the forest all out of the country, from every solitary beaver-swamp and mountain-side, as soon as possible.

We visited Veazie's mills, just below the island, where were sixteen sets of saws,—some gang saws, sixteen in a gang, not to mention circular saws. On one side, they were hauling the logs up an inclined plane by water-power; on the other, passing out the boards, planks, and sawed timber, and forming them into rafts. The trees were literally drawn and quartered there. In forming the rafts, they use the lower three feet of hard-wood saplings, which have a crooked and knobbed butt-end, for bolts, passing them up through holes bored in the corners and sides of the rafts, and keying them. In another apartment they were making fence-slats, such as stand all over New England, out of odds and ends,—and it may be that I saw where the picket-fence behind which I dwell at home came from. I was surprised to find a boy collecting the long edgings of boards as fast as cut off, and thrusting them down a hopper, where they were *ground up* beneath the mill, that they might be out of the way; otherwise they accumulate in vast piles by the side of the building, increasing the danger from fire, or, floating off, they obstruct the river. This was not only a saw-mill, but a grist-mill, then. The inhabitants of Oldtown, Stillwater, and Bangor cannot suffer for want of kindling stuff, surely. Some get their living exclusively by picking up the drift-wood and selling it by the cord in the winter. In one place I saw where an Irishman, who keeps a team and a man for the purpose, had covered the shore for a long distance with regular piles, and I was told that he had sold twelve hundred dollars' worth in a year. Another, who lived by the shore, told me that he got all the material of his out-buildings and fences from the river; and in that neighborhood I perceived that this refuse wood was frequently used instead of sand to fill hollows with, being apparently cheaper than dirt.

Page 256.

Everywhere [along the Penobscot] we saw signs of the great freshet, —this house standing awry, and that where it was not founded, but where it was found, at any rate, the next day; and that other with a water-logged look, as if it were still airing and drying its basement, and logs with everybody's marks upon them, and sometimes the marks of their having served as bridges, strewn along the road.

Page 307.

We soon after saw a splendid yellow lily (*Lilium Canadense*) by the shore, which I plucked. It was six feet high, and had twelve flowers, in two whorls, forming a pyramid, such as I have seen in Concord. We afterward saw many more thus tall along this stream, and also still more numerous on the East Branch, and, on the latter, one which I thought approached yet nearer to the *Lilium superbum*. The Indian asked what we called it, and said that the "loots" (roots) were good for soup, that is, to cook with meat, to thicken it, taking the place of flour. They get them in the fall. I dug some, and found a mass of bulbs pretty deep in the earth, two inches in diameter, looking, and even tasting, somewhat like raw green corn on the ear.

Page 158.

FLOWERS AND SHRUBS

The prevailing flowers and conspicuous small plants of the *woods*, which I noticed, were: *Clintonia borealis, Linnæa,* checkerberry (*Gaultheria procumbens*), *Aralia nudicaulis* (wild sarsaparilla), great round-leaved orchis, *Dalibarda repens, Chiogenes hispidula* (creeping snowberry), *Oxalis acetosella* (common wood-sorrel), *Aster acuminatus, Pyrola secunda* (one-sided pyrola), *Medeola Virginica* (Indian cucumber-root), small *Circæa* (enchanter's nightshade), and perhaps *Cornus Canadensis* (dwarf-cornel).

Of these, the last of July, 1858 [1857] only the *Aster acuminatus* and great round-leaved *orchis* were conspicuously in bloom.

The most common flowers of the *river* and *lake shores* were *Thalictrum cornuti* (meadow-rue), *Hypericum ellipticum, mutilum,* and *Canadense* (St. John's-wort), horsemint, horehound, *Lycopus Virginicus* and *Europaeus,* var. *sinuatus* (bugle-weed), *scutellaria galericulata* (skull-cap), *solidago lanceolata* and *squarrosa* East Branch (goldenrod), *Diplopappus umbellatus* (double-bristled aster) *Aster radula, Cicuta maculata* and *bullifera* (water-hemlock), meadow-sweet, *Lysimachia stricta* and *ciliata* (loose-strife), *Galium trifidum* (small bed-straw), *Lilium Canadense* (wild yellow-lily), *Platanthera peramaena* and *psycodes* (great purple orchis and small purple-fringed orchis), *Mimulus ringens* (monkey flower), dock (water), blue flag, *Hydrocotyle Americana* (marsh pennywort), *Sanicula Canadensis?* (black snake-root), *Clematis Virginiana?* (Common virgin's-bower),

Nasturtiun palustre (marsh cress), *Ranunculus recurvatus* (hooked crowfoot), *Ascelpias incarnata* (swamp milkweed), *Aster Tradescanti* (Tradescant's aster), *Aster miser,* also *longifolius Eupatorium purpureum* apparently, lake shores (Joe-Pye-weed), *Apocynum Canabinum* East Branch (Indian hemp), *Polygonum cilinode* (bindweed), and others. Not to mention among inferior orders wool-grass and the sensitive fern.

In the water, *Nuphar advena* (yellow pond-lily), some *potamogetons* (pond-weed), *Sagittaria variabilis* (arrowhead), *Sium lineare?* (water-parsnip).

Of these, those conspicuously in flower the last of July, 1857, were: rue, *Solidago lanceolata* and *squarrosa, Diplopappus umbellatus, Aster radula Lilium Canadense,* great and small purple orchis, *Mimulus ringens,* blue flag, virgin's-bower, &c.

The characteristic flowers in *swamps* were: *Rubus triflorus* (dwarf-raspberry), *Calla palustris* (water-arum), and *Sarracenia purpurea* (pitcher-plant). On *burnt grounds: Epilobium angustifolium,* in full bloom (great willow-herb), and *Erechthites hieracifolia* (fire-weed). On *cliffs: Campanula rotundifolia* (harebell), *Cornus Canadensis* (dwarf cornel), *Arctostaphylos uva-ursi* (bearberry), *Potentilla tridentata* (mountain cinquefoil), *Pteris aquilina* (common brake). At *old camps, carries, and logging-paths: Cirsium arvense* (Canada thistle), *Prunella vulgaris* (common self-heal), clover, herds-grass, *Achillea millefolium* (common yarrow), *Leucanthemum vulgare* (white-weed), *Aster macrophyllus, Halenia deflexa* East Branch (spurred gentian), *Antennaria margaritacea* (pearly everlasting), *Actæa rubra* and *alba,* wet carries (red and white cohosh), *Desmodium Canadense* (tick-trefoil), sorrel.

.   .   .   .

The prevailing underwoods were: *Dirca palustris* (moose-wood), *Acer spicatum* (mountain maple), *Virbunum lantanoides* (hobble-bush), and frequently *Taxus baccata,* var. *Canadensis* (American yew).

The prevailing shrubs and small trees along the shore were: *osier rouge* and alders (before mentioned); sallows, or small willows, of two or three kinds, as *Salis humilis, rostrata,* and discolor?, *Sambucus Canadensis* (black elder), rose, *Viburnum opulus* and *nudum* (cranberry-tree and withe-rod), *Pyrus Americana* (American mountain-ash), *Corylus rostrata* (beaked hazel-nut), *Diervilla trifida* (bush-honey-suckle), *Prunus Virginiana* (choke-cherry), *Myrica gale* (sweet-gale), *Nemopanthes Canadensis* (mountain holly), *Cephalanthus occiden-*

talis (button-bush), *Ribes prostratum,* in some places (fetid currant).

More particularly of shrubs and small trees in *swamps:* some willows, *Kalmia glauca* (pale laurel), *Ledum latifolium* and *palustre* (Labrador tea), *Ribes lacustre* (swamp gooseberry), and in one place *Betula pumila* (low birch). At *camps and carries:* raspberry, *Vaccinium Canadense* (Canada blueberry), *Prunus Pennsylvanica,* also along shore (wild red cherry), *Amelanchier Canadensis* (shad-bush), *Sambucus pubens* (red-berried elder). Among those peculiar to the *mountains* would be the *Vaccinium vitis-idæa* (cow-berry).

Of plants commonly regarded as *introduced* from Europe, I observed at Ansel Smith's clearing, Chesuncook, abundant in 1857; *Ranunculus acris* (buttercups), *Plantago major* (common plaintain), *Chenopodium album* (lamb's-quarters), *Capsella bursa-pastoris,* 1853 (shepherd's-purse), *Spergula arvensis,* also, north shore of Moosehead, in 1853, and elsewhere, 1857 (corn-spurry), *Taraxacum dens-leonis*—regarded as indigenous by Gray, but evidently introduced there—(common dandelion), *Polygonum Persicaria* and *hydropiper,* by a logging path in woods at Smith's (lady's-thumb and smart-weed), *Runex acetosella,* common at carries (sheepsorrel), *Trifolium pratense,* 1853, on carries, frequent (red clover), *Leucanthemum vulgare,* carries (white weed), *Phelum pratense,* carries, 1853–7 (herd's-grass), *Verbena hastata* (blue vervain), *Cirsium arvense,* abundant at camps 1857 (Canada thistle), *Rumex crispus?,* West Branch, 1853? (curled dock), *Verbascum thapsus,* between Bangor and lake, 1853 (common mullein).

Page 19.

OUTFIT FOR AN EXCURSION

The following will be a good outfit for one who wishes to make an excursion of *twelve* days into the Maine woods with a companion and one Indian, for the same purposes that I did.

Wear,—a check shirt, stout old shoes, thick socks, a neck ribbon, thick waistcoat, thick pants, old Kossuth hat, a linen sack.

Carry,—in an India-rubber knapsack, with a large flap, two shirts (check), one pair thick socks, one pair drawers, one flannel shirt, two pocket-handkerchiefs, a light India-rubber coat or a thick woolen one, two bosoms and collars to go and come with, one napkin, pins, needles, thread, one blanket, best gray, seven feet long.

Tent,—six by seven feet, and four feet high in middle, will do; veil and gloves and insect-wash, or, better, mosquito-bars to cover all at night; best pocket-map, and perhaps description of the route; compass; plant-book and red blotting-paper; paper and stamps, botany, small pocket spy-glass for birds, pocket-microscope, tape-measure, insect-boxes.

Axe, full size if possible, jackknife, fish-lines, two only apiece, with a few hooks and corks ready, and with pork for bait in a packet, rigged; matches (some also in a small vial in the waistcoat pocket); soap, two pieces; large knife and iron spoon (for all); three or four old news-papers, much twine, and several rags for dishcloths; twenty feet of strong cord, four-quart tin pail for kettle, two tin dippers, three tin plates, a fry-pan.

Provisions.—Soft hardbread, twenty-eight pounds; pork, sixteen pounds; sugar, twelve pounds; one pound black tea or three pounds coffee; one box or a pint of salt; one quart Indian meal, to fry fish in; six lemons, good to correct the pork and warm water; perhaps two or three pounds of rice, for variety. You will probably get some berries, fish, &c., beside.

A gun is not worth the carriage, unless you go as hunters. The pork should be in an open keg, sawed to fit; the sugar, tea or coffee, meal, salt, &c., should be put in separate water-tight India-rubber bags, tied with a leather string; and all the provisions, and part of the rest of the baggage, put into two large India-rubber bags, which have been proved to be water-tight and durable. Expense of preceding outfit is twenty-four dollars.

An Indian may be hired for about one dollar and fifty cents per day, and perhaps fifty cents a week for his canoe (this depends on the de-mand). The canoe should be a strong and tight one. This expense will be nineteen dollars.

Such an excursion need not cost more than twenty-five dollars apiece, starting at the foot of Moosehead, if you already possess or can borrow a reasonable part of the outfit. If you take an Indian and canoe at Old-town, it will cost seven or eight dollars more to transport them to the lake.

Page 208.

LIST OF BIRDS WHICH I SAW IN MAINE BETWEEN JULY 24 AND
AUGUST 3, 1857.

A very small hawk at Great Falls, on Webster Stream.

Haliætus leucocephalus (white-headed or bald-eagle), at Ragmuff, and above and below Hunt's, and on pond below Mattawamkeag.

Pandion haliætus (fish-hawk or osprey), heard, also seen on East Branch.

Bubo Virginianus (cat-owl), near Camp Island, also above mouth of Schoonis, from a stump back and forth, also near Hunt's on a tree.

Icterus phœniceus (red-winged blackbird), Umbazookskus River.

Corvus Americanus (American crow), a few, as at outlet of Grand Lake; a peculiar cawing.

Fringilla Canadensis (tree-sparrow), think I saw one on Mount Kineo July 24, which behaved as if it had a nest there.

Garrulus cristatus (blue-jay).

Parus atricapillus (chicadee), a few.

Muscicapa tyrannus (king-bird).

Muscicapa Cooperii (olive-sided fly-catcher), everywhere a prevailing bird.

Muscicapa virens (wood-pewee), Moosehead, and I think beyond.

Muscicapa ruticilla (American redstart), Moosehead.

Vireo olivaceus (red-eyed vireo), everywhere common.

Turdus migratorius (red-breasted robin), some everywhere.

Turdus melodus (wood-thrush), common in all the woods.

Turdus Wilsonii (Wilson's thrush), Moosehead and beyond.

Turdus aurocapillus (golden-crowned thrush or ovenbird), Moosehead.

Fringilla albicollis (white-throated sparrow), Kineo and after, apparently nesting; the prevailing bird early and late.

Fringilla melodia (song-sparrow), at Moosehead or beyond.

Sylvia pinus (pine warbler), one part of voyage.

Muscicapa acadica (small pewee), common.

Trichas Marylandica (Maryland yellow-throat), everywhere.

Coccyzus Americanus? (yellow-billed cuckoo), common.

Picus erythrocephalus (red-headed woodpecker), heard and saw, and good to eat.

Sitta Carolinensis (?) (white-breasted American nuthatch), heard.

Alcedo alcyon (belted kingfisher), very common.

Caprimulgus Americanus (night-hawk).

Tetrao umbellus (partridge), Moosehead carry, &c.

Tetrao cupido? (pinnated grouse), Webster Stream.

Ardea cærulea (blue heron), lower part of Penobscot.

Totanus macularius (spotted sandpiper or peetweet), everywhere.

Larus argentatus? (herring-gull), Heron Lake on rocks, and Chamberlain. Smaller gull on Second Lake.

Anas obscura (dusky or black duck), once in East Branch.

Anas sponsa (summer or wood duck), everywhere.

Fuligula albeola (spirit duck or dipper), common.

Colymbus glacialis (great Northern diver or loon), in all the lakes. A swallow; the night-warbler? once or twice.

Mergus Merganser (buff-breasted merganser or sheldrake), common on lakes and rivers.

Page 108.

A LIST OF INDIAN WORDS

Ktaadn, said to mean *Highest Land,* Rale puts for *Mt. Pemadene;* for *Grai, pierre à aiguiser, Kitadaügan.* (v. Potter.)

Mattawamkeag, place where two rivers meet. (Indian of carry.) (v. Williamson's *History of Maine,* and Willis)

Molunkus.

Ebeeme, rock.

Noliseemack; other name, Shad Pond.

Kecunnilessu, chicadee.

Nipsquecohossus, woodcock.

Skuscumonsuk, kingfisher. Has it not the pl. termination *uk* here, or *suk?*   } Joe.

Wassus, bear, *aouessous.* (Rale)

Lunxus, Indian-devil.

Upahsis, mountain-ash.

Moose (is it called, or does it mean, wood-eater?), *mous,* Rale.

Katahdinauguoh, said to mean mountains about Ktaadn.

Ebemena, tree-cranberry. *Ibibimin, nar,* red, bad fruit.
Rale. } Joe.

Wighiggin, a bill or writing, *aouixigan, "Livre, lettre, peinture, ceinture."* Rale. } Ind'n of carry.

Sebamook, Large-bay Lake, *Peqouasebem;* add *ar* for plural, *lac* or *étang.* Rale. *Ouaürinaügamek, anse dans un lac.* Rale. *Mspame,* large water. Polis. } Nicholai.

Sebago and *Sebec,* large open water.

Chesuncook, place where many streams empty in. (v. Willis and Potter.) } Tahmunt, &c.

Caucomgomoc, Gull Lake. (*Caucomgomoc,* the lake; *caucomgomoc-took,* the river, Polis.) }

Pammadumcook.

Kenduskieg, Little Eel River. (v. Willis.)   Nicholai.

Penobscot, Rocky River. *Puapeskou,* stone. (Rale v. Springer.) } Ind'n of carry.

Umbazookskus, meadow stream. (Much-meadow river, Polis.)

Millinocket, place of Islands.

Souneunk, that runs between Mountains. } Nicholai.

Aboljacarmegus, Smooth-ledge Falls and Dead-water.

Aboljacarmeguscook, the river there.

Muskiticook, Dead Stream. (Indian of carry.) *Meskikou,* or *Meskikouikou,* a place where there is grass. (Rale.) *Muskéeticook,* Deadwater. (Polis.)

Mattahumkeag, Sand-creek Pond. } Nicholai.

Piscataquis, branch of a river.

Shecorways, sheldrakes.

Naramekechus, peetweet. } Polis

Medawisla, loon.

Orignal, Moosehead Lake. (Montresor.)

Chor-chor-que, usnea.

Adelungquamooktum, wood-thrush. } Polis.

Bematruichtik, high land generally. (*Mt. Pemadené.* Rale.)

Maquoxigil, bark of red osier, Indian tobacco.

Kineo, flint (Williamson; old Indian hunter). (Hodge.)

Artoosoqu', phosphorescence.

Subekoondark, white spruce.

Skusk, black spruce.

Beskabekuk, the "Lobster Lake" of maps.

Beskabekukskishtuk, the dead-water below the island.

Paytaytequick, Burnt-Ground Stream, what Joe called ⎫Polis.
Ragmuff.

Nonlangyis, the name of a dead-water between the last and
Pine Stream.

Karsaootuk, Black River (or Pine Stream). *Mkazéouighen,*
black. Rale.

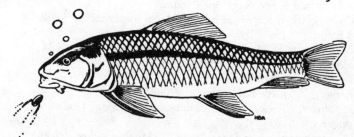

Michigan, fimus. Polis applied it to a sucker, or a poor, good-
for-nothing fish. *Fiante* (?) *mitsegan,* Rale. (Pickering puts the ?
after the first word.)

Cowosnebagosar, Chiogenes hispidula, means, grows where
trees have rotted.

Pockadunkquaywayle, echo. *Pagadaükoueouérré. Rale. Bo-
rorquasis,* moose-fly.

Nerlumskeechtcook (or *quoik?*), (or *skeetcook*), Dead-water,
and applied to the mountains near.

Apmoojenegamook, lake that is crossed.

Allegash, hemlock-bark. (v. Willis.)

Paytaywecongomec, Burnt-Ground Lake, *Telos.*

Madunkehunk, Height-of-land Stream (Webster Stream).

Madunkehunk-gamooc, Height-of-land Lake.

Matungamooc, Grand Lake.

Uncardnerheese, Trout Stream.

Wassataquoik (or -*cook*), Salmon River, East Branch. (v.
Willis.)

Pemoymenuk, Amelanchier berries, "*Pemouaimin, nak,* a
black fruit. Rale." Has it not here the plural ending?

Sheepnoc, Lilium Canadense bulbs. "*Sipen, nak,* white,
larger than *penak.*" Rale.

⎱Polis

⎱Polis

Paytgumkiss, Petticoat (where a small river comes into the⌉
Penobscot below Nickatow).   ⎬Polis
Burntibus, a lake-like reach in the Penobscot.   ⌋

Passadumkeag, "where the water falls into the Penobscot above the falls." (Williamson.) *Paüsidaükioui* is, *au dessus de la montagne.* Rale.

Olarmon, or *larmon* (Polis), red paint. "Vermilion, paint, *Ouramaü.*" Rale.

Sunkhaze, "See canoe come out; no, see 'em stream." (Polis.) The mouth of a river, according to Rale, is *Saüghedétegoue.* The place where one stream empties into another, thus ᴓ is *saüktaüoui.* (v. Willis.)

Tomhegan Br. (at Moosehead). "*Hatchet, temahigan.*" Rale.

Nickatow, "*Nicketaoutegué,* or *Niketoutegoue, rivière qui fourche.*" Rale.

From WILLIAM WILLIS, on the Language of the
Abnaquies, Maine Hist. Coll., Vol. IV.

Abalajako-megus (river near Ktaadn).

Aitteon (name of a pond and sachem).

Apmogenegamook (name of a lake).

Allagash (a bark camp). Sockbasin, a Penobscot, told him, "The Indians gave this name to the lake from the fact of their keeping a hunting-camp there."

Bamonewengamock, head of Allagash, Cross Lake. (Sockbasin.)

Chesuncook, Big Lake. (Sockbasin.)

Caucongamock (a lake).

Ebeeme, mountains that have plums on them. (Sockbasin.)

Ktaadn. Sockbasin pronounces this Ka-tah-din, and said it meant "large mountain or large thing."

Kenduskeag (the place of Eels).

Kineo (flint), mountain on the border, &c.

Metawamkeag, a river with a smooth, gravelly bottom. (Sockbasin.)

Metanawcook.

Millinoket, a lake with many islands in it. (Sockbasin.)

Matakeunk (river).

Molunkus (river).

Nicketow, Neccotoh, where two streams meet ("Forks of the Penobscot").

Negas (Indian village on the Kenduskeag).

Orignal (Montresor's name for Moosehead Lake).

Ponguongamook, Allagash, name of a Mohawk Indian killed there. (Sockbasin.)

Penobscot, Penobskeag, French *Pentagoet,* &c.

Pougohwaken (Heron Lake).

Pemadumcook (lake).

Passadumkeag, where water goes into the river above falls. (Williamson.)

Ripogenus (river).

Sunkhaze (river), Dead-water.

Souneunk.

Seboomook. Sockbasin says this word means "the shape of a Moose's head, and was given to the lake," &c. *Howard* says differently.

Seboois, a brook, a small river. (Sockbasin.)

Sebec (river).

Sebago (great water).

Telos (lake).

Telasiuis (lake).

Umbagog (lake), doubled up; so called from its form. (Sockbasin.)

Umbazookskus (lake).

Wassatiquoik, a mountain river. (Sockbasin.)

Judge C. E. Potter of Manchester, New Hampshire, adds in November, 1855:—

"*Chesuncook.* This is formed from *Chesunk,* or *Schunk* (a goose), and *Auke* (a place), and means 'The Goose Place.' Chesunk, or Schunk, is the sound made by the wild geese when flying."

Ktaadn. This is doubtless a corruption of *Kees* (high), and *Auke* (a place).

Penobscot, Penapse (stone, rock-place), and *Auke* (place).

Suncook, Goose-place, *Schunk-auke.*

The Judge says that *schoot* means to rush, and hence *schoodic* from this and *auke* (a place where water rushes), and that *schoon* means the same; and that the Marblehead people and others have derived the words *scoon* and *scoot* from the Indians, and hence schooner; refers to a Mr. Chute.